Download Forms on Nolo.com

You can download the forms in this book at:

 www.nolo.com/back-of-book/NNP.html

We'll also post updates whenever there's an important change to the law affecting this book—as well as articles and other related materials.

More Resources from Nolo.com

Legal Forms, Books, & Software

Hundreds of do-it-yourself products—all written in plain English, approved, and updated by our in-house legal editors.

Legal Articles

Get informed with thousands of free articles on everyday legal topics. Our articles are accurate, up to date, and reader friendly.

Find a Lawyer

Want to talk to a lawyer? Use Nolo to find a lawyer who can help you with your case.

NOLO
LAW for ALL

15th Edition

How to Form a
Nonprofit Corporation

Attorney Anthony Mancuso

FIFTEENTH EDITION	MAY 2021
Editor	DIANA FITZPATRICK
Cover Design	SUSAN PUTNEY
Book Design	SUSAN PUTNEY
Proofreading	SUSAN CARLSON GREENE
Index	VICTORIA BAKER
Printing	BANG PRINTING

ISSN 2327-2287 (Print)
ISSN 2327-2279 (Online)

ISBN 978-1-4133-2864-6 (pbk)
ISBN 978-1-4133-2865-3 (ebook)

This book covers only United States law, unless it specifically states otherwise.

Please note

We know that accurate, plain-English legal information can help you solve many of your own legal problems. But this text is not a substitute for personalized advice from a knowledgeable lawyer. If you want the help of a trained professional—and we'll always point out situations in which we think that's a good idea—consult an attorney licensed to practice in your state.

Acknowledgments

The author extends a special thanks to his editor, Diana Fitzpatrick, and Stan Jacobsen for invaluable and thorough research assistance, and to all the hardworking people at Nolo.

About the Author

Anthony Mancuso is a California attorney and a corporations and limited liability company expert. He graduated from Hastings College of the Law in San Francisco, is a member of the California State Bar, writes books and software in the fields of corporate and LLC law, and has studied advanced business taxation at Golden Gate University in San Francisco. He is currently employed by Google. He is the author of many Nolo books on forming and operating corporations (both profit and nonprofit) and limited liability companies. His titles include *Incorporate Your Business*, *How to Form a Nonprofit Corporation* (national and California editions), *Form Your Own Limited Liability Company*, *The Corporate Records Handbook*, *LLC or Corporation?*, and *Your Limited Liability Company: An Operating Manual*. His books and software have shown over 500,000 businesses and organizations how to form a corporation or an LLC. He also is a licensed helicopter pilot and a guitar player.

Table of Contents

Appendixes

Introduction

Forming a nonprofit corporation may sound like a daunting task that you should hand over to a lawyer as quickly as you can—after all, aren't there a lot of paperwork and filings, and complicated IRS nonprofit tax laws to learn? There is paperwork, and you will need to deal with the IRS, but the truth is, you can do it yourself. Forming a nonprofit corporation in any state is actually a fairly straightforward process. And, with the help of our line-by-line instructions, you can also obtain tax-exempt status from the IRS for your newly formed nonprofit corporation. Thousands of people have gone through the entire process of incorporating a nonprofit and obtaining 501(c)(3) tax-exempt status with this book to guide them.

Along the way, there may be decisions you need to make where you should seek professional advice. We'll let you know when you need outside help. And even if you do decide to hire a lawyer to handle some of the work for you, the information in this book will help you be an informed client—and get the most for your money.

This book explains, in plain English, how to incorporate your nonprofit in any state and obtain 501(c)(3) tax-exempt status from the IRS. We show you how to:

- prepare and file nonprofit corporation articles and bylaws in any of the 50 states
- apply for and obtain 501(c)(3) tax-exempt status from the IRS

- qualify as a 501(c)(3) public charity
- satisfy IRS conflict-of-interest and excess-benefit guidelines
- prepare minutes for your first board meeting, and
- take care of postincorporation filings and tasks.

We provide advice and instructions for both the streamlined IRS Form 1023-EZ tax exemption application and the standard IRS Form 1023 application. In Appendix B we explain how you can locate each state's secretary of state's office and state tax agency online to find state forms and additional information.

There are legal and tax technicalities that nonprofits must deal with in exchange for the substantial benefits they receive as nonprofits. We give you the information and tools you need both to form your tax-exempt nonprofit and understand the practical and ongoing issues related to running a nonprofit.

We know that any legal process can be challenging. We hope this book, with its step-by-step approach to incorporation and obtaining tax-exempt status from the IRS, will help you through the legal hoops and over the hurdles of incorporating your nonprofit in any state and obtaining tax-exempt status from the IRS. Congratulations on taking your first steps toward success in your new nonprofit endeavor!

PART

1

How Nonprofit Corporations Work

the process of incorporating and obtaining tax-exempt status. First, we'll help you create your corporate entity by showing you how to prepare and file articles of incorporation that meet your state's corporate law requirements. Then we'll show you how to obtain your state and federal nonprofit income tax exemptions for Section 501(c)(3) tax-exempt status.

Benefits of the Nonprofit Corporation

Now that you understand that this book is intended for nonprofit corporations organized for religious, charitable, scientific, literary, and/or educational purposes that want to qualify for a tax exemption under Section 501(c)(3) of the Internal Revenue Code (and hopefully your nonprofit is among them), let's look at the benefits you'll enjoy as a 501(c)(3) tax-exempt nonprofit corporation. The relative importance of each of the following benefits will vary from group to group, but at least one of them should be very significant for your organization.

If you finish this section and conclude that nothing here is very important for your group, you'll want to consider whether it makes sense to incorporate at all. Many groups accomplish their nonprofit purposes just fine as unincorporated nonprofit associations, without formal organizational paperwork or written operational rules. If you can continue to accomplish your nonprofit purposes and goals informally, you may be happier staying small.

Tax Exemptions

Nonprofit corporations are eligible for state and federal exemptions from payment of corporate income taxes, as well as other tax exemptions and benefits. At a federal corporate tax rate of 21%, it goes without saying—at least if you expect to earn a substantial amount of money (from services, exhibits, or performances, for example)—that you'll want to apply for an exemption. In states with a corporate income tax, a state income tax exemption is equally attractive, as are local, county, real property, and personal property tax exemptions. Chapters 3, 4, and 5 cover tax exemptions in detail.

SEE AN EXPERT

Get the help of a competent tax adviser as soon as you decide to incorporate. Make sure you choose someone experienced in the special field of nonprofit bookkeeping and reporting. Ask the adviser to help you (especially your treasurer) set up a good record-keeping system, which you can use to prepare your annual federal and state nonprofit tax forms and reports. Have the tax helper periodically review the system to be sure that you are maintaining your financial records properly and have filed your tax forms on time.

Receiving Public and Private Donations

One of the primary reasons for becoming a 501(c)(3) nonprofit corporation is that it increases your ability to attract and receive public and private grant funds and donations from sources such as:

- **Public sources.** Tax-exempt government foundations (like the National Endowment for the Arts, the National Endowment for the Humanities, or the Corporation for Public Broadcasting), as well as private foundations and charities (such as the Ford Foundation, the United Way, or the American Cancer Society), are usually required by their own operating rules and federal tax regulations to donate their funds to only 501(c)(3) tax-exempt organizations.

- **Individual private donors** can claim personal federal income tax deductions for contributions made to 501(c)(3) tax-exempt groups. At a donor's death, a federal estate tax exemption is available for bequests made to 501(c)(3) groups.

Nonprofit Moneymakers—The Latest in Hybrid Limited Liability Entities

A number of states allow the formation of hybrid limited liability entities (LLCs and/or corporations) that can make a profit yet also do good. For example, some states authorize the formation of low-profit LLCs (also called "L3Cs") for educational or charitable purposes as well as for making a profit. States initially created this special type of hybrid entity to allow foundations to more easily distribute funds to a qualified social purpose organization, although the IRS has not yet formally approved L3Cs for this purpose.

Some states authorize the formation of flexible purpose corporations or benefit corporations, which can be formed to do good works as well as to make money. The advantage of these hybrid entities is that they can allow the principals to spend time and money trying to do good without having to worry about stakeholders' being upset (and suing them) for not spending all their time trying to turn a profit.

These hybrid entities are sometimes loosely referred to as B corporations. However, this term really refers to a certification (issued by B Labs) that a socially responsive corporation, an LLC, or another entity can seek, not to a separate type of "corporation" or another distinct legal entity. Note that there are other sustainability certifications, including GRI (Global Reporting Initiative) and ULE 880 (a sustainability standard developed by UL Environment, an Underwriters Laboratories initiative). You can find websites of the organizations associated with these certifications online by searching these terms from your Internet browser.

All of these hybrids are profit-making entities, not pure nonprofit corporations organized and operated exclusively for nonprofit purposes. Therefore, it seems unlikely that the IRS would consider them qualified to obtain nonprofit 501(c)(3) income tax exemption.

In short, if you plan to ask people to give you significant amounts of money in furtherance of your nonprofit purpose, you need to demonstrate to your donors that you have 501(c)(3) tax-exempt status.

Protection From Personal Liability

Protecting the members of your group from personal liability is one of the main reasons for forming a corporation (either profit or nonprofit). Once you're incorporated, directors or trustees, officers, employees, and members of a corporation usually won't be personally liable for corporate debts or liabilities, including unpaid organizational debts and unsatisfied lawsuit judgments against the organization, as they normally would be if they conducted their affairs without incorporating. Creditors can go after only corporate assets to satisfy liabilities incurred by the corporation—not the personal assets (cars, homes, or bank accounts) of the people who manage, work for, or volunteer to help the nonprofit corporation.

EXAMPLE: A member of the audience sued a nonprofit symphony orchestra when the patron fell during a concert, claiming that the symphony (which also owned the concert hall) provided an unsafe ramp. The patron won a judgment that exceeded the orchestra's insurance policy limits. The amount of the judgment in excess of insurance is a debt of the corporation, but not of its individual directors, members, managers, or officers. By contrast, had the orchestra been an unincorporated association of musicians, the principals of the unincorporated group could be held personally liable for the excess judgment amount.

Corporation Basics

You don't have to understand all there is to know about corporations in order to follow this book or form your nonprofit. But there are a few basic concepts you'll want to have under your belt as we go through the process. Here they are, with special emphasis on any differences between for-profit corporations and nonprofits:

- **A corporation is a separate legal entity.** A corporation is a legal entity that allows a group of people to pool energy, time, and money for profit or nonprofit activities. It acquires legal existence after its founders comply with their state's incorporation procedures and formalities. The law treats a corporation as a separate person, distinct from the people who own, manage, or operate it. The corporation can enter into contracts, incur debts, and pay taxes. Corporations are either for-profit (business corporations) or nonprofits.

- **For-profit, or business, corporations versus nonprofits.** Business corporations can be formed for any legal purpose. They can issue shares of stock to investors in return for money or property, or services performed for the corporation. Shareholders receive a return on their investment if dividends are paid or if,

upon dissolution of the corporation, any corporate assets remain to be divided among the shareholders after payment of all creditors. Nonprofits, on the other hand, generally cannot issue shares of stock or pay dividends under state law (unless they are some type of hybrid such as consumer or producer co-ops). The federal tax code also prohibits 501(c)(3) tax-exempt nonprofit corporations from paying dividends or profits to their members or other individuals. When a 501(c)(3) tax-exempt nonprofit corporation dissolves, it must distribute its remaining assets to another tax-exempt nonprofit group.

- **In-state and out-of-state corporations.** A corporation formed in a particular state is known as a domestic corporation in that state. Corporations formed in other states, even if physically present and engaging in activities in a state, are called foreign corporations in that state. For example, a corporation formed in California is a domestic corporation as far as California is concerned, but a foreign corporation when considered by other states. We give more information on deciding whether to incorporate in a particular state below, in "Where Should You Incorporate?"

In a few situations, however, people involved with a nonprofit corporation may be personally liable for the corporation's liabilities. Here are some major areas of potential personal liability:

- **Taxes.** State and federal governments can hold the corporate employee who is responsible for reporting and paying corporate taxes personally liable for any unpaid taxes, penalties, and interest due for failure to pay taxes or file necessary returns (for example, the treasurer if the nonprofit board has given this officer full authority to pay all taxes as they become due). With proper planning,

your nonprofit corporation should be tax exempt, but you still have to file federal and state informational returns and annual reports to the secretary of state and state attorney general, as well as pay employee withholding and other payroll taxes and taxes on income unrelated to your nonprofit purposes. IRS penalties for delinquent tax payments and returns are substantial, so keep this exception to limited liability in mind—particularly if you will be the treasurer or a board member who specifically approves the payment of taxes on behalf of your corporation.

- **Dues.** Members of a nonprofit corporation are personally liable for any membership fees and dues they owe the corporation. In most cases, this is a minor obligation because dues are normally set at modest amounts.

- **Violations of statutory duties.** Corporate directors are legally required to act responsibly (not recklessly) when managing the corporation. They may be held personally financially liable if they fail to act responsibly. Personal liability of this sort is the exception, not the rule. Generally, as long as directors attend meetings and carry out corporate responsibilities conscientiously, they should have little to worry about: The corporate limited liability shield insulates directors from all but the most reckless and irresponsible decisions.

- **Intermingling funds or other business dealings.** A nonprofit corporation must act so that its separate existence is clear and respected. If it mixes up corporate funds with the personal funds of those in charge, fails to follow legal formalities (such as failing to operate according to bylaws, hold directors' meetings, or keep minutes of meetings), or risks financial liability without sufficient backup in cash or other assets, a court may disregard the corporate entity and hold the principals responsible for debts and other liabilities of the corporation. In legalese, this is known as piercing the corporate veil. Piercing the veil is the exception, not the rule, and only happens when a court decides that it is necessary to prevent a gross injustice or fraud perpetrated by the founders or principals of a corporation.

- **Private foundation managers.** If the nonprofit corporation is classified as a private foundation, foundation managers can be held personally liable for federal excise taxes associated with certain prohibited transactions. They may also be held personally liable for penalties and interest charged for failing to file certain tax returns or pay required excise taxes. (As explained in Chapter 4, a private foundation is a 501(c)(3) corporation that does not qualify as a public charity. You'll see that most 501(c)(3) nonprofits qualify as public charities and are not subject to the private foundation requirements.)

Does Incorporation Make Sense for Your Group?

A senior citizens' botany club began as an informal organization. Initially, six members took a monthly nature walk to study and photograph regional flora. Everyone chipped in to buy gas for whoever drove to the hike's starting point. Recently, however, membership increased to 15 and the group decided to collect dues from members to pay the increased expenses—gas money, guidebooks, maps, and club T-shirts—associated with more frequent field trips. To avoid mixing club monies with personal funds, a treasurer was designated to open a bank account on behalf of the organization. Several people suggest that it is time to incorporate the club.

Does incorporation make sense at this time? Probably not. There is no new pressing need to adopt the corporate form or to obtain formal recognition as a tax-exempt nonprofit. Most banks will allow an unincorporated group without a federal Employer Identification Number or IRS tax exemption to open up a non–interest-bearing account. However, should the club decide to seek funding and contributions to spearhead a drive to save open space in the community, it might be a good idea to incorporate.

- **Loans.** When a nonprofit corporation takes a loan to cover its operating costs or buys property subject to a mortgage, banks and commercial lending institutions sometimes insist on the personal guarantee of its directors or officers. If the directors or officers agree to personally guarantee the loan or mortgage, the protection that they would normally enjoy as a result of their organization's corporate status goes away. It is somewhat unusual for nonprofit directors or officers to sign a personal guarantee. Obviously, if they do, they will be liable to repay the loan if the corporation cannot do so.

Separate and Perpetual Legal Existence

A corporation is a legal entity that is separate from the people who work for it. Again, one benefit of this separate existence is that corporate liabilities are not the liabilities of the managers, officers, or members of the corporation (known as the corporate characteristic of limited liability). Another benefit is that this corporate legal person is, in a sense, immortal; the nonprofit corporation continues to exist as a legal entity despite changes in management or other corporate personnel caused by the resignation, removal, or death of the people associated with it. It may, of course, be dissolved or drastically affected by the loss of key people, but its inherent perpetual existence makes it more likely that the group's activities will continue, an attractive feature to the private or public donor who prefers funding activities that are organized to operate over the long term.

Employee Benefits

Another benefit of the nonprofit corporation is that its principals can also be employees and, therefore, eligible for employee fringe benefits not generally available to the workers in unincorporated organizations. These benefits include group term life insurance, reimbursement of medical expenses, and coverage by a qualified corporate employee pension or retirement income plan.

Formality and Structure

The formal corporate documents—the articles, bylaws, minutes of meetings, and board resolutions—that you'll prepare as a nonprofit will actually be quite useful to your organization. They'll outline the group's purposes, embody its operating rules, and provide structure and procedures for decision making and dispute resolution. This is important for any collective activity, but for nonprofit groups it is vital, especially if the board includes members of the community with diverse interests and viewpoints. Without the clear-cut delegation of authority and specific operating rules in the articles and bylaws, running the organization might be a divisive, if not futile, affair.

Miscellaneous Benefits

Additional advantages are available to nonprofits that engage in particular types of activities or operations. These benefits can be helpful, and in some cases are critical, to the success of a nonprofit organization. Here are examples of some of the benefits available to certain types of tax-exempt nonprofits:

- Your nonprofit may qualify for exemptions from county real and personal property taxes.
- 501(c)(3) organizations receive lower postal rates on third-class bulk mailings.
- Many publications offer cheaper classified advertising rates to nonprofit organizations.
- Nonprofits are the exclusive beneficiaries of free radio and television public service announcements (PSAs) provided by local media outlets.

- Many stores offer lower membership rates to nonprofit employees.
- Nonprofit employees are often eligible to participate in job training, student intern, work-study, and other federal, state, and local employment incentive programs (where salaries are paid substantially out of federal and state funds).

- 501(c)(3) performing arts groups are qualified to participate in the performance programs sponsored by federally supported colleges and universities.
- Certain 501(c)(3) educational organizations are eligible for a tax refund for gasoline expenses (for example, in running school buses).

The Disadvantages of Going Nonprofit

If your group has come together for 501(c)(3) tax-exempt purposes, and if reading about the benefits of becoming a nonprofit above prompted a "Wow! We would really like to be able to do *that!*" then chances are you've decided to tackle the rules and forms necessary to establish your status as a legal nonprofit. Before jumping in, however, take a minute to read the following descriptions of some of the hurdles and work you'll encounter along the way, especially if you have been operating informally (and successfully) without financial or employee record keeping or controls. If any of the following appear insurmountable to you, think again about incorporating.

Official Paperwork

One disadvantage in forming any corporation is the red tape and paperwork. You'll begin by preparing initial incorporation documents (articles of incorporation, bylaws, and minutes of the first meeting of the board of directors) and an IRS tax exemption application. Although this book will show you how to prepare your own incorporation forms and income tax exemption application with a minimum of time and trouble, the process will still take you a few hours. You and your compatriots must be prepared for some old-fashioned hard work.

After you've set up your corporation, you'll need to file annual tax and reporting returns with the state (the state tax or revenue office and the attorney general) as well as the Internal Revenue Service. Also, you will need to regularly prepare minutes of ongoing corporate meetings, and, occasionally, forms for amending articles and bylaws. The annual tax reporting forms will require the implementation of an organized bookkeeping system plus the help of an experienced nonprofit tax adviser as explained below. Fortunately, keeping minutes of these meetings is not all that difficult to do once someone volunteers for the task (typically the person you appoint as corporate secretary). Sample forms for amending nonprofit articles are usually available from the state corporate filing office online.

Annual nonprofit tax and information returns do present a challenge to a new group unfamiliar with state tax reporting forms and requirements. Other record-keeping and reporting chores, such as double-entry accounting procedures and payroll tax withholding and reporting, can be equally daunting. At least at the start, most nonprofits rely on the experience of a tax adviser, a bookkeeper, or another legal or tax specialist on the board or in the community to help them set up their books and establish a system for preparing tax forms on time. See Chapter 11 for recommendations on finding legal and tax professionals for your nonprofit.

Incorporation Costs and Fees

For nonprofit incorporators unwilling to do the job themselves, a main disadvantage of incorporating a nonprofit organization is the cost of paying an attorney to prepare the incorporation forms and tax exemption application. Putting some time and effort into understanding the material in this book can help you eliminate this added cost, leaving you with only the state and IRS filing fees. If you use IRS Form 1023-EZ, the streamlined federal tax exemption application, the total cost to form your tax-exempt nonprofit should be approximately $325 (for typical state incorporation fees and the IRS $275 streamlined tax exemption application fee). For nonprofits that use the longer Form 1023 application, the tax exemption application fee is $600. Check the IRS website (www.irs.gov) to get the latest fee information.

Time and Energy Needed to Run the Nonprofit

When a group decides to incorporate, the legal decision is often part of a broader decision to increase not just the structure, but the overall scope, scale, and visibility of the nonprofit. With a larger, more accountable organization come a number of new tasks: setting up and balancing books and bank accounts, depositing and reporting payroll taxes, and meeting with an accountant to extract and report year-end figures for annual informational returns. Although these financial, payroll, and tax concerns are not exclusively corporate chores, you'll find that most unincorporated nonprofits keep a low employment, tax, and financial profile and get by with minimum attention to legal and tax formalities.

EXAMPLE: A women's health collective operates as an unincorporated nonprofit organization. It keeps an office open a few days a week where people stop by to read and exchange information on community and women's health issues. The two founders donate their time and the office space and pay operating costs (such as phone, utilities, and photocopying) that aren't covered by contributions from visitors. The organization has never made a profit, there is no payroll, and tax returns have never been filed. There is a minimum of paperwork and record keeping.

The founders could decide to continue this way indefinitely. However, the founders want to expand the activities and revenues of the collective. They decide to form a 501(c)(3) nonprofit corporation in order to be eligible for tax-deductible contributions and grant funds from the city, and to qualify the group to employ student interns and work-study students. This will require them to prepare and file articles of incorporation and a federal corporate income tax exemption application. They must select an initial board of directors and prepare organizational bylaws and formal written minutes of the first board of directors' meeting.

After incorporation, the group holds regular board meetings documented with written minutes, sets up and uses a double-entry bookkeeping system, implements regular federal and state payroll and tax procedures and controls, files exempt organization tax returns each year, and expands its operations. A full-time staff person is assigned to handle the increased paperwork and bookkeeping chores brought about by the change in structure and increased operations of the organization.

This example highlights what should be one of the first things you consider before you decide to incorporate: Make sure that you and your coworkers can put in the extra time and effort that an incorporated nonprofit organization will require. If the extra work would overwhelm or overtax your current resources, we suggest you hold off on your incorporation until you get the extra help you need to accomplish this task smoothly (or at least more easily).

Restrictions on Paying Directors and Officers

As a matter of state corporation law and the tax exemption requirements, nonprofits are restricted in how they deal with their directors, officers, and members. None of the gains, profits, or dividends of the corporation can go to individuals associated with the corporation, including directors, officers, and those defined as members in the corporation's articles or bylaws. State self-dealing rules apply as well, regulating action by the board of directors if a director has a financial interest in a transaction.

Officers and staff can be paid a reasonable salary for work they do for the corporation. State laws often provide for this type of compensation, and even if nothing is specified, it is permissible. Directors can also be paid for their expenses and time for attending directors' meetings. In all cases, however, these payments should be reasonable. Lavish payments or undeserved payouts characterized as "salaries" or "compensation" can be challenged by the IRS and can lead to penalties and even a loss of tax exemption (see "Other Requirements for 501(c)(3) Groups" in Chapter 3).

Restrictions Upon Dissolution

One of the requirements for the 501(c)(3) tax exemption is that upon dissolution of the corporation, any assets remaining after the corporation's debts and liabilities are paid must go to another tax-exempt nonprofit, not to members of the former corporation.

Restrictions on Your Political Activities

Section 501(c)(3) of the Internal Revenue Code establishes a number of restrictions and limitations that apply to nonprofits. Here, we discuss a limitation that may be very significant to some groups—the limitation on your political activities. Specifically, your organization may not participate in political campaigns for or against candidates for public office, and cannot substantially engage in legislative or grassroots political activities except as permitted under federal tax regulations. (For more on this, see "Other Requirements for 501(c)(3) Groups" in Chapter 3.)

EXAMPLE: Society for a Saner World, Inc., has as one of its primary objectives lobbying hard to pass federal and local legislation that seeks to lessen societal dependency on fossil fuels. Since a substantial portion of the group's efforts will consist of legislative lobbying, the group's 501(c)(3) tax exemption probably will be denied by the IRS. Instead, the group should seek a tax exemption under IRC Section 501(c)(4) as a social welfare group, which is not limited in the amount of lobbying the group can undertake. Of course, the benefits of 501(c)(4) tax exemption are fewer too—contributions to the group are not tax deductible, and grant funds will be more difficult to obtain (see IRS Publication 557, Chapter 4, *Other Section 501(c) Organizations*).

Oversight by the Attorney General

Each state's attorney general has broad power to oversee the operations of 501(c)(3) non-profits. The attorney general can take the corporation to court to make sure it complies with the state corporation law. This usually doesn't happen, however, unless an organization commits a serious offense (such as the founders' diverting contributions for their personal use) and the organization is on the state attorney general's enforcement division radar (through a complaint filed by a disgruntled group or a member of the public who feels aggrieved by the nonprofit's actions or policies).

Religious 501(c)(3) nonprofit corporations have wider flexibility in managing their internal affairs. A state attorney general is less likely to step in and sue a religious nonprofit to enforce compliance with state corporate laws, except in the most extreme and unusual cases of fraud or misappropriation by the principals of a religious purpose nonprofit.

How Nonprofits Raise, Spend, and Make Money

Most nonprofits need to deal with money—indeed, being able to attract donations is a prime reason for choosing nonprofit status. Nonprofits can also make money. Nonprofit does not literally mean that a nonprofit corporation cannot make a profit. Under federal tax law and state law, as long as your nonprofit is organized and operating for a recognized nonprofit purpose, it can take in more money than it spends in conducting its activities. A nonprofit may use its tax-free profits for its operating expenses (including salaries for officers, directors, and employees) or for the benefit of its organization (to carry out its exempt purposes). What it cannot do under IRC Section 501(c)(3) is distribute any of the profits for the benefit of its officers, directors, or employees (as dividends, for example).

This section explains how nonprofits raise initial funds and how they make money on an ongoing basis.

Initial Fundraising

Under state corporate statutes, a nonprofit corporation is not legally required to have a specified amount of money in the corporate bank account before commencing operations. This is fortunate, of course, because many beginning nonprofits start out on a shoestring of meager public and private support.

So, where will your seed money come from? As you know, nonprofit corporations cannot issue shares, nor can they provide investment incentives, such as a return on capital through the payment of dividends to investors, bene-factors, or participants in the corporation (see "Corporation Basics," at the beginning of this chapter). Nonprofits have their own means and methods of obtaining start-up funds. Obviously, the most common method is to obtain revenue in the form of contributions, grants, and dues from the people, organizations, and governmental agencies that support the nonprofit's purpose and goals. Also, if you are incorporating an existing organization, the organization's assets are usually transferred to the new corporation. These assets may include the cash reserves of an unincorporated group, which can help your corporation begin operations. You can also borrow start-up funds from a bank, although for newly formed corporations, a bank will usually require that incorporators secure the loan with their personal assets—a pledge most nonprofit directors are understandably reluctant to make.

Often, of course, nonprofits receive initial and ongoing revenues from services or activities provided in the pursuit of their exempt purposes (ticket sales, payments for art lessons or dance courses, school tuition, or clinic charges). Section 501(c)(3) nonprofits are allowed to earn this type of revenue under federal and state tax laws and still maintain their tax-exempt status.

Making Money From Related Activities

Many nonprofits make money while they further the goals of the organization. The nonprofit can use this tax-exempt revenue to pay for operating expenses (including reasonable salaries) and to further its nonprofit purposes. For example, an organization dedicated to the identification and preservation of shorebirds might advertise a bird-watching hike for which they charge a fee; the group could then use the proceeds to fund their bird rescue operations. What it cannot do with the money, however, is distribute it for the benefit of officers, directors, or employees of the corporation (as the payment of a patronage dividend, for example).

EXAMPLE: Friends of the Library, Inc., is a 501(c)(3) nonprofit organized to encourage literary appreciation in the community and to raise money for the support and improvement of the public library. It makes a profit from its sold-out lecture series featuring famous authors and from its annual sale of donated books. Friends can use this tax-exempt profit for its own operating expenses, including salaries for officers and employees, or to benefit the library.

Making Money From Unrelated Activities (Unrelated Income)

Nonprofits can also make money in ways unrelated to their nonprofit purpose. Often this income is essential to the survival of the nonprofit group. This unrelated income, however, is usually taxed as unrelated business income under state and federal corporate income tax rules. While earning money this way is permissible, it's best not to let unrelated business activities reach the point where you start to look more like a for-profit business than a nonprofit one. This can happen if the unrelated income-generating activities are absorbing a substantial amount of staff time, requiring additional paid staff, or producing more income than your exempt purpose activities. If the unrelated revenue or activities of your tax-exempt nonprofit reach a substantial level, the IRS can decide to revoke the group's 501(c)(3) tax exemption—a result your nonprofit will no doubt wish to avoid. (For more information, see "Other Requirements for 501(c)(3) Groups" in Chapter 3.)

EXAMPLE: Many thousands of books are donated to Friends of the Library for its annual book sale, one of its major fundraising events. Although the sale is always highly successful, thousands of books are left over. Friends decides to sell the more valuable books by advertising in the rare and out-of-print books classified sections in various magazines. The response is overwhelming; soon, there are six employees cataloging books. In addition, Friends begins a business purchasing books from other dealers and reselling them to the public. Such a situation could attract attention from the IRS and prompt it to reconsider Friends' 501(c)(3) tax-exempt status.

Making Money from Passive Sources

Although it's not typical for the average nonprofit, a nonprofit corporation can make money from passive sources such as rents, royalties, interest, and investments. This income is nontaxable in some cases.

Your Path to Nonprofit Status

Nonprofit organizations first obtain nonprofit corporate status with the state corporate filing office—usually the corporations division of the secretary of state's office. This is a simple formality accomplished by filing articles of incorporation. Then they go on to obtain a corporate income tax exemption with the Internal Revenue Service. Once the IRS exemption is obtained, a copy of the federal tax exemption determination letter is filed with the state tax or revenue office. This automatically qualifies the nonprofit for a state corporate income tax exemption (assuming the state imposes a corporate tax). In a few states, you must apply for a separate state nonprofit corporate income tax exemption.

In sum, your path to nonprofit status is a usually a two-step process—first you incorporate with the state, then you apply for tax-exempt recognition from the IRS. When you're done with this book, you'll have completed each of these steps, plus additional follow-up steps to make sure your corporation is off to a good legal and tax start.

Where Should You Incorporate?

Corporations formed in a particular state are known in that state as domestic corporations. When viewed from outside that state, these corporations are considered foreign. A foreign corporation that plans to engage in a regular or repeated pattern of activity in another state must qualify to do business there by obtaining a certificate of authority from the secretary of state. For example, a corporation formed in Nevada that intends to do regular business in California is a foreign corporation in California, and must qualify with the California Secretary of State.

Incorporators who plan to operate in another state besides their home state might wonder whether it makes sense to incorporate in that other state. Maybe the incorporation fees or corporate taxes are lower than those in the home state or the nonprofit statutes are more flexible. Then, the reasoning goes, one could qualify the corporation in the home state as a foreign corporation. As tempting as this end run may appear, it's usually not worth it. This section explains why, and also advises you of out-of-state activities that you can engage in without worrying about qualifying in another state.

Qualifying as a Foreign Corporation in Your Home State Will Cost You More

The process of qualifying a foreign corporation to operate in your home state takes about as much time and expense as incorporating a domestic corporation in your home state. This means that you will pay more to incorporate out-of-state since you must pay the regular home state qualification fees plus out-of-state incorporation fees.

Two Sets of Tax Exemptions

Your corporation will still be subject to taxation in each state in which it earns or derives income or funds. If the state of incorporation, which we here assume is a "foreign" state, imposes a corporate income tax, then the nonprofit corporation will need to file for and obtain two state corporate tax exemptions—one for its home state (the state where the corporation will be active and qualify to do business) and one for the foreign state of incorporation. Similarly, double sales, property, and other state tax exemptions may often be necessary or appropriate.

Two Sets of State Laws

Your out-of-state corporation will still be subject to many of the laws that affect corporations in your home state. Many state corporate statutes that apply to domestic corporations also apply to foreign corporations.

Out-of-State Activities

For the above reasons, most readers who flirt with the idea of incorporating in a state other than their home state would be well advised to skip it. This doesn't mean, however, that you'll have to trim all of your activities to stay within your home state. Fortunately, there are many things a nonprofit can do as a foreign corporation in another state without obtaining a certificate of authority from the secretary of that state. Here are some activities that can be done in most states without qualifying to do business there:

- maintaining, defending, or settling any legal action or administrative proceeding, including securing or collecting debts and enforcing property rights

- holding meetings of corporate directors or of the membership and distributing information to members

- maintaining bank accounts and making grants of funds

- making sales through independent contractors and engaging in interstate or foreign commerce

- conducting a so-called isolated transaction that is completed within 30 days and is not one of a series of similar transactions, and

- exercising powers as an executor, administrator, or trustee, as long as none of the activities required of the position amount to transacting business.

When Out-of-State Incorporation Makes Sense

There may be a few of you for whom incorporation in another state makes sense. If you plan to set up a multistate nonprofit with corporate offices and activities in more than one state (a tristate environmental fund for example), you may want to consider incorporating in the state that offers the greatest legal, tax, and practical advantages. To help you decide where to incorporate, go online to each state's corporate filing office website. Another approach is to check a nonprofit resource center library. For nonprofit library resources online, type "nonprofit resource libraries" into your browser—you'll find a host of online libraries at your disposal. An experienced nonprofit lawyer or consultant can also help you determine which state is the most convenient and least costly to use as the legal home for your new nonprofit corporation.

Legal Rights and Duties of Incorporators, Directors, Officers, Employees, and Members

Even though a corporation is a legal person capable of making contracts, incurring liabilities, and engaging in other activities, it still needs real people to act on its behalf to carry out its activities. These people decide to incorporate, select those who will be responsible for running the organization, and actually manage and carry out the nonprofit's goals and activities.

This chapter explains the rights and responsibilities of those in your group who will organize and operate your nonprofit corporation. These incorporators, directors, officers, members, and employees have separate legal rights and responsibilities. Later, after your nonprofit is up and running, you may want to refer back to this chapter if you have questions regarding the powers and duties of these important people.

How Many People Are Needed to Form a Nonprofit Corporation?

In most states, more than one person is needed to organize and operate a corporation. Although most states allow just one person (who doesn't have to be a lawyer) to act as the incorporator, typically, at least three directors are needed to manage a nonprofit corporation, and at least two of the officer positions (usually the president, treasurer, or secretary) must be filled by different people. The easiest way to check your state's minimum-person requirement is to go to your state's filing office website and read the instructions for your state's nonprofit articles form. Usually, these instructions contain the latest state law requirements for the number of incorporators, directors, and officers. If they don't, look elsewhere on the website—many states maintain lists of basic organizational rules directly on their websites. As a last resort, you can check your state's nonprofit corporation law.

Even if your state allows the formation of a nonprofit by one person or a small number of people, the IRS probably will look askance at a "closely held" nonprofit that is founded, managed, and operated by so few people. Such small nonprofits may have a more difficult time convincing the IRS that they serve a public interest, not just the private interests and agendas of a close circle of nonprofit participants.

Incorporators and Their Role as Promoters

An incorporator is the person (or persons) who signs and delivers the articles of incorporation to the secretary of state for filing. In practice, the incorporator is often selected from among the people who serve as the initial directors of the corporation. Once the corporation is formed, the incorporator's legal role is finished. An attorney often serves as the incorporator for a corporation, although this is not required. Because you are doing the paperwork yourself with the help of this book, you won't need to pay a lawyer to act as your incorporator; one or more of your founders can act as the incorporator(s) of your nonprofit.

During the organizational phase, it's not unusual for an incorporator to become a "promoter" of the corporation. An incorporator's promotional activities can quickly go beyond enthusiastic talk about the organization. Promotional activities may involve obtaining money, property, personnel, and whatever else it takes to get the nonprofit corporation started. Arranging for a loan or renting office space will require signatures and promises— to repay the loan and pay the rent. But will the newly formed corporation automatically become responsible? Future directors may hesitate to join a new organization that is saddled already by contracts negotiated by an eager (but perhaps naive) promoter. The promoters themselves will naturally be nervous that they'll be personally responsible if the incorporation plans go awry. And what about the third parties? They may not be inclined to do business with promoters unless they are assured that there will be a responsible party at the other end. After explaining how a promoter must approach every transaction—with the corporation's best interests in mind—we'll show you how to address the concerns of the eventual directors, the promoters themselves, and the third parties with whom they do business.

A Promoter Must Act With the Corporation's Best Interests in Mind

When an incorporator acts as a promoter, he or she is considered by law to be its fiduciary. This legal jargon simply means the incorporator has a duty to act in the best interests of the corporation, and must make full disclosure of any personal interest and potential benefits he or she may derive from business transacted for the nonprofit.

> **EXAMPLE:** When the incorporator/promoter arranges to sell property to the nonprofit corporation, the promoter must disclose to the nonprofit's board of directors any personal ownership interest in the property and also any gain he or she stands to make on the sale.

Directors Must Ratify a Promoter's Actions

Most of the time, a nonprofit corporation will not be bound by an incorporator's preincorporation contract with a third party unless the board of directors ratifies the contract or the corporation accepts the benefits of the contract.

For example, if a nonprofit board votes to ratify the lease signed by an incorporator before the date of incorporation, the corporation will be bound to honor the lease. Similarly, if the nonprofit staff moves into its new offices and conducts business there, their actions will constitute a ratification and the nonprofit will be bound.

Promoters Can Avoid Personal Liability

Fortunately, if promoters carefully draft documents—such as any loan papers and leases—they can avoid the risk of personal liability in the event that the corporation doesn't ratify the deal (or if the corporation never comes into being). Incorporators will not be personally liable for these contracts if they sign in the name of a proposed corporation, not in their individual name, clearly inform the third party that the corporation does not yet exist and may never come into existence, and tell the third party that even if it does come into existence, it may not ratify the contract.

Convincing Third Parties to Do Business With a Promoter

As you might imagine, a cautious third party may balk at doing business with an individual whose yet-to-be-formed nonprofit may repudiate the deal. One way to provide some assurance to a third party is for an incorporator to be bound personally to the contract—in essence, become a guarantor for the loan, lease, or other contract. Understandably, few incorporators will be able or willing to put their personal finances on the line, unless they are absolutely sure that the corporation will in fact be formed and will ratify the deal. The other solution is to incorporate quickly—which you can do with the help of this book!

EXAMPLE: An incorporator/promoter enters into an agreement to lease office space for its organization. Six months later, the organization obtains nonprofit corporate status. The newly formed nonprofit is not bound by the lease agreement unless its board of directors ratifies the agreement or the organization used the office space during the preincorporation period.

Directors

Directors meet collectively as the board of directors, and are responsible—legally, financially, and morally—for the management and operation of your nonprofit corporation.

Before we discuss legalities, let's look at an overriding practical concern: how to select the best directors for your organization.

Ways to Reassure Potential Officers and Directors

Before you start looking for people to help run your nonprofit, take a moment for a reality check: Many potential helpers will hesitate to become involved because they've read in the press about a few notorious, high-visibility lawsuits where nonprofit directors have been held personally liable for misconduct by executives of the nonprofit (for example, the executive of a large, public membership nonprofit misappropriates program funds to buy a yacht or high-priced apartment for personal use). On a more down-to-earth level, a potential treasurer for your nonprofit may hesitate to serve if that person thinks he or she will be personally responsible for the organization's tax-reporting penalties, or a potential director may be worried about being personally sued by a fired employee of the nonprofit. Fortunately, these types of personal liability are extremely rare. Most nonprofits should be able to assure potential director and officer candidates that the nonprofit will be run accountably and sensibly without undue risk of tax or legal liability for the directors.

One obvious way to reassure candidates is to purchase directors' and officers' liability insurance from an insurance broker who handles nonprofit corporate insurance (called "D&O errors and omissions insurance"). This type of insurance, however, is expensive and usually beyond the reach of newly formed small nonprofits. Also, D&O coverage often excludes the sorts of potential liabilities that your directors and officers may be worried about (personal injury and other types of legal tort actions, claims of illegality, or intentional misconduct and the like). If you decide to investigate the cost of D&O insurance, you will want to make sure to go over the areas of coverage and exclusion in the policy very carefully before you buy in.

State legislators recognize that nonprofits often can't afford D&O liability insurance with adequate claim coverage, and many states have enacted nonprofit law provisions that help limit *volunteer* directors' and officers' exposure to liability. State laws also often require corporations to indemnify (advance or pay back) a director for legal expenses incurred in a lawsuit under certain conditions. These laws can provide added comfort to people considering serving as nonprofit corporation directors or officers. If you want more information about the laws in your state, browse your state's nonprofit laws (see Appendix B for information on how to locate your state's nonprofit law online) or consult with a nonprofit lawyer in your state. Again, we believe the best and most practical way to reassure directors and officers to hitch their wagons to your nonprofit organization's star is to be able to show them that you will operate your nonprofit fairly, responsibly, and safely without undue risk of lawsuits by employees or complaints by the public.

Selecting Directors

Choosing directors is one of the most important decisions you will make when organizing your nonprofit. Here are some important things to consider that will help you make the best possible choice for your organization.

Commitment to Your Nonprofit's Purpose

Your directors are a crucial link between your organization and its supporters and benefactors. Make sure that the members of the community that you plan to serve will see your directors as credible and competent representatives of your group and its nonprofit goals. Their status and integrity will be crucial to encouraging and protecting public trust in your organization, and their connections will be vital to attracting recognition, clients, donations, and other support. Use the following to guide your search:

- Consider members of the communities you will serve who have a proven commitment to the goals of your organization. There may be more than one community that you'll want to consider. For example, your draw may be local (city, county, or state), regional, or national. If you are an environmental group concerned with issues in the southern part of the state, you have both a geographic community (people in the area) and a community of interest (environmentalists generally). Your board should reflect a cross section of interested and competent people from both of these communities.

- Look for people with contacts and real-world knowledge and experience in the specific area of your nonprofit's interest. If you are starting a new private school or health clinic, someone familiar with your state's educational or public health bureaucracy would be a big help.

- If your organization is set up to do good works that will benefit a particular group, don't overlook the value of including a member of that recipient group. You may learn important things about your mission and get valuable buy-in from the beneficiaries of your hard work.

Business Knowledge and Expertise

Directors' responsibilities include developing and overseeing organizational policies and goals, budgeting, fundraising, and disbursing a group's funds. The board of directors may hire an administrator or executive director to supervise staff and daily operations, or it may supervise them directly. Either way, your board of directors should be a practical-minded group with strong managerial, technical, and financial skills. In making your selection, try to find people with the following skills and experience:

- **Fundraising experience.** While many large nonprofits have a staff fundraiser, smaller groups often can benefit from the advice of an experienced board member.

- **Experience managing money.** A professional accountant or someone with expertise in record keeping and budgeting can be a godsend. Many nonprofits get into difficulty because their record-keeping and reporting techniques aren't adequate to produce the information required by the federal and state governments. Many are simply inattentive to financial responsibilities, such as paying withholding taxes or accounting properly for public or private grant monies.

- **Useful practical skills.** Do you need the professional expertise of a doctor, a lawyer, or an architect; or operational assistance in areas such as public relations, marketing, or publishing? If so, make finding one of these professionals a high priority during your board search.

Public Officials Are a Good Choice

The IRS likes to see that you have a representative (and financially disinterested) governing body that reflects a range of public interests, not simply the personal interests of a small number of donors. While it's by no means required, the presence of a sympathetic public official on your board can enhance its credibility with both the IRS and the community.

Avoid Conflicts of Interest

When selecting board members, you may need to inquire about, or at least consider, a prospective member's agenda or motives for joining the board. Obviously, people who want to join for personal benefit rather than for the benefit of the organization or the public should not be asked to serve. This doesn't mean that everyone with a remote or potential conflict of interest should be automatically disqualified. It does mean that any slight or possible conflict of interest should be fully recognized and discussed. If the conflict is limited, the director may be able to serve constructively if he or she refrains from voting on certain issues. The bylaws included in this book have conflict of interest provisions that contain rules and procedures for avoiding or approving transactions, including compensation arrangements, that benefit the nonprofit's directors, officers, employees, or contractors. See Article 9 of the bylaws and "Limitation on Profits and Benefits," in Chapter 3, for more information on this topic.

Develop a Realistic Job Description

Your board of directors should be prepared to put time and energy into the organization. Make sure every prospective director has a realistic and clear understanding of what the job entails. Before you contact prospective candidates, we suggest that you prepare a job description that specifies at least the following:

- the scope of the nonprofit's proposed activities and programs
- board member responsibilities and time commitments (expected frequency and length of board meetings and extra duties that may be assigned to directors), and
- the rewards of serving on your board (such as the satisfaction of working on behalf of a cause you care about or the experience of community service).

A clear and comprehensive job description will help with decision making and will also help avoid future misunderstandings with board members over what is expected of them.

Train Your New Directors

The organizers of a nonprofit corporation often need to give initial directors orientation and training about the nonprofit's operations and activities. This training should continue so that board members can handle ongoing operational issues as well. For example, if your nonprofit corporation is organized to provide health care services, board members may need to learn city, state, and federal program requirements that impact your operations and should get regular updates on changes made to these rules and regulations.

 TIP

Choose the right number of directors. You'll want enough to ensure a wide basis of support (particularly with respect to fundraising), but not so many as to impede efficiency in the board's operation. Boards with between nine and 15 directors often work well.

Paying Your Directors

Nonprofit directors usually serve without compensation. We believe this is generally wise. Having nonprofit directors serve without pay reinforces one of the important legal and ethical distinctions of the nonprofit corporation: Unlike its for-profit counterpart, its assets are used to promote its goals, not for the private enrichment of its incorporators, directors, agents, members, or employees.

If you compensate directors, do so at a reasonable rate, related to the actual performance of services and established in advance by a board resolution. (See Article 9 of the bylaws included in this book for specific procedures to follow when approving compensation arrangements.) Most nonprofits reimburse directors only for necessary expenses incurred in performing director duties, such as travel expenses— typically a gas or mileage allowance—to attend board meetings. Sometimes directors are paid a set fee for attending meetings. In most cases, however, director compensation is minimal or nominal, if it is paid at all.

Special State Compensation Rules. Some states may restrict your ability to pay directors. For example, under California law, a majority of directors cannot be paid in a nondirector capacity nor can they be related to such a person (Cal. Corp. Code § 5227). Also, if you plan on paying your directors (whether in a director or nondirector capacity) or if you appoint relatives of paid people to your board, the IRS may decide that you are operated to serve the private interests (increase the personal wealth) of your directors or their relatives. If that happens, your IRS tax exemption application will be denied. If you plan on paying your board, check your state's nonprofit law to make sure it is allowed, or check with a lawyer.

Term of Office

The term of office for directors is usually specified in the corporation's bylaws. Some states set a maximum term for directors (typically one year) only if the term is not specified in the articles or bylaws; other states specify a maximum term in all cases. Most states let you specify any term for directors in your bylaws.

Staggered Elections for Board Members

In the interest of continuity, staggered elections of board members may be a good idea. For example, rather than replacing the entire board at each annual election, you may wish to reelect one-third of the board members each year to serve a three-year term. To start this staggered system out with a 15-member board, five of the initial directors would serve for one year, five for two years, and the remaining five for the full three-year term. At each annual reelection, one-third of the board would be elected to serve three-year terms.

Quorum Rules

For the board of directors to take action at a meeting, a specified number of directors of the corporation—called a quorum—must be present. Generally, state nonprofit statutes require a majority quorum. This means that a majority of the full board must be present to hold a meeting.

Voting Rules

Once a quorum is present at a meeting, a specified number of votes is needed to pass a board resolution. Unless otherwise stated in the articles or bylaws, a resolution normally must be passed by a majority vote of the directors present at a meeting where there is a quorum.

In some cases, the votes of interested directors cannot be counted. This is discussed more in "How to Avoid Self-Dealing," below.

> **EXAMPLE:** The bylaws of a corporation with ten board members specify that a quorum consists of a majority of the board and that action by the board can be taken by a majority of the directors present. This means that a quorum of at least six people (a majority of the ten-person board) must be present to hold a board meeting and, at the very least, four votes (a majority of the six members present at a meeting) are required to pass a resolution. If eight of the ten directors attend the meeting, action must be approved by at least five votes—a majority of those present at the meeting.

Director Action by Written Consent or Conference Call

Your board of directors doesn't necessarily have to meet in person to take action affecting the corporation. Many states authorize directors to take action by written consent or by a conference telephone call. In some states, the directors must consent unanimously, in writing, to this procedure; in others, only the number of directors needed to pass the resolution (normally a majority of a quorum) must consent. If you're interested in having your board take action without a meeting, check your state's nonprofit corporation law. Look for a section titled "Action by Written Consent" in the part dealing with "Directors."

If a quorum is present initially at a meeting and one or more board members leave, action can often still be taken even if you lose your quorum. As long you can still obtain the number of votes that represents a majority of the required quorum stated in the bylaws, the board normally can take action even though a quorum is no longer present at the meeting (this is known as the initial quorum rule). Going back to the example above, in a ten-director board, the required quorum for board action is six directors (a majority of the ten) and at least four votes (a majority of those present) are needed to take board action. Under the initial-quorum rule, two directors can leave the meeting and the four remaining votes will still be sufficient to pass a resolution. Why? Because a quorum was initially present and four board members, representing a majority of the required quorum of six, can vote to pass a resolution.

Executive Committees

The board of directors can delegate some or even a significant part of the board's duties to an executive committee, usually consisting of two or more directors. This arrangement is often used when some directors are more involved in running and managing the nonprofit's affairs and business than others.

Even the passive directors, however, should still keep an eye on what their more active colleagues are up to and actively participate in regular meetings of the full board. To encourage passive directors to stay involved, courts have held the full board responsible for the actions of the executive committee.

Fortunately, keeping the full board abreast of executive committee actions isn't very difficult. The full board should receive regular, timely minutes of executive committee meetings and should review and, if necessary, reconsider important executive committee decisions at each regularly scheduled meeting of the full board. The full board should retain the power to override decisions of the executive committee.

Under state law, there are certain actions that can't be delegated to an executive committee.

Typically, an executive committee cannot be given authority to do one or more of the following:

- approve action that requires approval by the membership
- fill vacancies on the board or other committees
- fix directors' compensation
- alter bylaws, or
- use corporate funds to support a nominee to the board after more people have been nominated than can be elected.

Don't confuse this special executive committee of directors with other corporate committees. The board typically appoints several specialized committees to keep track of and report on corporate operations and programs. These committees act as working groups that are more manageable in size and help make better use of the board's time and its members' talents. They may include finance, personnel, buildings and grounds, new projects, fundraising, or other committees. These committees, often consisting of a mix of directors, officers, and paid staff, do not normally have the power to take legal action on behalf of the corporation; their purpose is to report and make recommendations to the full board or the executive committee.

EXAMPLE: The board of directors appoints a finance committee charged with overseeing the organization's fundraising, budgeting, expenditures, and bookkeeping. The corporation's treasurer chairs the committee. Periodically, this committee makes financial recommendations to the full board. The board could also appoint a personnel committee to establish hiring and employment policies and to interview candidates for important positions. A plans and programs committee might be selected to put together the overall action plan for accomplishing the goals of the organization. Any action taken based on a committee's report or recommendation would be subject to approval by the board.

Directors' Duty of Care

Corporate directors and officers have a legal duty to act responsibly and in the best interests of the corporation: This is called their statutory "duty of care." The statutes defining this phrase use general, imprecise legal terms that are not very helpful in understanding what exactly it means. As a result, the meaning of the term has developed over time as judges and juries, faced with lawsuits, decide whether a director's acts did (or did not) live up to the duty of care. Fortunately, most of it boils down to common sense, as the following discussions show.

Personal Liability for Directors' Acts

In general, you shouldn't be overly concerned about the prospect of personal liability for your directors. Broadly speaking, courts are reluctant to hold nonprofit directors personally liable, except in the clearest cases of dereliction of duty or misuse of corporate funds or property. In the rare cases when liability is found, the penalties are usually not onerous or punitive—typically, the court orders directors to repay the losses their actions caused.

Ordinary negligence or poor judgment is usually not enough to show a director breached the duty of care. Instead, there generally must be some type of fraudulent or grossly negligent behavior. *Volunteer* directors and executive officers of nonprofits enjoy extra protection from personal liability. These personal immunity laws are discussed in detail in "Director Indemnification and Insurance," below.

EXAMPLE: A committee of the nonprofit advises the board of an unsafe condition on the corporation's property. The committee recommends certain remedial actions to get rid of the problem. If the board fails to implement any remedial measures or otherwise take steps to deal with the problem, a court could hold the directors personally liable for any ensuing damage or injuries.

Is Your Nonprofit a Socially Responsible Organization?

Do you need to certify your nonprofit as a socially sustainable organization? (For the names of popular certifications, in Chapter 1, see, "Nonprofit Moneymakers—The Latest in Hybrid Limited Liability Entities.") Many larger profit-making corporations are instituting socially responsible practices and processes and acquiring certifications in an attempt to satisfy a broader range of stakeholders—not only shareholders, but also employees, suppliers, creditors, and members of the community served or impacted by the organization. They commit to maintaining a low carbon footprint, and implementing fair labor practices, socially responsible investment practices, and long-range corporate planning strategies (as opposed to seeking short-term profits regardless of the long-term financial, social, and environmental impact of doing so). Strangely, perhaps, these socially responsible initiatives are being undertaken by large, publicly traded profit-making corporations, and not by midsized or smaller nonprofits. However, if your nonprofit interfaces with one of these sustainability-certified companies, it may be asked to obtain a certification too. More

specifically, if you are deemed to be in the "supply chain" of a certified company as a vendor of services, a creditor, or simply an organization to which it donates money, goods, or services, the certified company may be required, as part of its certification, to make sure you, too, are certified.

On the accounting front, sustainability standards similar to FASB (Financial Accounting Standards Board) rules are being developed by the SASB (Sustainability Accounting Standards Board) so that publicly traded and other entities can report their sustainability metrics to agencies such as the SEC (Securities and Exchange Commission) and to the public. If you interface with an SASB reporting company, you may be asked to prepare and report SASB metrics to it and to the public as well. Look up "SASB" online for more information. For more information on ESG (Environmental, Social, and Governance) disclosure developments, see the FASB, SEC, American Institute of CPAs (AICPA), and Governance and Accountability Institute (G & A Institute) websites. (Type any of these terms in your browser's search box to find more information.)

Although the risk of being held personally liable is small, there are some things a director can and should do to minimize the risk of personal liability. Most importantly, all directors, whether active participants or casual community observers, should attend board meetings and stay informed of, and participate in, all major board decisions. If the board makes a woefully wrongheaded or ill-advised decision that leads to monetary damages, the best defense for any board member is a "No" vote recorded in the corporate minutes.

Also, all boards should try to get an experienced financial manager on their board or use the services of a prudent accountant who demands

regular audited financial statements of the group's books. Legalities aside, what is most likely to put nonprofit directors at risk of personal liability is bad financial management, such as failing to pay taxes, not keeping proper records of how much money is collected and how it is disbursed, and commingling funds, mixing either directors' personal funds with corporate funds or restricted with nonrestricted funds.

Reliance on Regular Business Reports: A Safe Haven

To help directors accomplish their managerial duties, state law as well as IRS regulations and procedures often allow directors to rely on information from reliable, competent sources within the corporation (officers, committees, and supervisory staff), or on outside professional sources (lawyers, accountants, and investment advisers). If this information later turns out to be faulty or incorrect, the directors will not be held personally liable for any decision made in reliance on the information, unless the directors had good reason to question and look beyond the information presented to the board and failed to do so.

For example, if a nonprofit's treasurer tells the board that the organization has sufficient cash to meet ongoing payroll tax requirements, and the report seems reasonable (perhaps because the nonprofit has a budget surplus), the IRS will probably find that the individual board members were entitled to rely on the treasurer's report, even if there is not enough money to pay the taxes. However, if the board knows or should have known that the nonprofit is having a difficult time paying its bills despite reports to the contrary by the treasurer, and the board does not direct the treasurer to make sure to set money aside to pay payroll taxes, the IRS may try to hold board members personally liable for unpaid taxes.

Investment Decisions Involving Corporate Assets

Directors of 501(c)(3) nonprofit corporations must use more caution when making investment decisions than when they decide routine business matters. That's because when they make investment decisions involving corporate funds, directors usually have an added duty of care under state nonprofit law to avoid speculation and protect those funds—a stricter standard of care than the normal standard discussed above. A typical phrasing of this stricter standard of care, known as the directors' fiduciary duty to the corporation, is that the directors must "avoid speculation, looking instead to the permanent disposition of the funds, considering the probable income, as well as the probable safety of the corporation's capital."

> **EXAMPLE:** The treasurer of a performing arts group tells the group's directors that the group has a hefty surplus of funds because of its recent road tour. The board decides to invest this money in a stable asset mutual fund rather than one of several high-risk equity funds that reported double-digit declines in the last several quarters. If challenged by the state attorney general or a complaining member, the directors should be able to show that they've met their fiduciary duty to the corporation: They have attempted to preserve the capital of the corporation by investing in a stable fund with a predictable positive return track record rather than a riskier fund that was more likely to lose money.

Directors Must Be Loyal

A director has a duty of loyalty to the corporation. In most states, this is commonly understood to mean that the director must give the corporation a right of first refusal on business opportunities that the director becomes aware of in his or her capacity as director. If the corporation fails to take advantage of the opportunity after full disclosure, or if the corporation clearly would not be interested in the opportunity, the director can take advantage of the opportunity as an individual.

> **EXAMPLE:** Bob is a volunteer director on the board of Help Hospices, a nonprofit hospice and shelter organization. He agrees to shop around for a low-rent location in a reasonably safe neighborhood for the next nonprofit hospice site. He learns of three low-rent locations, one of which would also be ideal as a low-cost rental studio for his son who wants to move out of his parents' house as soon as possible. Bob reports all three locations to the

board and tells them that he plans to apply for a lease in his son's name on one of the rental units only if the board decides that it is not interested in leasing the space for nonprofit purposes. This type of specific disclosure is exactly what is required for Bob to meet his duty of loyalty to the nonprofit. Bob can apply for the lease for his son if the board gives him the go-ahead after deciding the nonprofit is not interested in leasing the space for itself.

How to Avoid Self-Dealing

Directors must guard against unauthorized self-dealing—that is, involving the corporation in any transaction in which the director has a material, or significant, financial interest—without proper approval. The self-dealing rules and proper approval requirements can arise in many different types of transactions, including the purchase or sale of corporate property, the investment of corporate funds, or the payment of corporate fees or compensation.

The nonprofit corporation laws of most states include special rules for validating self-interested director decisions of this sort. In most cases, the interest of the director must be disclosed prior to voting, and only disinterested members of the board may vote on the proposal.

> **EXAMPLE:** A board votes to authorize the corporation to lease or buy property owned by a director, or to purchase services or goods from another corporation in which a director owns a substantial amount of stock. Either of these could be considered a prohibited self-dealing transaction if not properly disclosed and approved, because a director has a material financial interest in each transaction and neither falls within one of the specific statutory exceptions.

See Article 9 of the bylaws included in this book for specific procedures to follow when approving transactions that benefit directors, officers, employees, or contractors associated with the nonprofit.

Loans and Guarantees

Most states expressly prohibit a nonprofit from making or guaranteeing a loan to a director, or require approval by special disclosure or voting rules. Because of the strict rules prohibiting individuals involved with a non-profit's operations from personally benefiting from the nonprofit, it's easy to see why a loan to a director from tax-exempt funds over which he or she exercises control might appear questionable. We suggest that you carefully review your state's nonprofit statutes before considering approval of loans or guarantees to directors—and, as always, ask a nonprofit lawyer for advice if you have questions.

Director Indemnification and Insurance

In addition to director and officer immunity statutes, most states have director indemnification laws. These laws typically require a corporation to indemnify (reimburse) a director for legal expenses incurred as a result of acts done on behalf of the corporation, if the director is successful in the legal proceeding.

Directors' (and officers') liability coverage (also called errors and omissions coverage) is, of course, one way to insulate directors from possible personal liability for their actions on behalf of the corporation. This type of insurance, however, is normally priced far beyond the reach of the average small nonprofit organization. Rather than worrying about trying to obtain this kind of coverage, it often makes more sense to do everything possible to minimize potential risks that might arise in the pursuit of your nonprofit purposes.

For example, try to make sure that employees perform their work in a safe manner and that anyone required to perform skilled tasks is properly trained and licensed. In addition, the corporation should obtain specific coverage for any likely risks: motor vehicle insurance to cover drivers of corporate vehicles, general commercial liability insurance to cover the group's premises, and so on.

Officers

Most states require a nonprofit corporation to have a president, secretary, and treasurer. Non-profits often appoint additional officers, such as a vice president, or use different titles for their officer positions, such as a chief operating officer instead of president, or chief financial officer instead of treasurer. One person can usually hold two or more offices, but some states prohibit one person from serving simultaneously as both the president and treasurer and/or secretary of the corporation. For proper nonprofit operation (and to help avoid an IRS implication that you are forming a "closely held" nonprofit to serve the interests of a small group of founders), it usually is best to appoint separate people to your nonprofit officer positions.

Duties and Responsibilities

The powers, duties, and responsibilities of officers are specified in the corporation's articles or bylaws, or by resolution of the board of directors. Generally, officers are in charge of supervising and implementing the day-to-day business of the corporation. This authority does not usually include the authority to enter into major business transactions, such as the mortgage or sale of corporate property. These kinds of major transactions are left to the board of directors. If the board wants the officers to have the power to make one or more major business decisions, special authority should be delegated by board resolution.

Officers have a duty to act honestly and in the best interests of the corporation. Officers are considered agents of the corporation and can subject the corporation to liability for their negligent or intentional acts if their acts cause damage and are performed in the scope of their employment.

Officers May Bind the Corporation

Generally, the actions and transactions of an officer are legally binding on the corporation. A third party is entitled to rely on the apparent authority of an officer and can require the corporation to honor a deal, regardless of whether the officer was actually empowered by the board to enter into the transaction. To avoid confusion, if you delegate a special task to an officer outside the realm of the officer's normal duties, it's best to have your board pass a resolution granting the officer special authority to enter into the transaction on behalf of the corporation.

And, of course, any action taken by an officer on behalf of a corporation will be binding if the corporation accepts the benefits of the transaction or if the board ratifies the action, regardless of whether or not the officer had the legal authority to act on the corporation's behalf.

Compensation of Officers

Officers can receive reasonable compensation for services they perform for a nonprofit corporation. It is appropriate to pay officers who have day-to-day operational authority, and not to pay the officers who limit themselves to presiding over the board of directors or making overall nonprofit policy decisions. In smaller nonprofits, it is more common for officers and directors to also assume staff positions and be paid for performing these operational tasks.

EXAMPLE: In a larger nonprofit organization, a paid executive director or medical director (these are staff positions, not board of director posts) might oversee routine operations of a medical clinic, and the paid principal or administrator (also staff positions) will do the same for a private school. However, in a smaller nonprofit, the corporate president or other officer may assume these salaried tasks.

See Article 9 of the bylaws included in this book for specific procedures to follow when approving transactions that benefit directors, officers, employees, or contractors associated with the nonprofit.

Loans, Guarantees, and Immunity Laws

Loans and guarantees to nonprofit officers are either prohibited or very strictly regulated, as they are with directors (see "Loans and Guarantees," above). Officers have a duty to act honestly and in the best interests of the corporation. Officers can be insured or indemnified against personal liabilities, and they can benefit from the same immunity statutes that relieve volunteer, and in some states paid, directors from personal liability for monetary damages. See your state nonprofit statutes before approving loans or guarantees to officers.

Employees

Employees of nonprofit corporations work for and under the supervision of the corporation and are paid a salary in return for their services. Paid directors and officers are considered employees for purposes of individual income tax withholding, Social Security, state unemployment, and other payroll taxes the employer must pay. Employees have the usual duties to report and pay their taxes, and the usual personal liability for failing to do so.

Employee Immunity

Employees are generally not personally liable for any financial loss their acts or omissions may cause to the corporation or to outsiders, as long as they are acting within the course and scope of their employment. If the harm is done to outsiders, it is the corporation, not the employees, which must assume the burden of paying for the loss.

CAUTION

Employees may be personally liable for taxes. An important exception to the rule of employee nonliability concerns the employee whose duty it is to report or pay federal or state corporate or employment taxes. The responsible employee (or officer or director) can be held personally liable for failure to report or pay such taxes. The IRS may take a broad view as to who is responsible for such duties—see "Federal Corporate Tax Returns" in Chapter 10.

Employee Compensation

Salaries paid to officers or regular employees should be reasonable and given in return for services actually performed. A reasonable salary is one roughly equal to that received by employees rendering similar services elsewhere. If salaries are unreasonably high, they are apt to be treated as a simple distribution of net corporate earnings and could jeopardize the nonprofit's tax-exempt status. Nonprofits should avoid paying discretionary bonuses at the end of a good year as it may look like a payment from the earnings and profits of the corporation, a no-no for 501(c)(3) tax-exempt nonprofits. In reality, since the pay scale for nonprofit personnel is usually lower than that of their for-profit counterparts, most of this cautionary advice shouldn't be needed for smaller nonprofits.

Employee Benefits

Among the major advantages associated with being an employee of a corporation are the employment benefits it can provide, such as corporate pension plans, corporate medical expense reimbursement plans, and term life insurance. Generally, amounts the corporation pays to provide these benefits are not included in the employee's individual gross income and therefore are not taxed to the employee. Also, the benefits themselves are often not taxed when the employee receives them.

The nonprofit itself enjoys a tax break when offering benefits in certain situations. Benefits are deductible by a nonprofit corporation if taxes are owed by the corporation in connection with an activity that uses the services of these employees. For example, if a nonprofit generates $20,000 in gross revenue unrelated to its exempt purposes, but pays wages of $10,000 plus benefits of $5,000 to generate this income, its net unrelated business income is reduced to $5,000.

Nonprofits may establish some of the employee benefit plans available to employees of business corporations. The rules are complicated, however. For information on setting up qualified employee plans and other benefits, consult your tax adviser or a benefit plan specialist.

Membership Nonprofits

If a nonprofit corporation establishes a formal membership structure in its articles of incorporation or bylaws, then members of the corporation will be granted basic rights to participate in the affairs and future of the nonprofit corporation. We refer to members who are given these special legal rights as formal members.

It is optional for a nonprofit corporation to have formal members with legal voting rights. To avoid the problems (including the paperwork and expense) of having to put elections of directors and other major corporate decisions to a vote of the members, most smaller nonprofits choose not to have formal membership structures.

Not having formal members is organizationally simpler than adopting a formal membership structure because only the directors are legally entitled to participate in the operation of the corporation. People interested in a non-membership nonprofit, although they may play fundamental advisory roles, need not be notified nor allowed to vote for directors or approve changes to the corporation's articles or bylaws. Normally this works well—because most people become involved in a nonprofit organization out of interest in the group's activities and purposes, or in some cases because they receive attendance privileges or discounts to nonprofit events or programs, not because they wish to participate in the legal affairs of the corporation.

Interested people who work with a nonprofit corporation to help it achieve its goals (and who may pay annual dues or fees) but are not formal members are often called supporters, patrons, contributors, or advisers. For example, a patron may be issued an informal museum membership that entitles the person to free admissions, participation in educational programs and events, use of a special facility, or attendance at exhibition previews, but does not give the person any say as a formal (legal) member in the museum's operation and management. We discuss the decision to set up (or do without) a formal membership structure and show you how to adopt membership or nonmembership bylaws in Chapter 7.

Classes of Membership

If you decide to set up a formal membership structure, you may establish different classes of membership, such as voting and nonvoting membership classes. If so, the rights, privileges, restrictions, and obligations associated with each class of membership must normally be stated in the articles of incorporation. (Again, most smaller corporations are better off without a formal membership structure and won't choose this option.)

Membership Quorum and Voting Rules

Most states allow nonprofits to set their own quorum requirement in the articles or bylaws for members' meetings. If the corporation does not adopt a membership quorum provision, some state statutes set a quorum for members' meetings at a low percentage of the full membership. Other states specify a limit (such as one-third of the membership) below which the quorum cannot be set in any case. Some states simply say that a quorum is the actual number of voting members that attend the meeting (under this circularly phrased rule, a meeting of members can always be held if one or more members show up for the meeting).

Despite this flexibility under state statutes, many membership nonprofits will wish to set the members' quorum requirement at a majority (or some higher percentage) of the voting membership to ensure that representational meetings are attended by a sufficient cross section of the voting membership.

The membership provisions in the bylaws included in this book provide a simple membership balloting procedure that allows members to elect directors and transact other business by mail without a meeting.

TIP

Use proxy voting with large membership groups. Larger membership nonprofits rarely call and hold meetings of the membership with the expectation that members will attend and vote at the meeting in person. Instead, membership proxies (written votes) are usually solicited by mail well in advance of the meeting. The corporate secretary tallies and reports these votes at the membership meeting. The main business of the membership— the reelection of the board—is usually accomplished through this proxy-by-mail or email procedure (or by relying on a specific nomination and balloting by mail procedure authorized by the state's nonprofit corporation statutes).

Unless the articles or bylaws state otherwise, each member is entitled to cast one vote on any matter submitted for approval to the members. Again, it's possible to have several classes of membership with different voting rights attached to each membership.

Formal Membership Rights in a Nonprofit Corporation

A formal (legally recognized) member of a nonprofit corporation is usually entitled, under the state's nonprofit corporation law, to vote on the following matters:

- election and removal of directors
- amendment of articles and bylaws
- approval of merger or consolidation with another corporation
- election to wind up or dissolve the corporation
- sale of corporate assets, and
- approval of a transaction involving an interested director or officer.

Requirements for Section 501(c)(3) Tax Exemption

Corporations, like individuals, are normally subject to federal and state income taxation. One reason to establish a nonprofit corporation is to obtain an exemption from corporate income taxes. Exemption is not automatic—a corporation must apply and show that it is in compliance with nonprofit exemption requirements to receive it. This chapter focuses on the basic federal tax exemption available to nonprofits under Section 501(c)(3) of the Internal Revenue Code and what is required to obtain tax-exempt status under this provision. In Chapter 8, we take you line by line through the federal tax exemption application.

You'll notice in going through the material in this chapter that many IRS tax exemption requirements are broad and seemingly applicable to a wide range of activities, both commercial and noncommercial. In fact, many commercial organizations are engaged in activities that could qualify for 501(c)(3) tax-exempt status. For example, there are for-profit scientific organizations that perform research that could qualify as 501(c)(3) scientific research. Similarly, many commercial publishing houses publish educational materials that could qualify the organization for 501(c)(3) status.

So why do only certain organizations obtain tax-exempt status? Because a corporation must choose to apply for tax-exempt status from the IRS. Many organizations that might be eligible for 501(c)(3) status prefer to operate as commercial enterprises because they do not want to be subject to the moneymaking, profit distribution, and other restrictions applicable to nonprofits. (See Chapter 1 for a discussion of these restrictions). By defining and organizing your activities as eligible for 501(c)(3) status and then seeking tax-exempt status from the IRS, you distinguish your organization from similar commercial endeavors.

Section 501(c)(3) Organizational Test

Under Section 501(c)(3) of the Internal Revenue Code, groups organized and operated exclusively for charitable, religious, scientific, literary, and educational purposes can obtain an exemption from the payment of federal income taxes. The articles of incorporation of a 501(c)(3) corporation must limit the group's corporate purposes to one or more of the allowable 501(c)(3) purposes and must not empower it to engage (other than as an insubstantial part of its activities) in activities that don't further one or more of these tax-exempt purposes. This formal requirement is known as the 501(c)(3) organizational test.

A group can engage in more than one 501(c)(3) tax-exempt activity. For example, a group's activities can be characterized as charitable and educational, such as a school for blind or physically handicapped children.

A nonprofit cannot, however, engage simultaneously in a 501(c)(3) exempt purpose activity and an activity that is exempt under a different subsection of Section 501(c). Thus, a group cannot be formed for educational *and* social or recreational purposes because social and recreational groups are exempt under Section 501(c)(7) of the Internal Revenue Code (see "Is Your Group a Nonprofit That Can Use This Book?" in Chapter 1, for a discussion of non-501(c)(3) tax-exempt groups). As a practical matter, this problem rarely occurs because the non-501(c)(3) subsections are custom-tailored to specific types of organizations, such as war veterans' organizations and cemetery companies.

Valid Purposes Under Section 501(c)(3)

Now let's take a closer look at the most common 501(c)(3) purposes—charitable, religious, scientific, literary, and educational—and the requirements for each of these purposes. In addition to the valid purpose requirements discussed in this section, there are other general requirements that all 501(c)(3) groups must comply with to obtain 501(c)(3) status. These are discussed below in "Other Requirements for 501(c)(3) Groups."

Humane Societies and Sports Organizations

There are other, less commonly used exemptions available under Section 501(c)(3), which we do not cover in this book. For example, groups organized to prevent cruelty to children or animals, or to foster national or international amateur sports competitions, can claim a tax exemption under Section 501(c)(3). However, these groups must meet narrowly defined 501(c)(3) requirements, and, for humane societies, special state requirements. See IRS Publication 557 for specifics on each of these special 501(c)(3) groups and contact your state attorney general's office for special incorporation requirements for humane societies.

Charitable Purposes

The charitable purpose exemption is the broadest, most all-encompassing exemption under Section 501(c)(3). Not surprisingly, it is also the most commonly used exemption.

Benefit to the Public

The word charitable as used in Section 501(c)(3) is broadly defined to mean "providing services beneficial to the public interest." In fact, other 501(c)(3) purpose groups—educational, religious, and scientific groups—are often also considered charitable in nature because their activities usually benefit the public. Even groups not directly engaged in a religious, educational, or scientific activity but whose activities indirectly benefit or promote a 501(c)(3) purpose can qualify as 501(c)(3) charitable purpose groups.

Groups that seek to promote the welfare of specific groups of people in the community (handicapped or elderly persons or members of a particular ethnic group) or groups that seek to advance other exempt activities (environmental or educational) will generally be considered organized for charitable purposes because these activities benefit the public at large and are charitable in nature.

Groups that advance religion, even if they do not have a strictly religious purpose or function, are often considered charitable purpose organizations under Section 501(c)(3). The IRS reasons that the advancement of religion is itself a charitable purpose. Examples of some of these charitable purposes include:

- **Monthly newspaper.** A group that published and distributed a monthly newspaper with church news of interdenominational interest was held to accomplish a charitable purpose because it contributed to the advancement of religion.

- **Coffeehouse.** A nonprofit organization formed by local churches to operate a supervised facility known as a coffeehouse was found to have a valid 501(c)(3) charitable purpose because it advanced religion and education by bringing together college-age people with church leaders, educators, and leaders from the business community for discussions and counseling on religion, current events, social, and vocational problems.

- **Genealogical research.** An organization formed to compile genealogical research data on its family members in order to perform religious observances in accordance with the precepts of their faith was held to advance religion and be a charitable organization under 501(c)(3).

- **Missionary assistance.** A missionary group established to provide temporary low-cost housing and related services for missionary families on furlough in the United States from their assignments abroad was held to be a charitable purpose organization under Section 501(c)(3).

Other examples of activities and purposes that have met the IRS organizational test for charitable purpose (and possibly another 501(c)(3) purpose as well) include:

- relieving the poor, distressed, or underprivileged
- advancing education or science
- erecting or maintaining public buildings, monuments, or works
- lessening the burdens of government
- lessening neighborhood tensions
- eliminating prejudice and discrimination
- promoting and developing the arts
- defending human and civil rights secured by law
- providing facilities and services to senior citizens
- maintaining a charitable hospital
- providing a community fund to support family relief and service agencies in the community
- providing loans for charitable or educational purposes, and
- maintaining a public-interest law firm.

Class or Group of Beneficiaries

A charitable organization must be set up to benefit an indefinite class of people, not particular persons. The number of beneficiaries can be relatively small as long as the benefited class is open and the beneficiaries of the group are not specifically identified.

> **EXAMPLE 1:** A charitable nonprofit corporation cannot be established under Section 501(c)(3) to benefit Jeffrey Smith, an impoverished individual. But Jeffrey Smith can be selected as a beneficiary of a 501(c)(3) charitable group whose purpose is to benefit needy individuals in a particular community (as long as he is a member of that community).

> **EXAMPLE 2:** A foundation that awards scholarships solely to undergraduate members of a designated fraternity was found to be a valid charitable organization under 501(c)(3), even though the number of members in the benefited group is small.

> **EXAMPLE 3:** A nonprofit formed to set up a free wireless local area network to help underprivileged and elderly members of the community connect to their community and get greater access to employment was found not to have a 501(c)(3) charitable purpose. The IRS viewed the nonprofit, which was founded and controlled by a for-profit technology company, as promoting the for-profit corporation's business brand and the commercial interests of businesses where the wireless hotspots would be located.

The following groups, all charitable in nature and benefiting a defined but indefinite group of people, were found to be valid charitable purpose organizations under Section 501(c)(3):

- an organization formed to build new housing and renovate existing housing for sale to low-income families on long-term, low-payment plans

- a day care center for children of needy, working parents

- a group created to market the cooking and needlework of needy women

- a self-help housing program for low-income families

- homes for the aged where the organization satisfies the special needs of an aged person for housing, health care, and financial security. (The requirements for housing and health care will be satisfied if the organization is committed to housing residents who become unable to pay and if services are provided at the lowest possible cost.)

- an organization that takes care of patients' nonmedical needs (reading, writing letters, and so on) in a privately owned hospital

- an organization that provides emergency and rescue services for stranded, injured, or lost persons

- a drug crisis center and a telephone hotline for persons with drug problems, and

- a legal aid society offering free legal services to indigent persons.

Health care nonprofits, whether hospitals or less formal, noninstitutional health care facilities or programs, can qualify as charitable 501(c)(3) organizations. However, the IRS is particularly concerned about conflicts of interest and business dealings between doctors who do work for the nonprofit and also rent space or have other commercial dealings with the nonprofit. The IRS recommends that the health care nonprofit form a community board and have conflict of interest provisions in its bylaws.

The Affordable Care Act added new requirements for charitable hospitals. (See Notice 2010-39 and Notice 2011-52 and ask your tax adviser for more information.)

Services Need Not Be Free

Section 501(c)(3) charitable organizations are not required to offer services or products free or at cost. Nevertheless, doing so, or at least providing services at a substantial discount from the going commercial rate, can help convince the IRS of your group's bona fide charitable intentions. Charging full retail prices for services or products does not usually demonstrate a benefit to the public. Other restrictions applicable to a nonprofit's ability to make money are discussed below in "Other Requirements for 501(c)(3) Groups."

Religious Purposes

For Section 501(c)(3) purposes, religious purpose groups can be either a loosely defined religious organization that practices or promotes religious beliefs in some way or a formal institutional church. Groups formed to advance religion often qualify as charitable purpose organizations under Section 501(c)(3).

Qualifying as a Religious Organization

Traditionally, the IRS and the courts have been reluctant to question the validity or sincerity of religious beliefs or practices held by a group trying to establish itself as a religious purpose organization. As long as the organization's beliefs appear to be "truly and sincerely held" and their related practices and rituals are not illegal or against public policy, the IRS generally does not challenge the validity of the religious tenets or practices. However, the IRS will question the nature and extent of religious activities (as opposed to religious beliefs) if they do not appear to foster religious worship or advance a religious purpose, or if they appear commercial in nature.

> **EXAMPLE:** A group that holds weekly meetings and publishes material celebrating the divine presence in all natural phenomena should qualify as a religious purpose group. However, an organization that sells a large volume of literature to the general public, some of which has little or no connection to the religious beliefs held by the organization, could be regarded by the IRS as a regular trade or business, not as a tax-exempt religious organization.

A religious group need not profess belief in a supreme being to qualify as a religious organization under Section 501(c)(3).

Religious corporations also have the widest flexibility in managing their internal affairs.

Qualifying as a Church

You can also qualify under the 501(c)(3) religious purpose category as a church, but doing so is more difficult than simply qualifying as a 501(c)(3) religious organization. One of the advantages of qualifying as a church is that a church automatically qualifies for 501(c)(3) *public charity status*—a status that all 501(c)(3) groups want to obtain, as we explain later, in Chapter 4.

FORMS AND RESOURCES
The IRS has a guide to assist churches and clergy in complying with the religious purpose requirement of the Internal Revenue Code. You can download the guide, IRS Publication 1828, *Tax Guide for Churches and Religious Organizations* from the IRS website. Most church and religious purpose groups will find the information in this publication extremely helpful when preparing their federal exemption application (see Chapter 8).

Under IRS rulings, a religious organization should have the following characteristics to qualify as a church (not all are necessary but the more the better):

- a recognized creed or form of worship
- a definite and distinct ecclesiastical government
- a formal code of doctrine and discipline
- a distinct religious history
- a membership not associated with any other church or denomination
- a complete organization of ordained ministers
- a literature of its own
- established places of worship
- regular congregations, and
- regular religious services.

Courts have used similar criteria to determine whether or not a religious organization qualifies as a church. In one case, the court looked for the presence of the following "church" factors:

- services held on a regular basis
- ordained ministers or other representatives
- a record of the performance of marriage, other ceremonies, and sacraments
- a place of worship
- some support required from members
- formal operations, and
- satisfaction of all other requirements of federal tax law for religious organizations.

All religious purpose groups that claim church status must complete a special IRS schedule with specific questions on some of the church characteristics listed above. We discuss this tax application and the special IRS schedule for churches in Chapter 8.

Traditional churches, synagogues, mosques, associations, or conventions of churches (and religious orders or organizations that are an integral part of a church and engaged in carrying out its functions) can qualify as 501(c)(3) churches without difficulty. Less traditional and less formal religious organizations may have a harder time. These groups often have to answer additional questions to convince the IRS that they qualify as tax-exempt churches.

> **EXAMPLE:** A nonprofit "online ministry" and "virtual church" that provided ministry materials and services (through online sales) was denied IRS classification as a church because, in the IRS's view, its website did not qualify as a "place of worship," nor did the persons who accessed the website constitute "a congregation assembled for worship."

Some churches stand a greater chance of being audited by the IRS than others. Not surprisingly, the IRS is more likely to examine and question groups that promise members substantial tax benefits for organizing their households as tax-deductible church organizations.

Scientific Purposes

Groups that engage in scientific research carried on in the public interest are also eligible for tax-exempt status under 501(c)(3). Under IRS regulations, research incidental to commercial or industrial operations (such as the normal inspection or testing of materials or products, or the design or construction of equipment and buildings) does not qualify as a scientific purpose under Section 501(c)(3). In an IRS case involving a pharmaceutical company, the company's clinical testing of drugs was held not to be "scientific" under Section 501(c)(3) because the clinical testing in question was incidental to the pharmaceutical company's commercial operations.

Generally, research is considered in the public interest if the results (including any patents, copyrights, processes, or formulas) are made available to the public; that is, the scientific research must be published for others to study and use. Research is also considered in the public interest if it is performed for the United States or a state, county, or city government, or if it is conducted to accomplish one of the following purposes:

- to aid in the scientific education of college or university students
- to discover a cure for a disease, or
- to aid a community or region by attracting new industry, or by encouraging the development or retention of an existing industry.

> **EXAMPLE:** An organization was formed by a group of physicians specializing in heart defects to research the causes and treatment of cardiac and cardiovascular conditions and diseases. The physicians practiced medicine in a private practice facility that was separate and apart from the organization's research facility that was used exclusively for the research program. Although some patients from the physicians' private practice were accepted for the research program, they were selected on the same criteria as other patients. The IRS found that the physician's research group met the scientific purpose organizational test for Section 501(c)(3) purposes.

If you are applying for a scientific exemption under Section 501(c)(3), your federal exemption application (covered in Chapter 8) should show that your organization is conducting public interest research, and you should provide the following information:

- an explanation of the nature of the research
- a description of past and present research projects

- how and by whom research projects are determined and selected, and
- who will retain ownership or control of any patents, copyrights, processes, or formulas resulting from the research.

RESOURCE

For a list of the specific information the IRS requires from scientific groups, see the "Scientific Organizations" section in IRS Publication 557.

Literary Purposes

This is a seldom-used Section 501(c)(3) category because most literary purpose nonprofits are classified as educational by the IRS. Nevertheless, valid 501(c)(3) literary purposes include traditional literary efforts, such as publishing, distribution, and book sales. These activities must be directed toward promoting the public interest as opposed to engaging in a commercial literary enterprise or serving the interests of particular individuals (such as the proprietors of a publishing house). Generally, this means that literary material must be available to the general public and must pertain to the betterment of the community.

A combination of factors helps distinguish public interest publishing from private publishing. If you publish materials that are clearly educational and make them available to the public at cost, or at least below standard commercial rates, then you might qualify as a 501(c)(3) literary purpose organization. However, if your material seems aimed primarily at a commercial market and is sold at standard rates through regular commercial channels, chances are that your literary organization will be viewed by the IRS as a regular business enterprise, ineligible for a 501(c)(3) tax exemption. For example, publishing textbooks at standard rates will probably not qualify as a tax-exempt literary purpose under Section 501(c)(3) because the activity is more private than public in nature. On the other hand, publishing material to promote highway safety or the education of handicapped children is likely to qualify as a bona fide 501(c)(3) literary purpose.

EXAMPLE: A publishing house that only published books related to esoteric Eastern philosophical thought applied for 501(c)(3) literary exemption. Their books were sold commercially but at modest prices. The IRS granted the tax exemption after requesting and reviewing the manuscript for the nonprofit's first publication. The IRS found that the material was sufficiently specialized to render it noncommercial in nature.

Educational Purposes

The type of educational activities that qualify as educational purpose under 501(c)(3) are broad, encompassing instruction both for self-development and for the benefit of the community. The IRS allows advocacy of a particular intellectual position or viewpoint if there is a "sufficiently full and fair exposition of pertinent facts to permit an individual or the public to form an independent opinion or conclusion. However, mere presentation of unsupported opinion is not (considered) educational."

If a group takes political positions, it may not qualify for an exemption (see discussion on political activities in "Other Requirements for 501(c)(3) Groups," below). An educational group that publishes a newsletter with a balanced analysis of issues, or at least with some room devoted to debate or presentation of opposing opinions, should qualify as a 501(c)(3) educational purpose group. If its newsletter is simply devoted to espousing one side of an issue, platform, or agenda, the educational purpose tax exemption may not be granted.

Examples of activities that qualify as educational purpose include:

- publishing public interest educational materials

- conducting public discussion groups, forums, panels, lectures, and workshops

- offering a correspondence course or a course that uses other media, such as television or radio

- operating a museum, zoo, planetarium, symphony, orchestra, or performance group

- serving an educational institution, such as a college bookstore, an alumni association, or an athletic organization, or

- publishing educational newsletters, pamphlets, books, or other material.

Formal School Not Necessary

To qualify as a 501(c)(3) educational organization, a group does not need to provide instruction in traditional school subjects or organize as a formal school facility with a regular faculty, established curriculum, and a regularly enrolled student body.

CAUTION

You may need formal school attributes for other reasons. People setting up nontraditional schools should remember that although they do not need a regular faculty, full-time students, or even a fixed curriculum to qualify for a 501(c)(3) educational purpose tax exemption, as a practical matter, they may need some or all of these things to qualify for state or federal support, participate in federal student loan programs, and obtain accreditation.

Child Care Centers

Providing child care outside the home qualifies as a 501(c)(3) educational purpose under special provisions contained in Internal Revenue Code Section 501(k) if:

- the care enables parent(s) to be employed, and

- the child care services are available to the general public.

A child care facility that gives enrollment preference to children of employees of a specific employer, however, will not be considered a 501(c)(3) educational purpose organization.

Private School Nondiscrimination Requirements

If you set up a 501(c)(3) private school, you must include a nondiscrimination statement in your bylaws and publicize this statement to the community served by the school. This statement must make it clear that the school does not discriminate against students or applicants on the basis of race, color, or national or ethnic origin.

Here is a sample statement taken from *IRS Revenue Procedure 75-50*:

Notice of Nondiscriminatory Policy as to Students

The [name of school] admits students of any race, color, national and ethnic origin to all the rights, privileges, programs, and activities generally accorded or made available to students at the school. It does not discriminate on the basis of race, color, national and ethnic origin in administration of its educational policies, admissions policies, scholarship, and loan programs, and athletic and other school-administered programs.

RESOURCE

Additional information on the history and status of 501(c)(3) private school nondiscrimination requirements is on the IRS website (www.irs.gov), in a tax topic update titled "Private School Update." For further information on IRS private school antidiscrimination rules and procedures, see IRS Revenue Procedure 75-50 and "Private Schools," in IRS Publication 557.

Other Requirements for 501(c)(3) Groups

In addition to being organized primarily for one or more allowable tax-exempt purposes, a nonprofit must not engage in other activities that conflict or substantially interfere with its valid 501(c)(3) purposes. This section discusses some of the requirements that keep a 501(c)(3) from straying too far from its exempt purpose activities. For more information on these unrelated business income rules (discussed generally below in the next section), see *Every Nonprofit's Tax Guide*, by Stephen Fishman (Nolo).

Unrelated Business Activities

To obtain 501(c)(3) status, a corporation cannot substantially engage in activities unrelated to the group's tax-exempt purposes. Or, put differently, your nonprofit corporation can conduct activities not directly related to its exempt purpose as long as these activities don't represent a substantial portion of your total activities. Some unrelated activity is allowed because as a practical matter, most nonprofits need to do some unrelated business to survive. For example, a nonprofit dance group might rent unused portions of its studio space to an outside group for storage. Another nonprofit might invest surplus funds to augment its income.

Most groups need not be overly concerned with this limitation unless activities unrelated to exempt purposes start to involve a significant amount of the group's energy or time, or if these activities produce "substantial" income. If the activities are themselves nonprofit, they should be included in the organization's exempt purposes and classified as related activities. The IRS keeps an eye out for tax-exempt groups that regularly engage in profit-making businesses with little or no connection to their exempt purposes (a church running a trucking company). Business activities necessary to further the group's exempt purposes, such as hiring and paying employees and paying rent for space used for the group's exempt purpose, are considered related activities.

Most new nonprofits work full time simply tending to their exempt purposes and do not explore unrelated moneymaking activities until later, if at all. However, if you plan to engage in unrelated business from the start, be careful. It's hard to pin down exactly when these activities become substantial enough to jeopardize the corporation's tax-exempt status. Also, income derived from unrelated business activities is subject to federal and state corporate income tax, even if it is not substantial enough to affect the group's 501(c)(3) tax-exempt status.

Limitation on Profits and Benefits

A 501(c)(3) nonprofit corporation cannot be organized or operated to benefit individuals associated with the corporation (directors, officers, or members) or other persons or entities related to, or controlled by, these individuals (such as another corporation controlled by a director). In tax language, this limitation is known as the prohibition on private inurement, and means that 501(c)(3) groups can't pay profits to, or otherwise benefit, private interests.

Two specific 501(c)(3) requirements implement this prohibition on self-inurement:

- No part of the net earnings of the corporation can be distributed to individuals associated with the corporation.

- Upon dissolution, the assets of a 501(c)(3) group must be irrevocably dedicated to another tax-exempt group (another 501(c)(3) or a federal, state, or local government for a public purpose).

These federal tax exemption requirements often are mirrored in a state's nonprofit corporation law. Note that the IRS and state law allow a nonprofit to pay reasonable salaries to directors, officers, employees, or agents for services rendered in furtherance of the corporation's tax-exempt purposes.

Excess Benefit Rules

The IRS has adopted strict rules and regulations regarding the payment of money, benefits, or property to nonprofit directors, officers, sponsors, donors, and others associated with the nonprofit. The main purpose for these rules, called the excess benefit rules, is to make sure nonprofit organizations do not pay out lavish benefits or skim off program funds to line the pockets or serve the private interests of individuals associated with the nonprofit. The excess benefit rules are also called the IRS intermediate sanctions, a euphemism that is meant to have an appropriately harsh ring. These rules are contained in Section 4958 of the Internal Revenue Code and Section 53.4958 of the IRS Regulations.

The excess benefit rules apply to individuals associated with 501(c)(3) nonprofit public charities. (As explained more fully in Chapter 4, in all likelihood you will be forming a public charity nonprofit.) The individuals subject to the rules include nonprofit directors, officers, and trustees, as well as major sponsors, donors, or anyone else in a position to exercise substantial influence over the affairs of the nonprofit. The rules also apply to family members and entities owned by any of the individuals subject to the rules.

Under the rules, an excessive benefit transaction is any transaction where the nonprofit gives cash, property, or anything of value to a recipient that exceeds the value of the services performed by the recipient (or the value of any other cash, property, or thing of value given to the nonprofit by the recipient). If a nonprofit pays $100 to an officer who has contributed $75 worth of services, the excess benefit is $25. Of course, the IRS is looking for much bigger numbers, sometimes in the realm of thousands, or hundreds of thousands of dollars worth of extra benefits paid by the nonprofit to directors, officers, consultants, sponsors, and donors.

The sanctions include a tax that must be paid by both the recipient of the excess benefit as well as the nonprofit managers (the directors and executive officers) who approved the excess benefit transaction. The recipient of the excess benefit can be assessed a 25% tax on the excess benefit, and the manager or managers who approved it can be assessed a 10% tax, with a limit on a manager's liability capped at $20,000 per transaction. A director must object to the transaction to be excluded from those considered to have approved it—silence or abstention at a board meeting that results in the excess benefit payment is not a defense. The recipient must repay or return the excess benefit to the nonprofit or the recipient will be charged an additional 200% tax. The message is clear—if you receive an undeserved benefit from your nonprofit, you and others in your nonprofit may have to pay large penalties.

The IRS regulations add detail about the scope and operation of the excess benefit rules. For example, disqualified persons are broadly defined to include all sorts of people paid by or associated with the nonprofit organization. Excess salaries, contract payments, benefits, privileges, goods, services, or anything else of value paid or provided to almost anyone associated with your nonprofit can potentially trigger the excess benefit tax rules.

The regulations also contain a safe harbor provision for deals or decisions that provide an economic benefit to a director, an officer, a contractor, or another key nonprofit person. To qualify for the protection of the safe harbor rule, a number of conditions must be met, including:

- Disinterested members of the board or committee must approve the transaction in advance.

- The decision must be based on "comparability" data reviewed and relied on by the board that shows the property is transferred at fair market value or compensation is paid at a rate similar to that paid by other organizations for comparable services.

- The decision must be documented in the corporate records at the time the transaction is approved.

Falling within the safe harbor provision creates a presumption that your deal or decision was fair. The IRS can rebut this presumption if it obtains evidence to the contrary.

Conflict of Interest Provisions

Article 9 of the bylaws included in this book contains rules and procedures for approving or avoiding conflict of interest transactions, including compensation arrangements. This bylaw provision contains the conflict of interest language recommended by the IRS (included in the sample conflict of interest policy in the instructions to IRS Form 1023). It also has language for the approval of compensation arrangements that attempts to comply with the safe harbor provisions of the excess benefit rules (See Article 9, Section 5). You will need to become familiar with Article 9 of your bylaws and refer to those provisions whenever your board, or a committee of your board, decides to set or increase salaries, enter into contracts, or approve deals with individuals or other organizations.

If you have any question about whether a transaction, contract, or compensation decision, or another economic decision is reasonable or whether it may be outside the safe harbor provisions of the excess benefit rules, ask a nonprofit lawyer for help. The last thing you want to have happen is to subject board members, officers, contractors, sponsors, donors, and others who deal with your nonprofit to the prospect of having to pay back money or the value of benefits previously paid out or provided by your nonprofit plus very hefty taxes, interest, and penalties.

Limitation on Political Activities

A 501(c)(3) corporation is prohibited from participating in any political campaigns for or against any candidate for public office. Participation in or contributions to political campaigns can result in the revocation of 501(c)(3) tax-exempt status and the assessment of special excise taxes against the organization and its managers. (See IRC §§ 4955, 6852, and 7409.)

Voter Education Activities

Section 501(c)(3) groups can conduct certain voter education activities if they are done in a nonpartisan manner (see IRS Revenue Ruling 78-248). If you want to engage in this type of political activity, we recommend you consult an attorney. Your organization can request an IRS letter ruling on its voter education activities by writing to the address listed in IRS Publication 557, Chapter 3, under "Political Activity."

Influencing Legislation

Section 501(c)(3) organizations are prohibited from acting to influence legislation, "except to an insubstantial degree." In the past, courts have found that spending more than 5% of an organization's budget, time, or effort on political activity was substantial. More recently, courts have tended to look at the individual facts of each case. Generally, if a nonprofit corporation contacts, or urges the public to contact, members of a legislative body, or if it advocates the adoption or rejection of legislation, the IRS considers it to be acting to influence legislation.

Lobbying to influence legislation also includes:

- any attempt to affect the opinions of the general public or a segment of the public, and
- communication with any member or employee of a legislative body, or with any government official or employee who might participate in the formulation of legislation.

However, lobbying to influence legislation does not include:

- making available the results of nonpartisan analysis, study, or research

- providing technical advice or assistance to a government body, or to its committee or other subdivision, in response to a written request from it, where such advice would otherwise constitute the influencing of legislation
- appearing before, or communicating with, any legislative body with respect to a possible decision that might affect the organization's existence, powers, tax-exempt status, or the deductibility of contributions to it, or
- communicating with a government official or employee, other than for the purpose of influencing legislation.

Also excluded from the definition of lobbying efforts are communications between an organization and its members about legislation (or proposed legislation) of direct interest to the organization and the members, unless these communications directly encourage members to influence legislation.

> **EXAMPLE:** A housing information exchange keeps its members informed of proposed legislation affecting low-income renters. This should not be considered legislative lobbying activity unless members are urged to contact their political representatives in support of, or in opposition to, the proposed legislation.

In determining whether a group's legislative activities are substantial in scope, the IRS looks at the amount of time, money, or effort the group spends on legislative lobbying. If they are substantial in relation to other activities, 501(c)(3) tax status might be revoked and, again, special excise taxes can be levied against the organization and its managers. (See IRC Section 4912.)

Political Expenditures Test

Under the political expenditures test in IRC Section 501(h), limitations are imposed on two types of political activities: lobbying expenditures and grassroots expenditures. Lobbying expenditures are those made for the purpose of influencing legislation, while grassroots expenditures are those made to influence public opinion.

For examples of these two types of activities, see IRS Publication 557, the "Lobbying Expenditures" section. The monetary limits are different for each of the categories, and the formulas for computing them are somewhat complicated.

If your 501(c)(3) nonprofit elects the political expenditures test, you must file IRS Form 5768, *Election/Revocation of Election by an Eligible Section 501(c)(3) Organization To Make Expenditures To Influence Legislation*, within the tax year in which you wish the election to be effective. This election is also available under similar rules at the state level.

The Alternative Political Expenditures Test

Since it is impossible to know ahead of time how the IRS will assess the substantiality of a group's legislative activity, the IRC allows 501(c)(3) public charities (most 501(c)(3) groups will qualify as public charities—see Chapter 4) to elect an alternative expenditures test to measure permissible legislative activity. Under this test, a group may spend up to 20% of the first $500,000 of its annual expenditures on lobbying, 15% of the next $500,000, 10% of the next $500,000, and 5% of its expenditures beyond that, up to a total limit of $1 million each year.

If your nonprofit corporation plans to do considerable lobbying activity, mostly by unpaid volunteers, then electing the expenditures

test might be a good idea. Why? Because the minimal outlay of money to engage in these activities will probably keep you under the applicable expenditure limits. If you didn't make this election, your 501(c)(3) tax exemption might be placed in jeopardy if the IRS considers your political activities to be a substantial part of your overall purposes and program.

CAUTION

Some groups can't use the political expenditures test. This expenditures test and its provisions for lobbying and grassroots expenditures are not available to churches, an integrated auxiliary of a church, a member of an affiliated group of organizations that includes a church, or to private foundations.

If you plan to engage in more than a minimum amount of political lobbying or legislative efforts, you need to decide whether it is to your advantage to elect the expenditures test based on the facts of your situation. If you find that these alternative political expenditures rules are still too restrictive, you might consider forming a social welfare organization or civic league under Section 501(c)(4) of the Internal Revenue Code, an exemption that requires a different federal exemption application, IRS Form 1024, and does not carry with it all the attractive benefits of 501(c)(3) status (access to grant funds, tax-deductible contributions, and so on). See "Is Your Group a Nonprofit That Can Use This Book?" in Chapter 1 and IRS Publication 557 for further information on 501(c)(4) organizations.

CAUTION

Additional limitations for certain groups. Federally funded groups may be subject to even more stringent political expenditure tests than those discussed here (for example, political activity and expenditure restrictions imposed by the federal Office of Management and Budget).

Political Action Organizations

The IRS can also challenge a 501(c)(3) group's political activities by finding that it is an action organization: one so involved in political activities that it is not organized exclusively for a 501(c)(3) tax-exempt purpose. Under these circumstances the IRS can revoke the organization's tax-exempt status. Intervention in political campaigns or substantial attempts to influence legislation, as discussed above, are grounds for applying this sanction. In addition, if a group has the following two characteristics, it will be classified as an action organization and lose its 501(c)(3) status:

- Its main or primary objective or objectives —not incidental or secondary objectives— may be attained only by legislation or defeat of proposed legislation.

- It advocates or campaigns for the attainment of such objectives rather than engaging in nonpartisan analysis, study, or research and making the results available to the public.

In determining whether a group has these characteristics, the IRS looks at the surrounding facts and circumstances, including the group's articles and activities, and its organizational and operational structure.

The point here is to be careful not to state your exempt purposes in such a way that they seem attainable only by political action. Even if you indicate that your activities will not be substantially involved with legislative or lobbying efforts, the IRS may decide otherwise and invoke this special classification to deny or rescind 501(c)(3) status.

If the IRS classifies a group as an action organization, the group can still qualify as a social welfare group under 501(c)(4).

EXAMPLE: A group that has a primary purpose of "reforming the judicial system in the United States" will likely sound like a political action organization to the IRS, because this sounds like a political goal that must be accomplished mostly by political means. However, if the group rephrases its primary purpose as "educating the public on the efficacy of mediation, arbitration, and other alternative nonjudicial dispute resolution mechanisms," it stands a better chance of having the IRS approve its application, even if it lists some political activity as incidental to its primary educational purpose.

CAUTION

Check the Federal Election Commission (FEC) website. Politically active groups should go to the FEC website at www.fec.gov to read about the ever-changing federal election laws and how they may impact their nonprofit's activities.

RESOURCE

IRS provides illustrations for clarification on what constitutes political campaign activities. IRS Revenue Ruling 2007-41 (included on the Nolo website) has 21 fact situations that help explain when the IRS will and will not consider a group to be conducting unpermitted political campaign activities.

Information for Specific Questions About Your Group's Activities

Even after reading through this chapter, you might still have some questions about whether your specific nonprofit activities meet the IRS definition of educational, charitable, or religious purposes under Section 501(c)(3) of the Internal Revenue Code. Or, after you take a closer look at Chapter 4, you might wonder whether your nonprofit can qualify for special public charity treatment as a school or church.

Answers to these types of questions used to be left to the expertise of highly paid lawyers and tax professionals—this is no longer true. It is remarkably easy to find out more about how the IRS might look at your nonprofit organization when it reviews your tax exemption application. The IRS website disseminates most of the material necessary to answer many technical questions as long as you are persistent enough to search the site thoroughly and uncover the material. Specifically, IRS publications and regulations, as well as the technical manuals the IRS examiners use when reviewing tax exemption applications, are available online.

There is a lot more helpful material on the IRS website, and we encourage you to browse it to learn as much as you'd like about nonprofit organization tax issues.

Following is one way to search the IRS site for nonprofit tax exemption answers.

Go to the main page of the IRS website at www.irs.gov and click the "Charities & Nonprofits" tab. This page contains special nonprofit tax topics, resources, and links to additional information. If you don't find what you're looking for, type a word or phrase in the search box which succinctly describes your question.

Another, more advanced approach is to type "Internal Revenue Manual" in the search box on the home page. This link takes you to a table that lists different sections of the internal IRS procedures manual used by IRS examiners and field agents. It contains a wealth of technical material about IRS procedures, rulings, and policies. Part 7 is the main area of interest for nonprofit groups applying for their 501(c)(3) tax exemption. Select this link, then scroll down the heading list until you see the heading, "7.25 Exempt Organizations Determinations Manual." Click on the link under this heading to "7.25.3, Religious, Charitable, Educational, Etc., Organizations." This chapter contains examples of groups that have and have not qualified under each of the 501(c)(3) tax-exempt purposes.

If you want to learn even more, you can examine any of the IRS rulings and cases that you uncover in your website search. Rulings are compiled in IRS *Cumulative Bulletins,* the most recent of which are available for browsing on the IRS website. Type "Internal Revenue Bulletins" in the search box and then select the volume for the year when the ruling was issued. Scroll through the beginning table of contents to find the page where the ruling begins (the first two numbers of a ruling indicate its year —for example, Ruling 2004-51 was issued in 2004, so you would look at the *Bulletin* for 2004 to find the text of the ruling). Most years have more than one *Bulletin* volume, and some rulings are placed in the next year's volume. It takes persistence to track down rulings, but they can be enormously helpful in understanding why the IRS accepted or rejected a nonprofit organization's application for a 501(c)(3) tax exemption. For more information on doing your own research, see Chapter 11.

RESOURCE

For an in-depth discussion and analysis of the requirements that apply to each type of 501(c)(3) nonprofit, supplemented annually with the latest IRS and court rulings in each area, see *The Law of Tax-Exempt Organizations*, by Bruce R. Hopkins, (John Wiley & Sons, Inc., Hoboken, NJ).

Public Charities and Private Foundations

In this chapter, we explain why it is not enough to simply obtain your 501(c)(3) tax-exempt status—you also need to be recognized as a 501(c)(3) public charity. Getting this extra recognition is essential to make your life as a nonprofit easier to manage. Even though the last thing you may be interested in at this point is delving into more tax technicalities, it will help you enormously to have a general understanding of the distinction between public charity and private foundation tax status before you do your federal tax exemption application. You will understand the importance of some of the most technical questions on the application and you'll know how to answer questions to show you qualify for public charity tax status.

We help you get through this information by explaining the different public charity classifications and requirements in plain English. You don't need to master this material. In fact, many nonprofits let the IRS decide which public charity category works for them. For now, simply read through the information to get a general understanding of the concepts. You can come back to this chapter when you do your federal tax exemption application and reread the sections that apply to you.

How to Start Out as a Public Charity

A new 501(c)(3) group can qualify as a public charity for the first five years if it reasonably expects to receive qualifying public support. We explain how to fill in your 501(c)(3) tax exemption application to apply for public charity status in Chapter 8.

Throughout this chapter, we refer to the Internal Revenue Code sections that apply to the different public charity classifications. You don't need to pay attention to these section references. They will be useful later as references when you prepare your federal tax exemption application.

The Importance of Public Charity Status

The IRS classifies all 501(c)(3) tax-exempt nonprofit corporations as either private foundations or public charities. Initially, most 501(c)(3) corporations are presumed to be private foundations. It's extremely important to understand that your group, too, will initially be viewed as a private foundation. The problem with this classification is that private foundations are subject to strict operating rules and regulations that don't apply to groups classified as public charities. You'll want to get yourself out from under this presumption because, like most 501(c)(3) groups, you would probably find it impossible to operate under the rules and restrictions imposed on private foundations. To avoid this classification, you will want to apply for public charity status when you apply for your federal 501(c)(3) tax exemption.

A few special groups are not presumed to be private foundations and do not have to apply for public charity status—the same groups that are not required to file a 501(c)(3) tax exemption application. We think it's foolhardy in most cases not to apply for, and obtain, official notification from the IRS that you are a public charity. (For a discussion of this issue, see "Do You Need to File Form 1023?" in Chapter 8.)

How to Qualify for Public Charity Status

As explained above, almost all 501(c)(3) nonprofits want to overcome the private foundation presumption and establish themselves as a public charity. There are three basic ways to do this:

- **Form one of the types of nonprofits that automatically qualify.** Particular types of nonprofit organizations, such as churches, schools, or hospitals, automatically qualify for public charity status because of the nature of their activities.

EXAMPLE: A church that maintains a facility for religious worship would most easily obtain automatic public charity status. A church qualifies for recognition as a public charity because of the nature of its activities rather than its sources of support.

- **Derive most of your support from the public.** If your group receives support primarily from individual contributions, government, or other public sources, you can qualify for public charity status as a publicly supported organization.

EXAMPLE: An organization formed to operate a center for rehabilitation, counseling, or similar services that plans to carry on a broad-based solicitation program and depend primarily on government grants, corporate contributions, and individual donations would most likely seek public charity status as a publicly supported organization.

- **Receive most of your revenue from activities related to your tax-exempt purposes.** If your group receives most of its revenue from activities related to its tax-exempt purposes, you can qualify under a special public charity support test (the exempt activities support test) that applies to many smaller nonprofits.

EXAMPLE: An arts group deriving most of its income from exempt purpose activities (lessons, performances, and renting studio facilities to other arts groups) would probably choose the support test. This public charity test, unlike those that apply to publicly supported organizations, allows groups to count income derived from the performance of their exempt purposes as qualified support.

You Can Let the IRS Decide Your Public Charity Classification

It's sometimes hard to figure out whether your organization will meet the public support test or the exempt activities test discussed below. To make this decision, an organization must second-guess future sources of support and tackle quite a few tax technicalities. Fortunately, if you have doubts, the IRS will help. If you are filling out the standard IRS Form 1023 application, simply check a box on the application and the IRS will decide this question for you based upon the financial and program information you submit with your application (see the Chapter 8 instructions to Part X, Line 5(i), of the Standard Form 1023 federal tax exemption application).

Automatic Public Charity Status

The IRS automatically recognizes certain 501(c)(3) groups as public charities because they perform particular services or engage in certain charitable activities. The following groups automatically qualify.

Churches

Religious purpose groups that qualify as churches for 501(c)(3) tax exemption purposes also automatically qualify as public charities. (IRC §§ 509(a)(1) and 170(b)(1)(A)(i).) Qualifying as a church under Section 501(c)(3) is more difficult than qualifying as a 501(c)(3) religious purpose organization. To qualify as a church, the organization must have the institutional and formal characteristics of a church. (See "Religious Purposes" in Chapter 3.) If your religious purpose 501(c)(3) group does not qualify as a church, it can still qualify for public charity status under one of the other public charity tests described below.

Schools

Certain educational institutions that have the institutional attributes of a school automatically qualify as public charities. (IRC §§ 509(a)(1) and 170(b)(1)(A)(ii).) Generally, these are educational organizations whose primary function is to present formal instruction. Such a school usually has a regular faculty and curriculum, a regularly enrolled body of students, and a place where its educational activities are carried on.

This school category for automatic public charity recognition is geared toward primary or secondary preparatory or high schools and colleges and universities with regularly enrolled student bodies. The farther an educational group strays from the institutional criteria mentioned above, the harder it will be for it to qualify as a public charity. This doesn't mean that less structured educational institutions can't automatically qualify for public charity status as schools—it just may be more difficult. Nontraditional groups have a better chance of obtaining automatic public charity status if they have some conventional institutional attributes, such as regional accreditation and a state-approved curriculum. If your educational purpose 501(c)(3) group does not fall within this school category for automatic recognition, it can still qualify for public charity status under the public support test or exempt activities support test, described below.

Hospitals and Medical Research Organizations

Nonprofit health care groups that operate charitable hospitals or facilities and whose main function is to provide hospital or medical care, medical education, or medical research automatically qualify as public charities. (IRC §§ 509(a)(1) and 170(b)(1)(A)(iii).) These charitable hospitals generally have the following characteristics:

- doctors selected from the community at large, who are part of the courtesy staff
- a community-oriented board of directors
- emergency room facilities available on a community access basis
- admission of at least some patients without charge (on a charitable basis)
- nondiscrimination with respect to all admissions (particularly Medicare or Medicaid patients), and
- a medical training and research program that benefits the community.

Other 501(c)(3) health care organizations, such as rehabilitation groups, outpatient clinics, community mental health programs, or drug treatment centers, can qualify as hospitals if their principal purpose is to provide hospital or medical care. A health organization that uses consultation services of certified medical personnel such as doctors and nurses will have an easier time meeting the hospital criteria. The IRS does not, however, recognize convalescent homes, homes for children or the aged, or institutions that provide vocational training for the handicapped as fitting within this public charity category.

Medical education and research organizations do not qualify under these IRC sections unless they actively provide on-site medical or hospital care to patients as an integral part of their functions. Medical research groups must also be directly and continuously active in medical research with a hospital, and this research must be the organization's principal purpose.

Public Safety Organizations

Groups organized and operated exclusively for public safety testing automatically qualify for public charity status. Generally, these organizations test consumer products to determine their fitness for use by the general public. (IRC § 509(a)(4).)

Government Organizations

Certain organizations operated for the benefit of a governmental college or university (e.g., state school) automatically qualify as public charities. (IRC §§ 509(a)(1) and 170(b)(1)(A)(iv).) Most likely, you won't be forming a corporation of this sort, but we mention it because this type of organization is included in the list of public charities on the federal tax exemption application form.

Supporting Organizations

Organizations operated solely for the benefit of, or in connection with, one or more of the above organizations, or publicly supported groups or groups that meet the exempt activities support test (described below in "Public Support Test" and "Exempt Activities Support Test"), are also automatically classified as public charities (except those that benefit a public safety organization). (IRC § 509(a)(3).)

RESOURCE

For further information on organizations listed above, see IRS Publication 557, *Tax-Exempt Status for Your Organization*, "Section 509(a)(1) Organizations." For supporting organizations, see Publication 557, "Section 509(a)(3) Organizations."

Public Support Test

To be classified as a publicly supported public charity, a group must regularly solicit funds from the general community. It must normally receive money from government agencies and/or from a number of different private contributors or agencies. (IRC §§ 509(a)(1) and 170(b)(1)(A)(vi).) The term "normally" has a special meaning in this context, which is explained below. We call this public charity test the public support test because the main requirement is that the organization must receive a substantial portion of its funds from broad-based public support sources.

In general, small nonprofits that expect most of their funding to come from a broad base of some combination of individual and corporate donors and small grants should qualify under this test. Museums, libraries, and community centers that promote the arts should also qualify under this public charity test if they rely on broad-based support from individual members of the community or from various public and private sources. Organizations that expect to rely primarily on a few private sources or occasional large grants to fund their operations will probably not meet the requirements of this section.

Nor will groups who expect to get most of their funding from income they receive from activities related to performing their tax-exempt related activities. These groups, which include some types of small grassroots organizations, would instead qualify under the exempt activities test described below.

To determine whether your group qualifies as a publicly supported public charity, you will need to do some basic math and understand some technical rules. Try not to get overwhelmed or discouraged by this technical material. For now, you can simply read through the information to get a sense of the basic criteria for this test and whether or not you might qualify. You can revisit anything that might seem applicable to you later when you fill in your federal tax exemption application.

More importantly, you may decide to let the IRS figure out which public support test works for you. In most cases, unless you know your nonprofit easily fits within the automatic public charity classification discussed above, the best and easiest approach is to let the IRS decide whether the public support test (covered in this section) or the exempt activities support test (discussed below) works for your nonprofit. After all, the technical experts on the IRS Exempt Organizations Determinations staff know this material inside out. Why not use their expertise and let them apply the public charity support tests to your group's past and projected sources of public support, which you will disclose in your federal tax exemption application?

RESOURCE

For more detailed information on qualifying as a public charity using the public support test, see IRS Publication 557, *Tax-Exempt Status for Your Organization,* "Publicly supported organizations." Also check the IRS website at www.irs.gov under the "Charities & Nonprofits" section for additional information.

How Much Public Support Do You Need?

The IRS will usually consider an organization qualified under the public support test if it meets one of the following tests:

- The group normally receives at least one-third of its total support from governmental units, from contributions made directly or indirectly by the general public, or from a combination of the two (including contributions from other publicly supported organizations).

- The organization receives at least one-tenth of its support from these sources *and* meets an additional "attraction of public support" requirement (we discuss the attraction of public support test, below).

We call this one-third or one-tenth figure public support. To keep your percentage high enough, you'll want the IRS to classify as much of your income as possible as public support (the numerator amount), and keep your total support figure (the denominator amount) as low as possible. This will make your final percentage of public support as high as possible. Of course, the IRS has many rules, and exceptions to the rules, to define public support and total support. We provide a guide to the basic technical terms used, below.

Some basic math must be used to estimate your organization's percentage of support. As we explain later, only certain types of support can be included in the numerator of the fraction—the support funds classified as qualified public support. The denominator of the fraction includes the organization's total support, which includes most sources of support received by the nonprofit. You will want as much support as possible to show up in the numerator as qualified public support. If some support received by the nonprofit does not qualify as public support, then it is better to have the support also excluded from the total support. This will keep the excluded support from reducing your public support percentage, since both the numerator and denominator will be left intact.

What Is Public Support?

Qualified public support (support included in the numerator of the fraction) includes funds from private and public agencies as well as contributions from corporate and individual donors. However, the IRS limits how much qualified support your group can receive from one individual or corporation. Also, some membership fees can be included as qualified support. We discuss these special rules in more detail, below.

What Does "Normally" Mean?

An organization must "normally" receive either one-third or one-tenth of its total support from public support sources. This means that one tax year won't make or break your chances of meeting the test—the IRS bases its decision on five years' cumulative receipts. Your organization will meet either the one-third or one-tenth support test for the current tax year if, during the current tax year and the four prior tax years (five years total), its cumulative public support equals one-third or one-tenth of its cumulative total support.

If your nonprofit meets the support test in the current year (based on support received over the five-year testing period, which includes the current tax year and the previous four tax years), it will be classified as a public charity for the current and the next tax year.

EXAMPLE 1: Open Range, Inc., is a nonprofit organization conducting medical research on the healthful effects of organic cattle ranching. ORI's cumulative total support was $60,000 for Year 1 through Year 5 (the current year), and its cumulative public support was $25,000. The organization will, therefore, be considered a publicly supported public charity for Year 5 and the following tax year. This remains true even if, for one or more of the previous four years or the current tax year (Year 5), public support did not equal one-third of the total support—it's the cumulative total that counts.

EXAMPLE 2: If World Relief, a 501(c)(3) nonprofit, meets the public support test for the current year because of grants and contributions received from the public for the previous four years through the end of current year (the five-year testing period that includes the current year), the nonprofit will be classified as a public charity for the current year and next year. Let's assume that in the next year World Relief fails the support test (using a new five-year testing period). It retains its public charity status for that year because it met the support test in the prior year. But if World Relief also fails the support test again in the following year (using a new five-year testing period), it will lose its public charity status as of the start of that tax year, and will be classified as a private foundation as of the beginning of that tax year.

What Is a "Government Unit"?

Money received from a government unit is considered public support. Government units include federal or state governmental agencies, county and city agencies, and so on. The most common example of governmental support is a federal or state grant.

The 2% Limit Rule

Direct or indirect contributions from the general public are considered public support. Indirect contributions include grants from private trusts or agencies also funded by contributions from the general public, such as grants from Community Chest or the United Way.

However, there is a major restriction applicable to these contributions. The total contributions from one individual, trust, or corporation made during the current year and preceding four tax years can be counted only to the extent that they do not exceed 2% of the corporation's total support for those five years. Contributions from government units, publicly supported organizations, and unusual grants are not subject to this 2% limit. These exceptions are discussed below.

> **EXAMPLE:** If your total support over the current year and previous four-year period was $60,000, then only $1,200 (2% of $60,000) contributed by any one person, private agency, or other source can count as public support.

Note that the total amount of any one contribution, even if it exceeds this 2%, five-year limitation, is included in the corporation's total support. Paradoxically, therefore, large contributions from an individual or private agency can have a disastrous effect on your status as a publicly supported charity. You get to include such contributions as public support

only to the extent of 2% of the current year and previous four years' total income, but the total income figure is increased by the full amount of the contribution. This makes it more difficult for you to meet the one-third or one-tenth public support requirement.

> **EXAMPLE:** On Your Toes, a ballet troupe, received the following contributions from Year 1 through Year 5:
>
> | Year 1 | $10,000 | from individual X |
> |---|---|---|
> | Year 2 | 20,000 | from individual Y |
> | Year 3 | 50,000 | from business Z, a one-owner unincorporated dance supply business |
> | Year 4 | 10,000 | as an additional contribution from individual X |
> | Year 5 | 10,000 | additional contribution from business Z |
> | | $100,000 | Total Support |

All support for the five-year period is from contributions, direct or indirect, from the general public. However, in view of the 2% limit, On Your Toes will have trouble maintaining its publicly supported public charity status. While all contributions count toward total support, only $2,000 (2% x $100,000) from any one contributor counts as public support.

Therefore, the troupe's public support for this period is only $6,000 ($2,000 from each contributor, X, Y, and Z), which falls $4,000 short of the minimum one-tenth public support requirement.

Now, suppose On Your Toes received $2,000 each from 50 contributors over the five-year period. It still has $100,000 total support, but because no one contributor gave more than 2% of the five years' total support, it can count the entire $100,000 as public support.

TIP

Increase your chances of qualifying as a publicly supported public charity. One way to do this is to solicit smaller contributions through a broad-based fundraising program and don't rely constantly on the same major sources. This way, you'll beat the 2% limit and have a better chance of qualifying contributions as public support.

Exceptions to the 2% Limit Rule

There are two major exceptions to the 2% limit, as described below.

Money From Government Units or Publicly Supported Organizations

Contributions received from a government unit or another publicly supported organization are not subject to the 2% limit, except those specifically earmarked for your organization by the original donor.

> **EXAMPLE:** Ebeneezer Sax gives $1 million to National Public Music, a national government foundation that promotes musical arts. NPM then gives your organization the million dollars as a grant. If Sax made the contribution to NPM on the condition that the foundation give it to your organization, it is considered earmarked for you and the 2% limit applies. If not, the limit doesn't apply—and you can count the whole donation as public support.

Except for earmarked contributions or grants, you can rely on large contributions or grants from specific government agencies or other publicly supported organizations every year, since all such contributions will be counted as public support.

Money From Unusual Grants

Another major exception to the 2% limit is for unusual grants from the private or public sector. A grant is unusual if it:

- is attracted by the publicly supported nature of your organization
- is unusual—this means you don't regularly rely on the particular grant and it is an unexpectedly large amount, and
- would, because of its large size, adversely affect the publicly supported status of your organization (as we've seen, because of the 2% limit, large grants can cause trouble).

If a grant qualifies as an unusual grant, you can exclude the grant funds from both your public support and total support figures for the year in which it is given.

> **EXAMPLE:** The National Museum of Computer Memorabilia, Inc., is a nonprofit corporation that operates a museum of computers and artificial intelligence memorabilia. Years 1 through 4 are difficult ones, and the museum raises very little money. But in Year 5, the organization receives an unexpected windfall grant. A look at the receipts helps illustrate the importance of the unusual grant exception. All amounts are individual contributions from the general public unless indicated otherwise:

Year 1	$1,000	from A
Year 2	1,000	from B
Year 3	1,000	from C
Year 4	1,000	from D
	1,000	from E
Year 5	100,000	from Z, a private grant agency
	$105,000	Total Receipts

Assume that the Year 5 grant qualifies as an unusual grant. The total support computation for the five-year period would be:

Year 1	$1,000	from A
Year 2	1,000	from B
Year 3	1,000	from C
Year 4	1,000	from D
	1,000	from E
Year 5	0	the $100,000 grant drops out from total support
	$5,000	Total Support

Because the total support is $5,000, the museum can only count a maximum of 2% times $5,000, or $100, received from any one individual during this period as public support. Therefore, the public support computation for this period looks like this:

Year 1	$100	from A
Year 2	100	from B
Year 3	100	from C
Year 4	100	from D
	100	from E
Year 5	0	the $100,000 contribution also drops out from the public support computation
	$500	Total Support

The museum meets the 10% support test because total public support of $500 equals 10% of the total support of $5,000 received over the five-year period. If the organization also meets the attraction of public support requirement (which must be met by groups whose public support is less than one-third of total support), it will qualify as a publicly supported public charity for Year 5 and Year 6. (If you meet the five-year support test, you qualify as a public charity for the current and next tax years.)

If the $100,000 contribution did not qualify as an unusual grant, the nonprofit would not meet the 10% public support test. Total support would equal total receipts of $105,000; a maximum of 2% times $105,000, or $2,100, from each individual and the grant agency would be classified as public support. Public support received over the five-year period would consist of $1,000 from individuals A, B, C, D, and E and the maximum allowable sum of $2,100 from the grant agency, for a total public support figure of $7,100. The percentage of public support for the five-year period would equal $7,100 divided by $105,000, or less than 7%, and the group would not meet the support test in Year 5. Again, you can see how a large grant can hurt you if it does not qualify as an unusual grant.

Membership Fees as Public Support

Membership fees are considered public support as long as the member does not receive something valuable in return, such as admissions, merchandise, or the use of facilities or services. If a member does receive direct benefits in exchange for fees, the fees are not considered public support. These fees are, however, always included in the total support computation.

What's Not Public Support?

We've already mentioned some sources of support that are excluded because of special circumstances (they exceed the 2% limit or are paid by members in return for something of value). There are additional types of support that are never included as public support. The following types of income are not considered public support and, in some cases, are also not included in the total support figure (in which case they would drop entirely from the percentage of one-third or one-tenth support calculation).

Unrelated Activities and Investment

Net income from activities unrelated to exempt purposes as well as gross investment income, which includes rents, dividends, royalties, and returns on investments, are not considered public support. Both these types of income are added to the total support figure (they stay in the denominator of your one-third or one-tenth support calculation).

Sales of Assets or Performing Tax-Exempt Activity

The following types of income are not considered as public support or part of total support (as with unusual grants, they drop out of both computations):

- **Gains from selling a capital asset.** Generally, capital assets are property owned by the corporation for use in its activities. Note that capital assets do not include any business inventory or resale merchandise, business accounts or notes receivable, or real property used in a trade or business. Gains from selling these noncapital asset items are characterized as gross investment income and are not considered public support, but are added to the total support figure.

- **Receipts from performing tax-exempt purposes.** Examples include money received from admissions to performances of a tax-exempt symphony, fees for classes given by a dance studio, and tuition, or other charges paid for attending seminars, lectures, or classes given by an exempt educational organization.

Since we're dealing with tax laws, you'd probably expect at least one complicating exception. Here it is. If your organization relies primarily on gross receipts from activities related to its exempt purposes (such as an educational

nonprofit that receives most of its support from class tuition), this exempt purpose income will not be considered public support. Instead it will be computed in total support (so it will decrease your percentage of support calculation by making the fraction smaller). If your group falls in this category, it will probably not be able to qualify as a publicly supported public charity and should attempt to qualify under the public charity exempt activities support test, discussed below.

Attraction of Public Support Test

Groups that can't meet the one-third public support requirements can qualify for public charity status if they receive at least one-tenth of their total support from qualified public income sources and meet the additional attraction of public support requirement. Only groups trying to qualify for public charity status using the one-tenth (as opposed to one-third) public support requirements must satisfy this attraction of public support test. The IRS considers a number of factors in determining whether a group meets the test. Only Factor 1, below, must be met; none of the other factors are required.

The IRS looks favorably on organizations that meet one or more of the attraction of public support factors listed below. Meeting as many of these factors as possible will not only help you obtain public charity status, it also shows that you satisfy the basic 501(c)(3) tax-exempt status requirements—namely, that your nonprofit is organized and operated in the public interest and has broad-based community support and participation.

Factor 1. Continuous Solicitation of Funds Program

Your group must continually attract new public or governmental support. You will meet this requirement if you maintain a continuous program for soliciting money from the general public, community, or membership—or if you solicit support from governmental agencies, churches, schools, or hospitals that also qualify as public charities (see "Automatic Public Charity Status," above). Although this factor concerns broad-based support, the IRS allows new groups to limit initial campaigns to seeking seed money from a select number of the most promising agencies or people.

Factor 2. Percentage of Financial Support

At least 10% of your group's total support must come from the public. However, the greater the percentage of public support, the better. Remember that if your public support amounts to one-third or more, you do not have to meet the attraction of public support factors listed in this section.

Factor 3. Support From a Representative Number of People

If your group gets most of its money from government agencies or from a broad cross section of people as opposed to one particular individual or a group with a special interest in your activities, it will more likely meet the attraction of public support requirement.

Factor 4. Representative Governing Body

A nonprofit corporation whose governing body represents broad public interests, rather than the personal interest of a limited number of donors, is considered favorably by the IRS. The IRS is more likely to treat an organization's governing body as representative if it includes:

- public officials
- people selected by public officials

- people recognized as experts in the organization's area of operations
- community leaders or others representing a cross section of community views and interests (such as members of the clergy, teachers, and civic leaders), or
- for membership organizations, people elected under the corporate articles or bylaws by a broad-based membership.

Factor 5. Availability of Public Facilities or Services

If an organization continuously provides facilities or services to the general public, the IRS will consider this favorably. These facilities and services might include a museum open to the public, an orchestra that gives public performances, a group that distributes educational literature to the public, or a senior citizens' home that provides nursing or other services to low-income members of the community.

Factor 6. Additional Factors

Corporations are also more likely to meet the attraction of public support requirement if any of the following apply:

- Members of the public with special knowledge or expertise (such as public officials, or civic or community leaders) participate in or sponsor programs.
- The organization maintains a program to do charitable work in the community (such as job development or low-income housing rehabilitation).
- The organization gets a significant portion of its funds from another public charity or a governmental agency to which it is, in some way, held accountable as a condition of the grant, contract, or contribution.

Factor 7. Additional Factors for Membership Groups Only

A membership organization is more likely to meet the attraction of public support requirement if any of the following apply:

- The solicitation for dues-paying members attempts to enroll a substantial number of people in the community or area, or in a particular profession or field of special interest.

- Membership dues are affordable to a broad cross section of the interested public.

- The organization's activities are likely to appeal to people with some broad common interest or purpose—such as musical activities in the case of an orchestra or different forms of dance in the case of a dance studio.

Exempt Activities Support Test

Don't worry if your Section 501(c)(3) group does not qualify as a public charity either automatically or through the one-third or one-tenth public support test described above. There is another way to qualify as a public charity. The exempt activities support test is likely to meet your needs if your 501(c)(3) group intends to derive income from performing exempt purpose activities and services (IRC § 509(a)(2)).

Although IRS publications sometimes include groups that meet the support test described in this section as publicly supported organizations, we do not in this chapter. For purposes of this chapter, publicly supported organizations are those that qualify under the public support test described above. We use the term "exempt activities support test" in this chapter to describe this test.

For more detailed information on this public charity category, see IRS Publication 557, *Tax-Exempt Status for Your Organization,* "Section 509(a)(2) Organizations."

> **TIP**
>
> **Let the IRS do the work for you.** You can let the IRS do the hard part of deciding how each of the special rules described below applies to your group's anticipated sources of financial support. We show you how to check a box on the federal exemption application to do this. For now, just read through this material and you can come back to a particular section if you need to later when you fill in your IRS tax exemption application.

What Type of Support Qualifies and How Much Do You Need?

To qualify under the exempt activities public charity support test, a 501(c)(3) nonprofit organization must meet two requirements:

1. The organization must normally receive more than one-third of its total support in each tax year as qualified public support. Qualified public support is support from any of the following sources:

   - gifts, grants, contributions (from individuals, corporations, or organizations), or membership fees, and

   - gross receipts from admissions, selling merchandise, performing services, or providing facilities in an activity related to the exempt purposes of the nonprofit organization.

2. The organization also must normally not receive more than one-third of its annual support from unrelated trades or businesses or gross investment income. Gross investment income includes rent from unrelated sources, interest, dividends, and royalties—sources of support far removed from the activities of most small nonprofit organizations. However, it does not include any taxes you pay on income from unrelated businesses or activities—these amounts are deducted before the one-third figure is calculated.

Again, the most important aspect of this test, and the one that makes it appropriate for many 501(c)(3) groups, is that it allows the one-third qualified public support amount to include the group's receipts from performing its exempt purposes. Hence, this public charity classification is appropriate for many self-sustaining nonprofits that raise income from their tax-exempt activities, such as performing arts groups, schools, and other educational purpose organizations, and nonprofit service organizations. School tuition, admissions to concerts or plays, or payments for classes at a pottery studio count as qualified public support under this public charity test.

Support Must Be From Permitted Sources

Qualified public support under this test must come from permitted sources including:

- individuals
- government agencies, and
- other 501(c)(3) public charities—generally, those that qualify as public charities under one of the tests described in "Automatic Public Charity Status" or "Public Support Test," above.

Permitted sources do not include disqualified persons (defined under IRC Section 4946)—people who would be considered disqualified if the organization were classified as a private foundation. These include substantial contributors, the organization's founders, and certain related persons.

Membership Fees and Dues Get Special Treatment

Dues paid to provide support for or to participate in the nonprofit organization, or in return for services or facilities provided only to members, are considered valid membership dues and can be counted in full as qualified public support. On the other hand, fees or dues paid in return for a discount on products or services provided to the public, or in return for some other monetary benefit, are not valid membership fees. However, these payments can still be counted as qualified public support if the fee entitles the member to special rates for exempt purpose activities—in which case the payments would qualify as receipts related to the group's exempt purposes, but the payments may be subject to the 1% or $5,000 limitation, discussed below.

EXAMPLE: People pay $50 to become members of All Thumbs, a nonprofit group dedicated to rebuilding interest in the unitar, a near-extinct one-stringed guitar-like musical instrument. All Thumbs' members are allowed $50 worth of reduced rate passes to all unitar concerts nationwide. Although these fees can't be counted as valid membership fees because they are paid in return for an equivalent monetary benefit (a $50 discount at unitar concerts), they still count as receipts related to the performance of the group's exempt purposes (putting on these concerts is an exempt purpose and activity of the group). Therefore, the fees can be counted by the organization as qualified public support (we assume the fees paid by each individual do not exceed the 1% or $5,000 limitation that applies to exempt purpose receipts, as discussed in the next section, below).

The 1% or $5,000 Limit for Exempt Purpose Income

There is one major limitation on the amount of income from exempt purpose activities that can be included in the one-third qualified public support figure. In any tax year, receipts from individuals or government units from the performance of exempt purpose services that exceed $5,000 or 1% of the organization's total support for the year, whichever is greater, must be excluded from the organization's qualified public support figure. This limitation applies only to exempt purpose receipts and not to gifts, grants, contributions, or membership fees received by the organization.

EXAMPLE: Van-Go is a visual arts group that makes art available to people around the nation by toting it around in specially marked vans. In one tax year, Van-Go derives $30,000 total support from the sale of paintings. The funds are receipts related to the performance of the group's exempt purposes. Any amount over $5,000 paid by any one individual cannot be included in computing Van-Go's qualified public support for the year, although the full amount is included in total support. Of course, if Van-Go's total support for any year is more than $500,000, then the limitation on individual contributions will be 1% of the year's total support, since this figure exceeds $5,000.

Are You Selling Services or Information That the Federal Government Offers for Free?

If your nonprofit plans to sell services or information, check to see if the same service or information is readily available free (or for a nominal fee) from the federal government. If so, you may need to tell potential clients and customers of this alternate source. This rule applies to all tax-exempt nonprofits (including any 501(c)(3) organization, whether classified as a public charity or private foundation). (IRC § 6711.) Failure to comply with this disclosure requirement can result in a substantial fine. For further information on these disclosure requirements, see IRS Publication 557.

Some Gifts Are Gross Receipts

When someone gives money or property without getting anything of value in return, we think of it as a gift or contribution. But when people give a nonprofit money or property in return for admissions, merchandise, services performed, or facilities furnished to the contributor, these aren't gifts. They are considered gross receipts from exempt purpose activities and are subject to the $5,000 or 1% limitation.

EXAMPLE: At its annual fundraising drive, the National Cormorant Preservation League rewards $100 contributors with a book containing color prints of cormorants. The book normally retails for $25. Only $75 of each contribution is considered a gift; the remaining $25 payments are classified as gross receipts from the performance of the group's exempt purposes and are subject to the $5,000 or 1% limitation.

Some Grants Are Gross Receipts

It is sometimes hard to distinguish money received as a grant from exempt purpose gross receipts. The IRS rule is that when the granting agency gets some economic or physical benefit in return for its grant, such as a service, facility, or product, the grant is classified as gross receipts related to the exempt activities of the nonprofit organization. This means that the funds will be subject to the 1% or $5,000 limitation that applies to exempt purpose receipts. Money contributed to benefit the public will be treated as bona fide grants by the IRS, not as exempt purpose receipts. This type of bona fide grant is not subject to the 1% or $5,000 limitation.

EXAMPLE 1: A pharmaceutical company, Amalgamated Mortar & Pestle, provides a research grant to a nonprofit scientific and medical research organization, Safer Sciences, Inc. The company specifies that the nonprofit must use the grant to develop a more reliable childproof cap for prescription drug containers (the results of the nonprofit research will be shared with the commercial company). The money is treated as receipts received by Safer Sciences in carrying out its exempt purposes and is subject to the $5,000 or 1% limitation.

EXAMPLE 2: Safer Sciences gets a grant from the federal Centers for Disease Control and Prevention to build a better petri dish for epidemiological research. Since the money is used to benefit the public, the full amount will be included in the nonprofit organization's qualified public support figure.

Unusual Grants Drop Out of the Support Computation

To be included as qualified support (in the numerator of the support fraction), the support must be from permitted sources. Disqualified persons include founders, directors, or executive officers of the nonprofit. A large grant from one of these sources could undermine the ability of the nonprofit to qualify under this public charity test.

To avoid this result for nonprofits that would otherwise qualify under the exempt activities support test, unusual grants are ignored—that is, they drop out of both the numerator and denominator of the support calculation. (There is a similar exclusion for unusual grants under the public support test, discussed above.) A grant will be classified as unusual if the source of the grant is not regularly relied on or actively sought out by the nonprofit as part of its support outreach program and if certain other conditions are met. If you want to learn more about these unusual grant requirements for groups that qualify as a public charity under the exempt activities support test, see IRS Publication 557.

Rents Related to Exempt Purposes Are Not Gross Investment Income

Rents received from people or groups whose activities in the rented premises are related to the group's exempt purpose are generally not considered gross investment income. This is a good thing. Why? Remember: Under this public charity test, the organization must normally not receive more than one-third of its total support from unrelated trades or businesses or from gross investment income.

EXAMPLE: Good Crafts, Inc., a studio that provides facilities for public education in historic crafts, rents a portion of its premises to an instructor who teaches stained glass classes. This rent would probably not fall into the gross investment income category. However, if the tenant's activities in the leased premises were not related to the nonprofit's purposes, then the rent would be included as gross investment income and, if all the unrelated and investment income of the nonprofit exceeded one-third of its total support, the nonprofit could lose its public charity status under the exempt activities support test.

Keep this exception in mind if your group owns or rents premises with extra space. It may be important to rent (or sublease, if you are renting, too) to another person or group whose activities are directly related to your exempt purposes. (If you're renting, be sure the terms of your lease allow you to sublease; most of the time, you'll need your landlord's permission.)

SEE AN EXPERT

When to consult a tax expert. If you plan to supplement your support with income from activities unrelated to your exempt purposes (as more and more nonprofits must), check with your tax adviser. You'll want to make sure this additional income will not exceed one-third of your total support and jeopardize your ability to qualify under this public charity category.

There's That Word "Normally" Again

To qualify as a public charity under the support test, groups must "normally" meet the one-third qualified support requirements set forth in "Public Support Test," above. As with publicly supported organizations, this means that the IRS looks at the total amount of support over the current tax year and previous four years to decide if the organization meets the support text for the current tax year. (See "What Does 'Normally' Mean?" above.)

Private Foundations

Initially, the IRS will classify your 501(c)(3) corporation as a private foundation. As we mentioned at the beginning of this chapter, almost all nonprofits will want to overcome this presumption and establish themselves as a public charity instead. Because you are probably interested in public charity status, you can skip this section or read through it quickly if you want learn about private foundations and the operating limitations and restrictions applicable to them. If you want to form a private foundation, you can use this book as an introduction to the subject, but you will probably also need the help of a nonprofit

lawyer or tax specialist with experience setting up private foundations. The rules that apply to private foundations are very complicated and the penalties for not obeying the rules are stiff.

RESOURCE

Need more information on private foundations? See IRS Publication 4221-PF, *Compliance Guide for 501(c)(3) Private Foundations*, available at the IRS website at www.irs.gov.

Background

Broadly speaking, the reason that private foundations are subject to strict operating limitations and special taxes, while public charities are not, is to counter tax abuse schemes by wealthy individuals and families. Before the existence of private foundation restrictions, for example, a person with a lot of money could set up his own 501(c)(3) tax-exempt organization (such as The Jonathan Smith Foundation) with a high-sounding purpose (to wipe out the potato bug in Northern Louisiana). The potato bugs, though, were never in any danger, because the real purpose of the foundation was to hire all of Jonathan Smith's relatives and friends down to the third generation. Instead of leaving the money in a will and paying heavy estate taxes, Jonathan Smith neatly transferred money to the next generation tax free by use of a tax-exempt foundation that just happened to hire all of his relatives.

To prevent schemes such as this, Congress enacted the private foundation operating restrictions, special excise taxes, and other private foundation disincentives discussed in the next section.

Operating Restrictions

Private foundations must comply with operating restrictions and detailed rules, including:

- restrictions on self-dealing between private foundations and their substantial contributors and other disqualified persons

- requirements that the foundation annually distribute its net income for charitable purposes

- limitations on holdings in private businesses

- provisions that investments must not jeopardize the carrying out of the group's 501(c)(3) tax-exempt purposes, and

- provisions to assure that expenditures further the group's exempt purposes.

Violations of these provisions result in substantial excise taxes and penalties against a private foundation and, in some cases, against its managers, major contributors, and certain related persons. Keeping track of and meeting these restrictions is unworkable for the average 501(c)(3) group, which is the main reason why you'll want to avoid being classified by the IRS as a private foundation.

Limitation on Deductibility of Contributions

Generally, a donor can take personal income tax deductions for individual contributions to private foundations of up to only 30% of the donor's adjusted gross income. Donations to public charities, on the other hand, are generally deductible up to 60% of the donor's adjusted gross income (AGI). With exceptions, the federal CARES Act raised the limit to 100% for 2020.

Of course, the overwhelming number of individual contributors do not contribute an amount even close to the 30% limit, so this limitation is not very important. The real question of importance to contributors is whether you are a qualified 501(c)(3) organization so that charitable contributions to your group are tax deductible.

RESOURCE

For more on IRS rules about deduction limitations. IRS Publication 526, *Charitable Contributions*, discusses the rules limiting deductions to private foundations (called 30% limit organizations) and public charities (60% limit organizations), including special rules that apply to donations of real estate, securities, and certain types of tangible personal property. You can search for qualifying 501(c)(3) organizations (both public charities and private foundations) and other qualified groups eligible to receive tax-deductible charitable contributions using the IRS Tax Exempt Organization Search tool, which can be found online at www.irs.gov/charities-non-profits/tax-exempt-organization-search.

Special Types of Private Foundations

The IRS recognizes two special types of private foundations that have some of the advantages of public charities: private operating and private nonoperating foundations. We mention them briefly below because they are included in IRS nonprofit tax publications and forms. Few readers will be interested in forming either of these special organizations.

Private Operating Foundations

To qualify as a private operating foundation, the organization generally must distribute most of its income to tax-exempt activities and must meet one of three special tests (an assets, a support, or an endowment test). This special type of 501(c)(3) private foundation enjoys a few benefits not granted to regular private foundations, including the following:

- **More generous deductions for donors.** As with public charities, individual donors can deduct up to 60% of adjusted gross income for contributions to the organization.

- **Extended time to distribute funds.** The organization can receive grants from a private foundation without having to distribute the funds received within one year (and these funds can be treated as qualifying distributions by the donating private foundation).

- **No excise tax.** The private foundation excise tax on net investment income does not apply.

All other private foundation restrictions and excise taxes apply to private operating foundations.

Private Nonoperating Foundations

This special type of private foundation is one that either:

- distributes all the contributions it receives to public charities and private operating foundations (discussed just above) each year, or

- pools its contributions into a common trust fund and distributes the income and funds to public charities.

Individual contributors to private nonoperating foundations that make qualifying distributions can deduct their donations up to 60% of their AGI. However, these organizations are subject to all excise taxes and operating restrictions applicable to regular private foundations.

Other Tax Benefits and Reporting Requirements

In this chapter we discuss additional federal tax issues that affect nonprofits, such as the deductibility of contributions made to 501(c)(3) nonprofits and what happens if a 501(c)(3) makes money from activities not related to its tax-exempt purposes. We also cover nonprofit tax benefits and tax and nontax requirements that apply to 501(c)(3) nonprofits under state law.

Federal and State Tax Deductions for Contributions

A donor (corporate or individual) can claim a personal federal income tax deduction for contributions made to a 501(c)(3) tax-exempt organization. These contributions are called charitable contributions. Generally, states follow the federal tax deductibility rules for charitable contributions made to nonprofit corporations.

Corporations can make deductible charitable contributions of up to 10% of their annual taxable income. Individuals can deduct up to 60% of their adjusted gross income (AGI) in any year for contributions made to 501(c)(3) public charities and to some types of 501(c)(3) private foundations, as explained in Chapter 4. Donations to most types of private foundations are limited to 30% of an individual's adjusted gross income in each year.

What Can Be Deducted

A donor can deduct the following types of contributions:

- **Cash.**
- **Property.** Generally, donors can deduct the fair market (resale) value of donated property. Technical rules apply to gifts of appreciated property (property that has increased in value) that may require donors to decrease the deduction they take for donating appreciated property—see IRS Publication 526, *Charitable Contributions*, "Giving Property That Has Increased in Value."
- **Unreimbursed car expenses.** These include the cost of gas and oil incurred by the donor while performing services for the nonprofit organization.
- **Unreimbursed travel expenses.** These include expenses incurred by the donor while away from home and performing services for the nonprofit organization, such as the cost of transportation, meals, and lodging.

What Cannot Be Deducted

Certain types of gifts cannot be deducted as charitable contributions. Nondeductible gifts include:

- **The value of volunteer services.** For example, if you normally are paid $40 per hour for bookkeeping work, and you volunteer ten hours of your time to a nonprofit to help them prepare their annual financial statements, you cannot claim a charitable deduction for the value of your time donated to the nonprofit (you can't claim a charitable deduction of $400).
- **The right to use property.** If you rent out office space for $1,000 per month and allow a nonprofit to use one-tenth of the total space for a small office, you cannot claim a charitable deduction of $100 per month for letting the nonprofit use the space for free.
- **Contributions to political parties.** These contributions, however, can be taken as a tax credit, subject to dollar and percentage limitations.
- **Direct contributions to needy individuals.**
- **Tuition.** Even amounts designated as donations, which must be paid in addition to tuition as a condition of enrollment, are not deductible.

- Dues paid to labor unions.
- The cost of raffle, bingo, or lottery tickets, or other games of chance.
- Child care costs paid while performing services for a nonprofit organization.

Donations That Can Be Partially Deducted

Contributions that a nonprofit receives in return for a service, a product, or another benefit (such as membership fees paid in return for special membership incentives or promotional products, or donations charged for attending a performance) are only partially deductible. Donors may deduct for these only to the extent that the value of the contribution exceeds the fair market value of the service, product, or benefit received by the donor.

> EXAMPLE: If a member of a 501(c)(3) organization pays a $30 membership fee and receives a record album that sells for $30, nothing is deductible. But if a $20 product is given in return for the $30 payment, $10 of the fee paid is a bona fide donation and may be deducted by the member as a charitable contribution.

501(c)(3) nonprofit groups should always clearly state the dollar amount that is deductible when receiving contributions, donations, or membership fees in return for providing a service, product, or discount or another benefit to the donor.

Reporting Requirements

Individuals can claim deductions for charitable contributions by itemizing the gifts on IRS Schedule A and filing this form with their annual 1040 income tax return. IRS rules require donors to obtain receipts for all charitable contributions claimed on their tax returns. Receipts must describe the contribution and show the value of any goods or services received from the nonprofit by the donor as part of the transaction. See IRS publications mentioned below for more information on how to prepare donor receipts for your organization.

RESOURCE

The IRS requirements for deducting and reporting charitable contributions change from year to year. For current information, see IRS Publication 526, *Charitable Contributions*. For information on valuing gifts, see IRS Publication 561, *Determining the Value of Donated Property*.

Federal Estate and Gift Tax Exemptions

Gifts made as part of an individual's estate plan (through a will or trust document) can be an important source of contributions for 501(c)(3) nonprofits. When the individual dies, the 501(c)(3) organization receives the money and the money is excluded from the taxable estate of the individual. This can provide significant tax savings for donors. Hence, many people are motivated to engage in estate planning, including making charitable gifts to nonprofit organizations.

Traditionally, colleges and universities and larger environmental and health organizations have actively solicited estate charitable giving by providing information to members and donors about estate planning and the benefits of charitable bequests. Increasingly, smaller nonprofits are starting to understand the game and are pursuing similar strategies in their fundraising efforts. If you understand how charitable giving affects the donor's taxes, you'll be better able to persuade potential donors to give to your cause.

CAUTION

Check with your tax adviser for the latest estate and gift tax rules; they change often.

Generally, an individual does not pay taxes on gifts made during his or her lifetime. However, gifts to an individual (who isn't the giver's spouse) or to a nonqualified organization will reduce the donor's unified estate and gift tax credit to the extent the gifts exceed a set amount each year (the current gift tax exclusion rules are posted on the IRS website). On the other hand, gifts made to a 501(c)(3) nonprofit that qualifies as a public charity (even if they exceed the exclusion amount) do not reduce this federal and estate gift tax credit. Hence, tax-wise you might be better off giving the money to a literary nonprofit that, in turn, gives grants to promising writers, rather than directly donating the money to a writer. (Unfortunately, you may not earmark the money donated to a literary nonprofit for a particular writer, as explained in "Charitable Purposes," in Chapter 3.) There are many twists and turns to finding the best way to gift funds to deserving individuals and organizations. Consult a knowledgeable tax adviser or financial planner before deciding on a charitable or estate gifting plan.

RESOURCE

For further information on federal and state estate and gift taxes and individual estate planning techniques, see *Plan Your Estate*, by Denis Clifford (Nolo).

Federal Unrelated Business Income Tax

All tax-exempt nonprofit corporations, whether private foundations or public charities, may have to pay tax on income derived from activities unrelated to their exempt purposes. The first $1,000 of unrelated business income is not taxed. After that, the normal federal corporate tax rate of 21% applies.

CAUTION

Be careful with unrelated income. As explained in "Unrelated Business Activities," in Chapter 3, if unrelated income is substantial, it may jeopardize the organization's 501(c)(3) tax exemption.

Activities That Are Taxed

Unrelated business income comes from activities that are not directly related to a group's exempt purposes. An unrelated trade or business is one that is regularly carried on and not substantially related to a nonprofit group's exempt purposes. It is irrelevant that the organization uses the profits to conduct its exempt purpose activities.

EXAMPLE 1: Enviro-Home Institute is a 501(c)(3) nonprofit organized to educate the public about environmentally sound home design and home construction techniques. Enviro-Home develops a model home kit that applies its ideas of appropriate environmental construction and is very successful in selling the kit. The IRS considers this unrelated business income because it is not directly related to the educational purposes of the organization.

EXAMPLE 2: A halfway house that offers room, board, therapy, and counseling to recently released prison inmates also operates a furniture shop to provide full-time employment for its residents. This is not an unrelated trade or business because the shop directly benefits the residents (even though it also produces income).

Activities That Are Not Taxed

A number of activities are specifically excluded from the definition of unrelated trades or businesses. These include activities in which nearly all work is done by volunteers, and those that:

- are carried on by 501(c)(3) tax-exempt organizations primarily for the benefit of members, students, patients, officers, or employees (such as a hospital gift shop for patients or employees)

- involve the sale of mostly donated merchandise, such as thrift shops

- consist of the exchange or rental of lists of donors or members

- involve the distribution of low-cost items, such as stamps or mailing labels worth less than $5, in the course of soliciting funds, and

- involve sponsoring trade shows by 501(c)(3) groups—this exclusion extends to the exempt organization's suppliers, who may educate trade show attendees on new developments or products related to the organization's exempt activities.

Some of these exceptions have been hotly contested by commercial business interests at congressional hearings. The primary objection is that nonprofits receive an unfair advantage by being allowed to engage, tax free, in activities that compete with their for-profit counterparts. Expect more hearings and future developments in this volatile area of nonprofit tax law.

Also excluded from this tax is income not derived from services (termed gross investment income in the Internal Revenue Code). Remember, this tax applies to unrelated activities, not necessarily to unrelated income. Examples of nontaxable income include:

- dividends, interest, and royalties

- rent from land, buildings, furniture, and equipment (some forms of rent are taxed if the rental property was purchased or improved subject to a mortgage, or if the rental income is based on the profits earned by the tenant), and

- gains or losses from the sale or exchange of property.

See Section 512(b) of the Internal Revenue Code for the complete list of these untaxed sources of income and the exceptions that exist for certain items.

SEE AN EXPERT

It is often difficult to predict whether the IRS will tax an activity or income as unrelated business. Furthermore, IRS regulations and rulings and U.S. Tax Court decisions contain a number of rules classifying specific activities as unrelated businesses that are subject to tax. In short, you should do more research or consult a tax specialist if you plan to engage in activities or derive income from sources not directly related to your exempt purposes. Please note, this isn't the same thing as saying you shouldn't engage in an unrelated activity—many nonprofits must engage in commercial businesses unrelated to their exempt purposes to survive. But to avoid jeopardizing your 501(c)(3) tax-exempt status and to understand the tax effects of engaging in unrelated business, you simply need good tax advice.

State Corporate Income Tax Exemptions

Most states have a corporate income tax, but nonprofit groups are eligible to apply for an exemption in all cases. Fortunately, in the overwhelming majority of states, there is little or nothing to do, as state authorities will rely on your federal 501(c)(3) exemption determination as proof that you are also entitled to a state corporate income tax exemption.

In many states, a nonprofit corporation that has received its federal exemption is automatically exempt from state corporate income taxes. A few states exempt nonprofits if they file nonprofit articles with the secretary of state (obtaining a federal tax exemption is not necessary to obtain the state tax exemption).

Some states require you to notify the department of revenue or complete a separate exemption application, but their decision is based on the federal determination. Finally, only a handful of states make an independent evaluation of nonprofit purposes, activities, and financial statements to determine whether to grant an exemption.

Generally, a corporation that has filed for its federal tax exemption need not pay state corporate income taxes prior to receiving a federal determination, which can take a few months or more in special cases. If the federal application is denied—and the state exemption determination is based upon obtaining the federal exemption—the corporation may have to pay the state income taxes it would have paid as a for-profit corporation while the application was pending. Check with a tax adviser for the rules in your state.

Even if your organization receives a state tax exemption, it may still be required to file an informational tax return yearly. For forms and information about your state's exemption requirements, contact your state tax agency online.

Also keep in mind that just as at the federal level, there are state taxes on unrelated business income generated by a regular activity that has nothing to do with your exempt purposes. If you will have unrelated business income, you might wish to see a tax accountant in your state to be certain about your state corporate tax liabilities and necessary state filings.

 TIP

Don't forget about state unrelated business income taxes. Like the IRS, each state with a corporate income tax scheme normally will assess regular state corporate income tax on income earned by a nonprofit within the state from activities that are unrelated to the nonprofit's tax-exempt purposes. Your state tax office can provide the specific details of your state's unrelated business income tax.

Other State Taxes

Each state imposes additional taxes that may apply to your nonprofit activities and operations. In many cases, your tax-exempt 501(c)(3) can apply for an exemption from one or more of these additional taxes.

Most states have enacted a sales tax. Some states exempt nonprofits from payment when purchasing goods. Only a few exempt nonprofits from collecting sales tax when selling goods, and then only under restricted circumstances, such as fundraising events—bake sales, crafts fairs, benefit dinners, or performances, for example—that take place occasionally during the year.

In addition, a nonprofit corporation may be eligible to apply for exemption from state and local use, excise, and property taxes, hotel and meal taxes, and business license fees.

Some States Require an Advance Tax Payment

In a small number of states, incorporators must make a franchise tax, a trust fund, or another advance payment when filing nonprofit articles of incorporation with the secretary of state. Check with your state tax agency by going to its online website.

Contact your state's tax agency online to learn more about your tax responsibilities—and exemption possibilities.

State Solicitation Regulations

Fundraising is a way of life for most nonprofit organizations, which must depend either on public or private grants, or on contributions solicited from the general public, for all operating funds. This activity—solicitation of contributions from the general public by a 501(c)(3) public charity—is regulated by most states.

Generally, state regulation of charitable solicitations is meant to serve two purposes:

- to curb fundraising abuses by monitoring the people involved and their activities, and

- to give the public access to information on how much an organization spends to raise whatever ultimately goes into funding its charitable, educational, religious, or other nonprofit purposes.

A majority of states require groups that solicit within the state to register, usually with the attorney general. Most of these states also require the registration of paid fundraisers and solicitors, both the people who administer the programs and those who go door-to-door or use the telephone or other media to solicit money. A registration fee, a bond, or both, may also be required for solicitors, ranging from as little as $15 to $800 or more.

The U.S. Supreme Court has decided several cases affecting how much information solicitors must disclose about their methods of solicitation and what happens to the money they collect. At present, states may require professional solicitors to tell prospective donors where to check for financial information on their campaigns, including what percentage of the money collected actually goes to charity, but fundraisers needn't submit scripts of their pitches to the state for review.

In addition to solicitor regulation, many states have detailed contribution reporting requirements, and demand information on the amount spent (on paid solicitors, advertising and promotion, mailings, and so on) to raise the total amount solicited. The organization may have to supply this information either annually or for each individual fundraising campaign.

While large-scale fundraising operations—those that use telemarketing and massive direct mail solicitation—are the targets of these regulations, all organizations must comply with these rules. Find out what your obligations are by checking with your city government. At the state level, the attorney general's office is usually in charge of solicitation registration; if not, find out from your secretary of state what registration and reporting requirements, if any, you must meet.

Regulation of charitable solicitation is currently an active area of both legislation and litigation. At the federal level, the Federal Trade Commission (FTC) participates in litigation against fraudulent multistate charitable solicitation schemes. Many state legislatures have enacted laws or tightened existing ones regulating charitable solicitation.

RESOURCE

For more information on fundraising registration requirements, see *Nonprofit Fundraising Registration: Nolo's 50-State Digital Guide,* by Stephen Fishman and Ronald Barrett (Nolo).

Exceptions to State Solicitation Regulations

Typically, grants, unrestricted gifts, bona fide membership fees, and payments for goods and services not received in connection with a solicitation are exempted from state solicitation rules and regulations.

State Nonprofit Corporate Report Requirements

Nonprofit corporations in most states must periodically file reports with the secretary of state, in effect reregistering their existence. Generally this is an annual report, but in a few states a report is required less frequently.

The contents of the state corporate report—generally submitted on a form supplied by the secretary of state—vary. Most states want only a simple recital of minimal information to confirm that a corporation is still operating, under the same name, at the same address, and for the purposes stated in its articles of incorporation.

Sometimes the names and addresses of directors and/or officers must be included, and the report must be signed by one of these people. Many states also collect a filing fee with the annual report.

A few states, however, require more detailed financial and other information, such as:

- salaries, loans, guarantees, and other payments or benefits made to or conferred on directors and officers

- the amount of money invested in real or personal property in the state, or

- a complete financial statement listing all assets and liabilities, revenues and receipts, and expenses and disbursements (except for the smallest nonprofits; your accountant or treasurer should prepare a balance sheet and income statement at least annually).

Each state has its own filing date or period; you can get this information from your secretary of state. Although completing the corporate report is a mere formality in most states, requiring the submission of very little information, compliance is important. Failing to file may, in some cases, result in the imposition of a fine and the suspension of corporate powers by the secretary of state.

PART

2

Incorporating Your Nonprofit

Choose a Name and File Your Articles of Incorporation

This chapter shows you how to form your nonprofit corporation in a sequence of small, manageable steps. Fortunately, most incorporation steps are relatively easy and straightforward. For the most part, you will fill in blanks on standard incorporation forms based on information you already have at your fingertips. Take your time and relax—you'll be surprised at how easy it all is when you follow our instructions one step at a time.

TIP

Forming your corporation will be the first step you take to obtain nonprofit status. Your corporation must be in existence when you apply for your federal tax exemption. We recommend, however, that before you file your articles, you read through and prepare some of the other documents required later in the process, such as your bylaws and tax exemption application. That way you'll know what is required to complete the process before you form your corporation. (See the discussion in "Check Your State Filing Office Website," below.)

Because the content and format of certain corporate documents differ from state to state, it's essential that you contact your secretary of state or another corporate official to obtain official incorporation forms and information. We show you how to do this. We provide sample clauses, forms, and information designed to show you how to use this state-specific information to prepare your nonprofit incorporation forms.

As you begin the process of forming your corporation, we suggest that you use the Incorporation Checklist, in Appendix C (or, access the checklist file online at the Nolo website; see Appendix A for the link). This will help you chart your way through the incorporation steps in Chapters 6 through 10 and can greatly simplify the incorporation process for you.

Nonprofit Nomenclature

Different states use different words in their nonprofit statutes, regulations, and bureaucracies. We have tried to use the most common terms to describe nonprofit forms, procedures, and officials. For example, we refer to the charter document used to form the nonprofit corporation as the articles of incorporation. In some states, this document is given another name such as the certificate of incorporation. Similarly, we refer to the office that handles corporate filings as the secretary of state's office—this is the official designation used in most states for this function. Just keep in mind that your state may occasionally use different corporate terminology than we use in the text.

CAUTION

We strongly recommend you go to the IRS website, at www.irs.gov, and browse IRS Form 1023-EZ, the streamlined tax exemption application many groups will be able to use, IRS Form 1023, the regular 501(c)(3) exemption application, IRS Form 990, the annual exempt organization information return, and the instructions to these forms. Looking over the forms will give you a sense of the amount of organizational and financial work required to form a tax-exempt nonprofit. We help you get through the exemption application in Chapter 8, but you will need all the additional help and expertise you can get to be able to gather and report the detailed program, fundraising, and financial data required on the annual 990 return and its associated schedules. We are not trying to scare you off—we just want you to make a realistic assessment of your ability to handle the required level of record keeping and reporting before you form your nonprofit.

Setting up procedures to assemble and report the required information on your annual federal 990 return is one of the prices you pay for tax exemption (unless you are exempt from filing a 990 return). Your workload will be lessened if you qualify to file Form 990-EZ.

View Materials From Your Secretary of State

To get started, you will need to view nonprofit incorporation information and forms provided by your secretary of state's office. You can go online to your state's filing office to see your state's nonprofit forms, instructions, and other information.

Most states' corporate filing office websites provide a nonprofit articles of incorporation form with instructions for filling it in, and a link to the nonprofit corporation statutes that contain the technical requirements for organizing and operating a nonprofit corporation in your state. In most states, the nonprofit laws are contained in a separate nonprofit statute or act. In a few states, the nonprofit laws are mixed in with, and can be obtained as part of, the state's regular business corporation act or law. In Appendix B we explain how you can locate your state's statute online. This is the fastest and most efficient way to access your state's nonprofit law. You may need to refer to these statutes when completing your articles of incorporation and corporate bylaws.

Most secretary of state's websites also provide:

- a fee schedule showing current charges for filing, copying, and certifying various corporate forms
- forms and instructions to check corporate name availability and reserve a corporate name, and
- forms and instructions for postincorporation procedures. These may include materials to amend articles, change the corporation's registered office or registered agent, or register an assumed corporate name (one that is different from the corporate name shown in the incorporation papers).

Many states also allow you to check name availability, reserve a corporate name, and prepare and file your articles online. If your state's website provides these services, we recommend you use them as an efficient alternative to using the mail.

To Obtain Your Nonprofit Material

Check your state's website. The site probably has everything you need online.

You can call your secretary of state for special questions. The phone number of the corporations division or similar office in your state is listed on the state corporate filing office website.

Choose a Corporate Name

Your first step in forming your corporation is to choose a name that you like and one that also meets the requirements of state law. The state corporate filing office (typically the secretary of state) will approve your corporate name when you file your articles of incorporation. As explained more below, you can check name availability and reserve a corporate name before you file your articles.

The Importance of Your Corporate Name

As a practical matter, your corporate name is one of your most important assets. It represents the goodwill of your organization. We don't use the term goodwill here in any legal, accounting, or tax sense; rather, your name is significant because people in the community and at grant agencies and other nonprofits, and those with whom you do business will identify your nonprofit primarily by its name. For this reason, as well as to avoid having to print new stationery, change promotional literature, or create new logos, you should pick a name you'll be happy with for a long time.

> ### Keeping or Changing Your Name
>
> If you are incorporating an existing organization, you may want to use your current name as your corporate name, particularly if it has become associated with your group, its activities, fundraising efforts, products, or services. Many new corporations do this by simply adding "Inc." to their old name (for example, The World Betterment Fund decides to incorporate as The World Betterment Fund, Inc.). Using your old name is not required, however. If you have been thinking about a new name for your organization, this is your chance to change it.

Corporate Name Legal Requirements

Let's look at the basic legal name requirements applicable in most states for nonprofit corporations.

Your Name Must Be Unique

Your proposed corporate name (the name stated in your articles of incorporation) must not be the same as, or confusingly similar to, a name already on file with the secretary of state.

The list of names maintained by the secretaries of state includes:

- existing corporations formed in your state
- out-of-state corporations qualified to do business in your state
- names reserved for use by individuals planning to incorporate in your state (name reservation periods vary from 30 to 120 days and often can be renewed at least once)
- names registered in your state by out-of-state corporations, and
- in some states, names registered as trademarks or service marks and those registered as assumed corporate names (we discuss these special types of business names below).

In deciding whether a corporate name is too similar to one already on file, the secretary's office will usually look only at similarities between the names themselves, not at similarities in the types and locations of the businesses using the names. If you attempt to form a corporation with a name that is similar in sound or wording to the name of another corporation on the corporate name list, the secretary's office may reject your name and return your articles of incorporation to you.

EXAMPLE: Your proposed corporate name is Open Spaces Society, Inc. If another corporation has filed the name Open Spaces International, Inc., with the secretary of state, your name will probably be rejected as too similar.

Corporate Designator Requirements

In many states, your corporate name must include a corporate designator, such as Incorporated, Corporation, Company, Limited, or one of their abbreviations.

Although corporate designators are typically included at the end of a corporate name (The Foundation for Health, Incorporated), the designator may generally be placed anywhere in your corporate name (The Incorporated Healthcare Foundation).

RESOURCE

Corporate name requirements. See the instructions to your state's articles form to determine the nonprofit corporate name requirements in your state.

Prohibited Names

The statutes of various states forbid the use of specific words in the name of a nonprofit corporation. Mostly, prohibited names are those associated with specialized business, nonprofit, professional or governmental entities, or corporations. Try to avoid names from each of these categories—here are several examples of specialized corporate names whose use is limited by state laws:

Accounting	Insurance
Attorney	Physician
Banking	Reserve
Cooperative	Trust
Engineering	United States
Federal	

Of course, if you are forming a specialized nonprofit corporation, such as a consumers' or producers' cooperative or a nonprofit organization named "Solar Engineering Data Sciences" that collects research on solar engineering, you may be entitled to use one of these special words in your corporate name.

Using Two Names and Changing Your Name

If you want to adopt a formal corporate name in your articles that's different than the one you have used (or plan to use) to identify your nonprofit organization, you can do so. You'll need to file a fictitious business name statement (also known as an assumed business name statement or a dba statement in some states) with the local county clerk.

You can also change your corporate name after you've filed your articles. After making sure that the new name is available for use (as explained further, below), you can amend your articles and file the amendment with the secretary of state.

> **CAUTION**
>
> **Having your name approved by the corporate filing office when you file your articles of incorporation does not guarantee that you will have the absolute legal right to use that name.** As explained in more detail below, another organization or business may already be using the name as its business name or may be using it as a trademark or service mark. If someone else is using the name, that organization may be able to prevent you from using it, depending on its location, type of business, and other circumstances. We show you how to do some checking on your own to be relatively sure that no one else has a prior claim to your proposed corporate name based on trademark or service mark.

Practical Suggestions When Selecting a Name

Now that we've looked at the basic legal requirements related to your choice of a corporate name, here are some practical suggestions to help you do it.

> **RELATED TOPIC**
>
> **For a listing of these special tax-exempt nonprofit groups and a brief description of each group,** see IRS Publication 557, Chapter 4, "Other Section 501(c) Organizations."

Use Common Nonprofit Terms in Your Name

There are a number of words that broadly suggest 501(c)(3) nonprofit purposes or activities. Choosing one of these names can simplify the task of finding the right name for your organization and will alert others to the nonprofit nature of your corporate activities. Here are just a few:

Aid	Human
American	Humane
Appreciation	Institute
Assistance	International
Association	Learning
Benefit	Literary
Betterment	Mission
Care	Music
Center	Orchestra
Charitable	Organization
Coalition	Philanthropic
Community	Philharmonic
Congress	Program
Conservation	Project
Consortium	Protection
Council	Public
Cultural	Refuge
Education	Relief
Educational	Religious
Environmental	Research
Exchange	Resource
Fellowship	Scholarship
Foundation	Scientific
Friends	Service
Fund	Shelter
Health	Social
Help	Society
Heritage	Study
Home	Troupe
Hope	Voluntary
Hospice	Welfare
Hospital	

Names to Avoid

When selecting a corporate name, we suggest you avoid, or use with caution, the types of words described in this section. Of course, there are exceptions. If one of these words relates to your particular nonprofit purposes or activities, it may make sense to use the word in your name.

Avoid words that, taken together, signify a profit-making business or venture, such as Booksellers Corporation, Jeff Baxter & Company, Commercial Products, Inc., or Entrepreneurial Services Corp.

Avoid words that describe or are related to special types of nonprofit organizations (those that are tax exempt under provisions of the IRC other than Section 501(c)(3)), such as Business League, Chamber of Commerce, Civic League, Hobby, Recreational or Social Club, Labor, Agricultural or Horticultural Organization, Political Action Organization, Real Estate Board, or Trade Group.

These Names Are Already Taken

Here is a small sampling of some well-known —and off-limits—nonprofit names and abbreviations:

AAA

American Ballet Theatre or ABT

American Conservatory Theater or ACT

American Red Cross

Audubon

Blue Cross

Blue Shield

Environmental Defense Fund

National Geographic

National Public Radio or NPR

Public Broadcasting System or PBS

Sierra Club

EXAMPLE: The name Westbrook Social Club, Inc., would clearly identify a social club, tax exempt under IRC Section 501(c)(7). For this reason, you shouldn't use this type of name for your 501(c)(3) nonprofit. However, The Social Consciousness Society might be an appropriate name for a 501(c)(3) educational purpose organization. Also, although The Trade Betterment League of Pottersville would identify a 501(c)(6) business league, and The Millbrae Civic Betterment League a 501(c)(4) civic league, The Philanthropic League of Castlemont might be a suitable name for a 501(c)(3) charitable giving group.

Avoid words or abbreviations associated with nationally known nonprofit causes, organizations, programs, or trademarks. You can bet that the well-known group has taken steps to protect its name as a trademark or service mark. Steer clear of the names in "These Names Are Already Taken," above.

Avoid words with special symbols or punctuation that might confuse the secretary of state's computer name search software, such as: @ # $ % ^ & * () + ? > or <.

Pick a Descriptive Name

It's often a good idea to pick a name that clearly reflects your purposes or activities (for example, Downtown Ballet Theater, Inc.; Good Health Society, Ltd.; or Endangered Fish Protection League, Inc.). Doing this allows potential members, donors, beneficiaries, and others to easily locate and identify you. More fanciful names (The Wave Project, Inc., or Serendipity Unlimited, Inc.) are usually less advisable because it might take a while for people to figure out what they stand for, although occasionally their uniqueness can provide better identification over the long term.

EXAMPLE: Although the name Northern Counties Feline Shelter, Inc., will alert people at the start to the charitable purposes of the nonprofit group, Cats' Cradle, Inc., may stay with people longer once they are familiar with the activities of the organization.

Limit Your Name Geographically or Regionally

If you use general or descriptive terms in your name, you may need to further qualify it by geographic or regional descriptions to avoid conflicts or public confusion.

EXAMPLE 1: Your proposed name is The Philharmonic Society, Inc. Your secretary of state rejects this name as too close to a number of philharmonic orchestras on file. You refile using the proposed name, The Philharmonic Society of East Creek, and your name is accepted.

EXAMPLE 2: Suppose you are incorporating the Diabetes Support Group, Inc. Even if this name does not conflict with the name of another corporation on file in your state, it is still a good idea to limit or qualify the name to avoid confusion by the public with other groups in other parts of the country that share the same purposes or goals. You could do this by changing the name to the Diabetes Support Group of Middleville.

Choose a New Name Instead of Trying to Distinguish Yourself

Instead of trying to distinguish your proposed name from another established group by using a regional or other identifier, it's usually better to choose a new and different name if the public is still likely to confuse your group with the other group.

EXAMPLE: Your proposed nonprofit name is The Park School, Inc. If another corporation (specializing in a nationwide network of apprentice training colleges) is already listed with the name Park Training Schools, your secretary of state may reject your name as too similar.

You may be able to limit your name and make it acceptable (The Park Street School of Westmont, Inc.) but this may not be a good idea for two reasons: First, members of the public who have heard of the Park Training Schools might think that your school is simply a Westmont affiliate of the national training program. Second, you might still be infringing the trademark rights of the national group (they may have registered their name as a state or federal trademark).

Check Name Availability

The secretary of state will reject your articles of incorporation if the name you've chosen for your corporation is not available. Any name already being used by another corporation on file with the secretary of state's office is considered unavailable. To avoid having your articles rejected, it's often wise to check if the name you want is available before you try to file your articles.

Check Online or by Phone

In many states, you can check corporate name availability online by going to the state filing office website, or you can call the main number of the corporate filings office listed on the state website and ask to speak to someone in the corporate name availability section.

If your proposed corporate name is not the same as or similar to an existing name listed online, you may decide it's safe to go ahead and file your articles without formally checking name availability or reserving your name with the secretary of state. If you discover a match to your proposed name, and the corporation is still active (the name search tells you whether the corporation is active or not), you need to look for another name. If you discover a similar corporate name, the secretary of state may find that it is too similar to your proposed name to let you use it. The only way to tell whether the secretary of state will allow you to use a name that is similar to an existing corporate name is to do a formal name availability check or try to reserve the name. If the secretary of state reports that the name is not available or won't reserve it for your use, you know the name was too similar to the existing corporation's name.

Do You Want to Bypass Name Checking Procedures?

Even if your proposed corporate name is available when you check with the secretary of state, this does not guarantee that your name will be available when you later file your articles of incorporation. For this reason, you may wish to dispense with a written name availability check and attempt to reserve your corporate name, as explained below, or file your articles and hope that your name is available for use.

Filing your articles without preliminary name checking or reservation makes sense if your state allows you to form your corporation online—if your proposed name is unavailable, the website will tell you. Also, if your state offers an expedited (24-hour) filing procedure for a small additional fee, you'll know in a day or two if your proposed name is available and if your articles were filed. Of course, if your state allows you to check a proposed corporate name online or over the phone, we suggest you take the time to do this in all cases.

TIP

Don't use an LLC name for your corporation. Even though the corporate filing office may let you use a corporate name that conflicts with an LLC name, we advise against doing this. To avoid legal disputes, it's best to stay clear of any business name (whether a corporate, an LLC, or an unincorporated business name) that is the same as or similar to your proposed corporate name. The fact that an LLC name has a different ending than your corporate name (for example, "Racafrax, LLC" and you want to use "Racafrax" as your corporate name) does not mean you will be allowed to use your proposed name. If the names are substantially similar, a court may stop you from using your proposed name, even if you use it for a corporation and the competing business name is used by an LLC.

What to Do When There's a Name Conflict

If using your proposed name is crucial to you and the secretary of state's office tells you that it is too similar to an existing corporate name already on file, there are a few things you can do, as explained below.

Appeal the Decision

You can ask the corporate filing office's legal counsel to review the staff's determination regarding your name's acceptability. This will involve filing a written request, and you may decide to seek the help of a lawyer. Here's why: The legal question of whether or not a name is so close to another name so as to cause confusion to the public is a difficult one, and involves looking at a number of criteria contained in court decisions. Factors such as the nature of each trade name user's business (the term trade name simply means a name used

in conjunction with the operation of a trade or business), the geographical proximity of the two businesses, and other factors work together in ways that are difficult to predict. We cover trade name issues in more detail below but, for now, we simply note that if you do get into this sort of debate, you will probably want to see a lawyer who is versed in the complexities of trade name or trademark law or do some additional reading on your own.

Get Permission

An obvious resolution would be to obtain the written consent of the other corporation. Sometimes, profit corporations that have registered a name similar to the proposed name of a nonprofit corporation will be willing to allow the nonprofit corporation to use the similar name. We think this is too much trouble. Besides, most businesses jealously guard their names, and it is unlikely any business or organization will let you ride on the coattails of its existing name. If you are told your proposed corporate name is too similar to another name, we recommend you move on and choose another name that is available for your use.

Pick Another Name

You may decide that it's simpler (and less trouble all the way around) to pick another name for your nonprofit corporation. We usually recommend this approach.

CAUTION

A name check is just a preliminary indication of the availability of your proposed corporate name. Don't order your stationery, cards, or office signs until the secretary of state has formally accepted your name by approving a reservation of corporate name or filing your articles of incorporation.

Reserve Your Corporate Name

Most states allow you to reserve an available corporate name with the secretary of state. During the reservation period, only you may file articles with this name or a similar name. The reservation period and the fees vary. In many states, you can renew your reservation if you don't get around to filing your articles during the first reservation period.

Once you have decided on a corporate name and established its availability, it makes sense to reserve it if you will not be filing your articles immediately for two reasons:

- Available corporate names are becoming hard to find, particularly in states with a lot of corporate filing activity.

- Reserving a name allows you to hold on to it while you complete your initial paperwork.

To reserve a corporate name, follow the instructions on your secretary of state website —most states provide an online reservation of name form, which you can download. Some even let you reserve your name online and pay for the reservation by credit card. If you have no information, call the corporations filings office of your secretary of state and ask for instructions. If the secretary does not provide a form, you can use the reservation of corporate name letter, shown below.

FORMS AND RESOURCES

You can download a copy of the Application for Reservation of Corporate Name form from the Nolo website; see Appendix A for the link. Appendix C includes a blank copy of the form.

CAUTION

Reservation fees are subject to change. To be sure the fee amounts are correct, call your secretary of state's office or check current fee information at your state's website.

CAUTION

The person who signs the letter must also sign the articles. Make sure that the person signing this reservation letter will be available to sign articles of incorporation on behalf of your organization: The corporate name is reserved for this person's use only.

Perform a Name Search

Approval by the secretary of state's office doesn't necessarily mean that you have the legal right to use a name; it simply means that your name does not conflict with that of another corporation already on file with the secretary of state and that you are presumed to have the legal right to use it within your state. Another organization (corporate or noncorporate, for-profit or nonprofit) may, in fact, already have the legal right to use this same name as a federal or state trademark or service mark used to identify its goods or services. Most secretaries of state do not check state trademark/service mark registration lists to see if your proposed corporate name is available; none check the federal trademark register. Also, another organization may already be presumed to have the legal right to the name in a particular county if it is using it as a trade name (as the name of its business or organization) and has filed an assumed (or fictitious) business name statement with its county clerk. The secretaries of state of many states do not register or check assumed names, even assumed corporate names; this is most often done at the county level.

Who Needs to Do a Name Search

In many circumstances, you will know that your name is unique and unlikely to infringe on another organization's name. This would probably be the case, for example, if you called your group the Sumner County Crisis Hotline, or the Southern Wisconsin Medieval Music

Application for Reservation of Corporate Name

[Date] _____

[Name and address of secretary of state office] _____

_____

_____

Re: Corporate Name Reservation

Please reserve the following corporate name for my use for the allowable period specified under the state's corporation statutes.

[your proposed corporate name] _____

I enclose the required payment of $ ____[fee]_____. My name, address, and phone number are included below if you wish to contact me regarding this request.

Name: _____

Address: _____

Phone: _____

Thank you for your assistance.

[your signature] _____

Society. By qualifying your name this way, you know that you are the only nonprofit in your area using the name. However, in some circumstances you may be less sure of your right to use a name. For example, the names Legal Rights for All or The Society to Cure Lyme Disease may be in use by a group in any part of the country.

Who Gets to Use a Name

The basic rule is that the ultimate right to use a particular name will usually be decided based on who was first in time to actually use the name in connection with a particular trade, business, activity, service, or product. In deciding who has the right to a name, the similarity of the types of businesses or organizations and their geographical proximity are usually taken into account.

Do Your Own Search

Below we list self-help name-checking procedures you may want to use to be more certain that your proposed corporate name is unique. Use these name search procedures before you file your articles. Obviously, you can't be 100%

certain—you can't possibly check all names in use by all other groups. However, you can check obvious sources likely to expose names similar to the one you wish to use. Here are some places to start:

- **State and county assumed business name files.** Your secretary of state website should indicate whether assumed (or fictitious) corporate names (different from the name a corporation uses in its articles) are registered with your secretary of state's office, at the county level, or both. If they are registered at the state level, call the assumed name section at the secretary of state's office and ask whether your proposed corporate name is the same as or similar to a registered assumed (or fictitious) corporate name. Also, call your local county clerk's office to ask how you can check assumed business name filings. In most states, noncorporate assumed or fictitious business name statements, or "doing business as" (dba) statements, are filed with the county clerk's office. In most cases, you will have to go in and check the assumed business name files in person and it takes just a few minutes to do this.

- **State trademarks and service marks.** Call the trademark section of your secretary of state's office and ask if your proposed corporate name is the same as or similar to trademarks and service marks registered with the state (some offices may ask for a written request and a small fee before performing this search).

- **Directories.** Check major metropolitan phone book listings, nonprofit directories, business and trade directories, and other directories to see if another company or group is using a name similar to your proposed corporate name. Large public libraries keep phone directories for many major cities throughout the country, as well as trade and nonprofit directories. A local nonprofit resource center or business branch of a public library may have a special collection of nonprofit research materials—check these first for listings of local and national nonprofits. One commonly consulted national directory of nonprofit names is the *Encyclopedia of Associations* published by Gale Research Company (www.gale.cengage.com).

- **Trademark Database.** If your name is the type that might be used to market a service or product or to identify a business activity of your nonprofit corporation, you should check federal trademarks and service marks. You can check the United States Patent and Trademark Office's trademark database for free at www.uspto.gov. You can also go to a large public library or special business and government library in your area that carries the *Federal Trademark Register*, which lists trademark and service mark names broken into categories of goods and services.

- **Internet databases.** Most of the business name listings mentioned above, including yellow page listings, business directory databases, and the federal and state trademark registers, are available as part of several commercial computer databases. For example, the federal and state registers can be accessed through the TrademarkScan databases using SAEGIS, Dialog, or Westlaw online services. (Use your browser's search engine to find links to these services.) Subscription databases charge fees for your research time (unlike the www.uspto.gov site, which is free).

Outside Help

Of course, if you wish to go farther in your name search, you can pay a private record search company to check various databases and name listings. Alternatively, or in conjunction with your own efforts or search procedures, you can pay a trademark lawyer to oversee or undertake these searches for you (or to render a legal opinion if your search turns up a similar name). Most organizers of smaller nonprofits, particularly those who believe that a specialized or locally based name is not likely to conflict with anyone else's name, will not feel the need to do this and will be content to undertake the more modest self-help search procedures mentioned above.

The Consequences of Using Another's Name

To avoid problems, we suggest using the name selection techniques and performing the kind of commonsense checking described earlier. Disputes involving trade names, trademarks, and service marks tend to arise in the private, commercial sector. It is unlikely that your nonprofit will wish to market products and services as aggressively as a regular commercial concern and thereby run afoul of another business's trademark or service mark (you'd also be jeopardizing your tax-exempt status by engaging in a substantial amount of commercial activity). Nonetheless, as a matter of common sense, and to avoid legal disputes later on, you should do your best to avoid names already in use by other profit and nonprofit organizations, or in use as trademarks or service marks.

Legal remedies for violation of trade name or trademark rights vary under federal and state laws and court decisions. Most of the time, the business with the prior claim to the name can sue to enjoin (stop) you from using your name or can force you to change it. The court may also award the prior owner money damages for loss of sales or goodwill caused by your use of the name. If you violate a trademark or service mark registered with the U.S. Patent and Trademark Office, the court may award treble damages (three times the actual money damages suffered as a result of the infringement), any profits you make from using the name, and court costs; and may order that the goods with the offending labels or marks be confiscated and destroyed.

EXAMPLE: A company called Foul Weather Gearheads has been in business for ten years selling foul weather gear such as rain slicks and hip boots via catalogs and the Internet. For the first seven to eight years, Foul Weather averaged gross annual sales of approximately $2 million. Another company, calling itself Rainy Day Gearheads, starts selling competing products, and Foul Weather's gross revenues slip by about 25% over the next two years. If Foul Weather can prove that the Rainy Day Gearheads trademark likely caused customer confusion that resulted in Foul Weather's decrease in sales, Foul Weather can recover its lost profits. Or if, prior to the infringement, Foul Weather had registered its name on the Principal Trademark Register maintained by the U.S. Patent and Trademark Office, it could choose to go after Rainy Day's profits (instead of recovering its own losses), attorneys' fees, and treble damages.

RELATED TOPIC

For further information, see *Patent, Copyright & Trademark: An Intellectual Property Desk Reference*, by Richard Stim (Nolo).

Protect Your Name

Once you have filed your articles of incorporation, you may want to take some additional steps to protect your name against later users. For example, if your name is also used to identify your products or services, you may wish to register it with your state of incorporation and the United States Patent and Trademark Office as a trademark or service mark. You may also want to register in other states if you plan to conduct operations there.

Applying for a Federal Trademark

To apply for a federal trademark, go to the website of the Patent and Trademark Office (PTO) at www.uspto.gov and download a trademark application. Fill out the form following the instructions. A month or so after mailing the form, you should hear from the PTO. If there are any problems, you will receive a written list of questions together with the telephone number of a trademark examiner. The examiner should be able to address any questions and issues you can't handle yourself and should help you finalize your application without undue difficulty or delay.

You can register your name with the U.S. Patent and Trademark Office if either of the following apply:

- You have actually used the name in interstate commerce (that is, in two or more states) in connection with the marketing of goods or services.
- You intend to use the name in interstate commerce in connection with the marketing of goods or services.

If you specify the second ground in your trademark application, you must file an affidavit (sworn statement) within six months stating that the name has been placed in actual use—and pay an additional fee. This six-month period may be extended for additional six-month periods (at an additional fee for each extension), up to a total extension of two-and-one-half years. To obtain these extensions, you have to convince the Patent and Trademark Office that you have good cause for delaying your use of the name. Because trademark application procedures are relatively simple and inexpensive, you may wish to tackle this task yourself; your local county law library should have practice guides available to help you handle state and federal trademark and service mark filing formalities.

Prepare Your Articles of Incorporation

The next step in organizing your nonprofit corporation is to prepare articles of incorporation. This is your primary incorporation document: Your corporation comes into existence on the date you file your articles with your secretary of state. You must complete this step before you send in your federal tax exemption application because the IRS requires a filed copy of your articles with your tax exemption application.

Check Your State Filing Office Website

Most secretaries of state provide sample or ready-to-use forms for articles of incorporation that meet the statutory requirements. You can download these forms from their websites. Before you do anything else, check your state's corporate filing office website. Here's what you may find:

- **Sample articles forms and instructions.** Many secretaries of state provide a sample articles form with instructions. You will need to retype your final form using the format and content of the sample form.
- **Ready-to-use articles.** Some states provide a form that you can print, fill in, and file with the secretary of state. Instructions for filling in the blanks are often provided on the printed form.
- **Online filing.** Some states let you prepare and file articles online. If this option is available, we suggest you use it—it's fast and efficient.

- **Links to nonprofit statutes.** Most state web-sites provide a link to the state's nonprofit corporation laws.
- **Filing checklist.** Some websites include a checklist showing both the filing require-ments and some common reasons for rejection of articles. This information can help you comply with some of the less obvious substantive and formal require-ments of your secretary of state's office (such as whether you can show a P.O. box as an address, how to properly sign and acknowledge the form, how much space to leave at the top of the first page for the secretary's file stamp, and so on).

RESOURCE

If you prefer to form your nonprofit corporation through an online service, you can use Nolo's Online Nonprofit formation service. This easy-to-use service includes preparation and filing of the articles of incorporation with your secretary of state's office, minutes of the first meeting of the board of directors, and more. For additional information, see Nolo's website (www.nolo.com/lander/entry/np/nonprofit-name).

Some States Require Special Nonprofit Articles Forms

Some states classify nonprofit corporations as public benefit, religious, or mutual benefit corporations and provide a separate articles form for each type of nonprofit; others provide one form and ask you to specify the type of nonprofit you are organizing. (See your state's filing office website for instructions on completing any special articles form.) In these states, most 501(c)(3) tax-exempt nonprofit corporations organized for charitable, educational, literary,

or scientific purposes are classified as public benefit corporations. Religious purpose 501(c)(3) nonprofits are, naturally, classified as religious corporations. The articles of incorporation form and the instructions provided on your state's filing office website will tell you if your state classifies nonprofits into different categories, and, if so, which articles form to use to form a 501(c)(3) tax-exempt nonprofit corporation.

Typical Secretary of State Guidelines for Retyping Articles

- Write all text in English (no foreign language characters, punctuation, or diacritical marks).
- Type your responses to blank items (or retype your form) using a black ink ribbon. Some secretaries may allow hand-printed responses—check your secretary of state's instructions.
- Use letter-sized (8½" × 11") paper.
- Fasten pages with staples, not rivet-type fasteners.
- Make sure all typing and signatures (and any hand-printed responses) are of sufficient contrast to be legibly photocopied by the secretary's office; black ink is usually specified.

Preparing Articles of Incorporation in Iowa and Nebraska

Only Iowa and Nebraska do not provide a complete or sample articles form for you to follow or use. If you are forming a nonprofit in either state, first go online to the state's filing office website to see if they now provide a form. If not, follow our instructions below to prepare an articles form from scratch.

Iowa

Go to the Nonprofits section of the Iowa Secretary of State website. Under Forms & Fees, you will see Articles of Incorporation and a link to Section 504.202 of the Iowa Nonprofit Corporation Act. This section of the Iowa Nonprofit Corporation Act specifies the mandatory and optional contents of nonprofit articles of incorporation. The statute says that the articles must contain the name of the corporation, the address of the corporation's registered agent and the name of the registered agent at this office, the name and address of each incorporator (only one is needed), whether the corporation will have members, and provisions regarding the distribution of assets of the corporation upon its dissolution.

Additional optional provisions also are listed in the statue. To draft these, use our sample clauses in this chapter for each of these provisions: Article 1. Name of Corporation, Article 2. Registered Agent and Office, Article 5. Names and Addresses of Incorporators, Article 7. Membership Provisions, and the dedication of assets clause shown in the "Additional Federal Tax Exemption Language" section later in this chapter. Also include any other provisions you wish or that we recommend to obtain your federal tax exemption. The Iowa nonprofit corporation name requirements are contained in Section 504.401 of the Iowa statutes. Just insert this section name in the search box to see the requirements.

Nebraska

The Nebraska nonprofit corporation articles statute is contained in Section 21-1921 of the Revised Nebraska Statutes (search for "21-1921 Nebraska Legislature" in your browser to get a link to the statute). Articles must state the name of the corporation; whether the corporation is a public benefit, religious, or mutual benefit corporation; the street address of the registered office and the name of the registered agent at that office; the name and street address of each incorporator; whether the corporation will have members; and an asset dedication clause.

To complete your own Nebraska articles, see the following sample articles in this chapter: Article 1. Name of Corporation, Article 2. Registered Agent and Office, Article 5. Names and Addresses of Incorporators, Article 7. Membership Provisions, and the dedication of assets clause shown in the "Additional Federal Tax Exemption Language" section later in this chapter. Also include any other provisions you wish or that we recommend to obtain your federal tax exemption. The Nebraska nonprofit corporation name requirements are contained in Section 21-1931 of the Nebraska statutes (enter "21-1931 Nebraska Legislature" in your browser to get a link to the statute).

Generally, most Nebraska 501(c)(3) nonprofits are formed for either religious purposes (as a religious corporation), or as a public benefit corporation (formed for charitable, educational, or other public benefit 501(c)(3) purposes).

You can file a PDF version of your articles online using the state's eDelivery service (see the information on the state filing office website).

Complete Your Articles

The basic clauses various states require in articles of incorporation are similar. By following the material below and referring to the specific instructions for preparing articles provided by your secretary of state, you should be able to prepare your form without undue difficulty. Here are some hints to make this job easier:

- Scan the following information to get a general idea of the various types of clauses and provisions traditionally included in standard articles of incorporation. This information will help you understand the specific form and instructions provided by your secretary of state.

- If your secretary provides a sample form that must be retyped, type or write out a draft copy first.

- Complete as much of the form as you can, following your secretary of state's form and specific instructions. If you get stuck with a particular article or provision, refer to our instructions below.

- To locate a particular incorporation requirement in your state (for example, the number of directors to be named in your articles) see the instructions to the state's form. If you want more information, browse your state's nonprofit corporation statute.

Sample Article Provisions

Below we provide sample language and explanations of the provisions you are likely to find in the articles of incorporation provided by your secretary of state. An article number and heading identifies the subject matter of the provision or clause and explanatory text follows each sample article. Blanks indicate information that needs to be inserted in the text of the provision or clause.

Heading and Format of Articles

Articles of Incorporation

Article 1. ....
Article 2. ....
Article 3. ....

State law does not normally specify any format for the heading or body of the articles. Typically, only the name of the document (Articles of Incorporation) is shown in the heading, and each provision is numbered sequentially. Your secretary of state's office may provide guidelines for retyping articles.

Statement of Statutory Authority

The undersigned incorporator(s), in order to form a corporation under the _[name of state's nonprofit corporation law]_ , adopt the following Articles of Incorporation:

Although not required in many states, a statement of statutory authority often is included at the beginning of the articles stating the name or section numbers of the state's nonprofit corporation act under which the corporation is being formed.

In some states, it is customary to recite that the incorporators or the corporation meet specific statutory requirements (for example, that the incorporators are of legal age or that the corporation is not formed for pecuniary profit).

Here is an example of a statutory authority clause taken from an official state form:

> The undersigned natural person(s) of the age of eighteen years or more for the purpose of forming a corporation under the _____ Nonprofit Corporation Act adopt(s) the following Articles of Incorporation.

RESOURCE

Specific forms and instructions for forming a California nonprofit are contained in *How to Form a Nonprofit Corporation in California*, by Anthony Mancuso (Nolo). Use this more specialized book if you are incorporating in California.

Article 1. Name of Corporation

The name of this corporation is _____

_____.

The first article of incorporation normally specifies the name of the corporation. See "Choose a Corporate Name," above, to select a name for your corporation. If you have reserved a corporate name, make sure to use the exact spelling of the reserved name in your articles.

Article 2. Registered Agent and Office

The name and address of the registered agent of this corporation are: _____

_____.

Most states require that articles include the name and address of the corporation's initial registered agent (or agent for service of process). The agent is the person authorized to receive legal papers on behalf of the corporation; the agent's office is also known as the registered office of the corporation. Generally, the agent must be a resident of the state and at least 18 years of age. Although the registered office may be different from the principal office of the corporation in many states, most nonprofits keep things simple and appoint one of the directors as the initial agent, showing the principal address of the corporation as the registered office of the corporation.

TIP

You must usually use a street address, not a post office box, as your agent's address. Also, some states require the filing of a separate designation of registered agent form with the articles. See your state's instructions to the official article's form.

Article 3. Statement of Purpose

The purposes for which this corporation is organized are: _____

_____.

A statement of purpose clause is a standard feature in nonprofit articles of incorporation. Your statement of purpose should be used to satisfy state corporate law and federal 501(c)(3) tax exemption requirements. Let's look at the federal requirements first.

Federal 501(c)(3) Tax-Exempt Purpose Clause

In the purpose clause in your articles of incorporation, you must include language stating that your corporation is organized for 501(c)(3) tax-exempt purposes. We refer to this language in later discussions as your *statement of tax-exempt purposes*.

Here is the standard IRS-approved language (see IRS Publication 557) for this statement of tax-exempt purposes:

> Article 3. The purposes for which this corporation is organized are:
>
> This corporation is organized exclusively for charitable, religious, educational, and scientific purposes, including, for such purposes, the making of distributions to organizations that qualify as exempt organizations under Section 501(c)(3) of the Internal Revenue Code, or the corresponding section of any future federal tax code.

This general statement authorizes the corporation to engage in one or more 501(c)(3) tax-exempt purposes, including making distributions to other 501(c)(3) organizations.

While this general statement will satisfy IRS requirements, we think it makes more sense (and also meets IRS requirements) to specify the real 501(c)(3) purpose or purposes of your nonprofit in a brief tax-exempt purpose statement. Here is an example of a specific tax-exempt purpose statement that we prefer instead of a general statement:

> Article 3. The purposes for which this corporation is organized are:
> This corporation is organized and operated exclusively for [*state one or more of your actual tax-exempt purposes, such as "charitable," "religious," "educational," "literary," and/or "scientific"*] purposes within the meaning of 501(c)(3) of the Internal Revenue Code.

This specific tax-exempt purpose statement eliminates the purpose related to distributing funds to other 501(c)(3)s. The additional purpose is usually only relevant to feeder organizations set up to support other nonprofits. This specific purpose statement also makes it clear that the nonprofit is organized and operated for 501(c)(3) purposes—the IRS likes to see this additional "operational" language.

The official form of articles promulgated by your secretary of state may already contain a boilerplate or fill-in statement of tax-exempt purposes (or a slight variation on one of the clauses shown above). Some official forms include this clause in a statement of purposes article; others include it under a space set aside on the form for "additional provisions." In all cases, if this (or similar) tax-exempt purpose language does not appear in your articles, make sure to include it somewhere on the form. You'll need it to get your federal income tax exemption.

RELATED TOPIC

Your secretary of state form may include other tax exemption provisions. See Article 8, below, for a discussion of additional federal tax exemption language that is required, or may be included, in your articles.

Additional Statements of Purpose Required Under State Law

In many states, a statement of 501(c)(3) tax-exempt purposes will be all you need to satisfy the requirements for completing the purpose clause in your articles. Some states, however, have their own unique requirements for purpose clause wording in the articles. Below we look at the most common types of statements required under state statutes.

TIP

These special statements of purpose satisfy state law requirements. To satisfy the federal 501(c)(3) tax requirements, make sure to also include a statement of your federal tax-exempt purposes somewhere in your articles (see above).

If You Get Stuck on Your Statement of Nonprofit Purposes

We provide instructions for dealing with the types of purpose clauses required in the majority of states. However, if you encounter special language or special format requirements not covered in our discussion, here are two suggestions:

- Rely primarily on the instructions to the sample and printed forms on your secretary of state's website—these will usually show you how to cope with any special state statutory requirements.
- For further assistance, check your state's articles statute for the special statutory language you must include or special requirements you must follow to complete your purpose clause.

Statement of Lawful Purpose

Some states require that the articles contain specific statutory wording indicating that the corporation is formed for a lawful purpose under the laws of the state (we call this a *statement of lawful purposes*).

A typical statement of lawful purposes reads as follows:

> The purpose of the corporation is to engage in any lawful act or activity for which corporations may be organized under the Nonprofit Corporation Law of _____ .

If your articles include this lawful purpose statement (in addition, of course, to a tax-exempt purpose statement, as explained above), we recommend that you add language to limit it to make it clear that your nonprofit will only pursue lawful activities that satisfy the IRC 501(c)(3) requirements. Here's one way to do this (see the language in italics added to the end of the standard lawful purpose statement below):

> The purpose of the corporation is to engage in any lawful act or activity for which corporations may be organized under the Nonprofit Corporation Law of _____, *provided, however, that the corporation shall only engage in acts or activities that are consistent with and in furtherance of its 501(c)(3) tax-exempt purposes, which are described in other provisions of these articles.*

Statement of Specific Purposes

Some states also require a brief, one- or two-sentence description of the purposes and activities of your corporation in the purpose clause of the articles (we call this a *statement of specific purposes*). If you can't determine whether your state requires a statement of specific purpose by reading your state's instructions, we suggest you include one just to be safe.

Environmental Education. Here is a sample statement of specific purposes for an environmental group:

> Article 3. The specific purposes for which this corporation is organized are:
> to publish a newsletter providing information to the public on preserving tropical rain forests.

Publishing and Lectures. Here is a sample specific purpose clause for a group that wishes to publish books and give public lectures:

> Article 3. The specific purposes for which this corporation is organized are:
> to develop an institution to teach and disseminate educational material to the public, including, but not limited to, material relating to   *[the areas of instruction are mentioned here]* , through publications, lectures, or otherwise.

Dance Group. The following sample specific purpose clause is for a group that wishes to set up studios where it can teach dance and hold performances. The educational purposes of the group are clearly identified in the specific purpose clause and the general public is identified as the recipient of these services. For future flexibility, the group leaves itself the option of teaching and promoting other art forms.

> Article 3. The specific purposes for which this corporation is organized are:
> to educate the general public in dance and other art forms. The means of providing such education includes, but is not limited to, maintaining facilities for instruction and public performances of dance and other art forms.

Housing Improvement. Here is a sample clause for a group planning to get grants and tax exemptions to improve housing conditions for low- and moderate-income people by organizing a housing information and research exchange.

Note that the following example simply and succinctly states the group's specific purposes, characterizing them as charitable and educational purposes in the interests of the general public— no further embellishment or narrative in the specific purpose clause is needed here.

> Article 3. The specific purposes for which this corporation is organized are:
> to provide education and charitable assistance to the general public by organizing a housing information and research exchange.

Medical Clinic. This sample specific purpose clause is for a community health care clinic for low-income individuals.

> Article 3. The specific purposes for which this corporation is organized are:
> to establish and maintain a comprehensive system of family-oriented health care aimed primarily at the medically underserved areas of ___[city and county]___ .

Religious Teachings and Publishing. Here is a specific purpose statement that is appropriate for a religious group devoted to the teachings and works of a particular religious leader or religious order:

> Article 3. The specific purposes for which this corporation is organized are:
> to establish a religious organization to promote the teachings of, and publish materials of and concerning, [_name of spiritual leader or religious order_] .

Scientific Research. Sometimes, a reference to the tax-exempt purposes of the group will suffice as a specific purpose statement, as follows:

> Article 3. The purposes for which this corporation is organized are:
> to engage in scientific research in the public interest.

Tips on Preparing a Statement of Specific Purposes

Make sure to keep your specific purpose statement brief—one or two short sentences is best (for example, to set up a child care center, home for the aged, mental health hotline, or dance or musical troupe; to provide scholarships to needy students or establish a book fair; and so on). The secretary of state usually doesn't want much detail or narrative here. You will provide a fuller description of your nonprofit purposes and activities in your bylaws and on your federal tax exemption application.

If possible, describe the kinds of activities you pursue in language that will clearly identify them as ones that the IRS considers to be tax-exempt.

For example, if your specific purpose is to set up a hospital, indicate that you are forming a _charitable hospital_; if establishing a child care center, state that _it is open to the general public and will allow parents to be gainfully employed_; if setting up a scientific organization, that _scientific research will be carried on in the public interest_.

Avoid using keywords, terms, or phrases associated with organizations exempt from taxation under other (non-501(c)(3)) sections of the Internal Revenue Code, such as _social_, _fraternal_, _recreational_, _political_, and so on.

Article 4. Number, Names, and Addresses of Initial Directors

The number of initial directors of this corporations is

_____.

Their names and addresses are as follows: _____
_____.

Many states require you to include the number of persons who will serve on the first board of directors, followed by their names and addresses. In some states, this information is not (or is only optionally) included in the articles provided by the secretary of state.

RELATED TOPIC

Directors. The instructions to your state's articles should indicate the minimum number of directors required in your state. Also see "How Many People Are Needed to Form a Nonprofit Corporation?" in Chapter 2.

To fill in this article, type the number of directors of your corporation, then list the names and addresses (street, not P.O. box) of the persons appointed to your initial board. Initial board members serve until the first meeting held to reelect directors and the date of this meeting will be specified in your bylaws.

Article 5. Names and Addresses of Incorporators

The names and addresses of the incorporators of this corporation are: _____

_____.

The incorporator is the person or persons who form the corporation by signing and filing articles of incorporation. Although more than one incorporator may be used, most nonprofits, if allowed, designate one person to assume this responsibility. Most articles of incorporation require the name and address of the incorporator (or incorporators) of the corporation either in the body of the articles or at the end of the document after the signature line.

Although the incorporator is usually one of the initial directors of the corporation, usually any person may be designated the incorporator and prepare, sign, and file articles on behalf of your corporation.

RELATED TOPIC

Incorporators. Your state's articles instructions should indicate any special incorporator requirements in your state (for example, if you must have more than one incorporator). Also see "How Many People Are Needed to Form a Nonprofit Corporation?" in Chapter 2.

Article 6. Duration of Corporation

The period of duration of this corporation is: _____

_____.

In some states, the articles include a provision specifying the duration of the corporation. Almost all nonprofit corporations wish to continue into the indefinite future and will insert the word "perpetual" in this provision. In the extremely rare circumstance that you wish to limit the duration of your corporation's existence, insert a specific period or date in this clause.

Article 7. Membership Provisions

The classes, rights, privileges, qualifications, and obligations of members of this corporation are as follows: _____

_____.

In some states, the articles of incorporation include a membership clause similar to the sample shown below.

As explained in Chapter 2, most smaller nonprofit corporations will not wish to set up a formal membership structure and will indicate "No Members" if this clause appears in their articles. If you do decide to adopt a formal membership structure, it's usually best to indicate here that "The membership provisions of this corporation shall be stated in the bylaws of this corporation." This approach gives you the most flexibility—bylaw provisions may be repealed, changed, and added with relative ease, while amendments to articles must be filed with the secretary of state.

Finally, if you wish to adopt membership provisions and your state requires you to summarize these provisions in your articles, here is some standard language you may wish to use that provides for one class of dues-paying membership in the corporation:

> This corporation shall have one class of membership. Any person shall be qualified to become a member upon payment of the initial dues and shall continue as a member upon paying the annual dues. The amount, method, and time of payment of dues shall be determined, and may be changed, from time to time, by the board of directors. Additional provisions specifying the rights and obligations of members shall be contained in the bylaws of this corporation pursuant to, and in accordance with, the laws of this state.

RELATED TOPIC

For further information and suggested language to set up a formal membership structure in your bylaws, see Chapter 7.

Article 8. Additional Provisions

Insert additional provisions for operating the corporation in the space provided below:

[Insert required and optional 501(c)(3) tax exemption provisions, special language from state statutes for the operation of the corporation, and so on].

In many states, a blank article for additional provisions is included in the standard articles form. In some states, this blank article begins with wording similar to the language shown above (with suggestions for the types of optional clauses that may be inserted given in parentheses).

Below, we discuss some required and optional federal and state language you should include in this portion of your articles if it is not already included on your state's form.

Additional Federal Tax Exemption Language

To be eligible for your 501(c)(3) tax exemption, your articles must dedicate the assets of the corporation to exempt purposes. Technically, this dedication clause is not required in a few states (including Arkansas, California, Louisiana, Massachusetts, Minnesota, Missouri, Ohio, and Oklahoma—see Part III of the instructions to Form 1023: _Application for Recognition of Exemption_). Nonetheless, we recommend all incorporators make sure a dedication of assets clause appears in their articles. This will help you to minimize delay in the processing of your federal tax exemption and avoid problems if your state laws change in the future. Here is a general dedication of assets clause you can include in the Additional Provisions article (adapted from example language in the IRS Instructions to Form 1023):

> Article 8. Additional Provisions
> Upon the dissolution of this corporation, its assets remaining after payment, or provision for payment, of all debts and liabilities of this corporation shall be distributed for one or more exempt purposes within the meaning of Section 501(c)(3) of the Internal Revenue Code or shall be distributed to the federal government, or to a state or local government, for a public purpose.

CAUTION

Always include a dedication statement. Make sure to include this dedication of assets statement in your articles if one does not already appear on your form.

Alternative Wording for Specific Dedication Clause: The sample dedication language above dedicates the assets of the nonprofit corporation to one or more allowable 501(c)(3) tax-exempt purposes. Most nonprofits, however, prefer using a clause that dedicates its assets to one or more of its specific 501(c)(3) purposes. Here is an example of a specific dedication clause of this type:

> The property of this corporation is irrevocably dedicated to [*state one or more of your actual tax-exempt purposes, such as "charitable," "religious," "educational," "literary," and/or "scientific"*] purposes. Upon the dissolution or winding up of the corporation, its assets remaining after payment, or provision for payment, of all debts and liabilities of this corporation shall be distributed to a nonprofit fund, foundation, or corporation which is organized and operated exclusively for [*repeat the same purpose or purposes stated in the first blank*] purposes and which has established its tax-exempt status under Section 501(c)(3) of the Internal Revenue Code.

There is one other type of dedication of assets clause you can use in your articles—one which dedicates your assets to a specific nonprofit organization. Of course, the organization should be a qualified 501(c)(3) and you should provide that the assets will be distributed to another 501(c)(3) in case the named organization is not in existence or tax exempt when your nonprofit dissolves. If you want to specify a named organization to which you will dedicate your assets, see the instructions to Form 1023 and IRS Publication 557.

Optional 501(c)(3) Tax Exemption Language

Now let's look at optional federal tax exemption language which is commonly included in nonprofit articles. We recommend that all nonprofits include the first three optional paragraphs shown below (if these federal tax exemption provisions are not already included on your secretary's sample or printed form). Many states allow you to expand the portion of the articles set aside for additional provisions by attaching a typewritten page to your form.

Limitation on Political Activities. The following clause shows that your nonprofit group will comply with the 501(c)(3) limitation on political activities as discussed in "Limitation on Political Activities," in Chapter 3:

> No substantial part of the activities of this corporation shall consist of carrying on propaganda, or otherwise attempting to influence legislation (except as otherwise provided by Section 501(h) of the Internal Revenue Code), and this corporation shall not participate in, or intervene in (including the publishing or distribution of statements), any political campaign on behalf of, or in opposition to, any candidate for public office.

Limitation on Private Inurement (Private Benefits). Below is standard IRS-approved language prohibiting private inurement—private or personal benefit to individuals associated with the nonprofit corporation, such as directors, officers, employees, and so on, as discussed in Chapter 3. The last portion of this clause indicates that reasonable compensation for services rendered is allowed under federal tax law.

> No part of the net earnings of this corporation shall inure to the benefit of, or be distributable to, its members, directors, officers, or other private persons, except that this corporation shall be authorized and empowered to pay reasonable compensation for services rendered and to make payments and distributions in furtherance of the purposes set forth in these articles.

General Limitation on Nonprofit Activities. The statement below limits the activities of the corporation to those permitted to 501(c)(3) organizations and those allowed to corporations to which contributions are deductible under Section 170(c)(2) of the Internal Revenue Code:

> Notwithstanding any other provision of these articles, this corporation shall not carry on any other activities not permitted to be carried on (1) by a corporation exempt from federal income tax under Section 501(c)(3) of the Internal Revenue Code or (2) by a corporation contributions to which are deductible under Section 170(c)(2) of the Internal Revenue Code.

RELATED TOPIC

For a discussion of the deductibility of charitable contributions made to 501(c)(3) organizations, see Chapter 4.

Private Foundation Restrictions. The following language relates to technical aspects of the 501(c)(3) tax exemption and states that the corporation will comply with all the operating restrictions that apply to private foundations if the corporation is classified as a private foundation by the IRS. Because you will want your nonprofit to be classified as a 501(c)(3) public charity rather than a private foundation, you do not need to include this language in your articles. We mention it only because it may appear in the official form promulgated by your secretary of state (it is required only for private foundations formed in Arizona and New Mexico).

> In any taxable year in which this corporation is a private foundation as described in Section 509(a) of the Internal Revenue Code, the corporation (1) shall distribute its income for said period at such time and manner as not to subject it to tax under Section 4942 of the Internal Revenue Code; (2) shall not engage in any act of self-dealing as defined in Section 4941(d) of the Internal Revenue Code; (3) shall not retain any excess business holdings as defined in Section 4943(c) of the Internal Revenue Code; (4) shall not make any investments in such manner as to subject the corporation to tax under Section 4944 of the Internal Revenue Code; and (5) shall not make any taxable expenditures as defined in Section 4945(d) of the Internal Revenue Code.

RELATED TOPIC

For a discussion of private foundation and public charity tax status, see Chapter 4.

Sample Completed Articles

We've covered a lot of ground in the individual sample articles of incorporation and explanations above. To help you tie all this information together, we include a sample completed articles below together with our comments (which appear in italicized type).

FORMS AND RESOURCES

Articles of incorporation. You can download a copy of a blank articles of incorporation form from the Nolo website (see Appendix A for the link). A copy has also been included in Appendix C.

File Your Articles of Incorporation

File your articles with your secretary of state following the instructions on your secretary of state's website. Most corporations file by mail, although many offices will accept articles in person. Some states allow you to fill in and file your articles online (see your state filing office website for any online filing information). Some states provide their own articles filing letter. If your state does and you file by mail, use it instead of ours, below.

Use eDelivery or online filing of articles if available on your state filing office website.

Some state filing office websites allow you to file a PDF version of your articles online after paying the filing fees with a credit card. We recommend you use this service if available since it avoids the weeks of delay necessary to file your articles by mail.

FORMS AND RESOURCES
You can download a copy of the Articles Filing Letter from the Nolo website (see Appendix A for the link). Also, there is a blank copy of the form in Appendix C. You may wish to use (or modify) it to submit your articles of incorporation by mail to the secretary of state. Complete it as indicated on the following sample and special instructions, below.

Special Instructions for the Articles Filing Letter

❶ A person who signs your articles should prepare and sign this cover letter if you are filing your articles by mail and your state filing office does not provide you with a cover letter to use.

   Note: If you have reserved a corporate name, the person who reserved the corporate name should prepare and sign this letter—the corporate name will be reserved for this person's use only.

❷ In some states, you need only submit an original of the articles—the secretary will file the original and send you a certificate of incorporation as proof of filing. In other states, you need to submit the original and one or more copies. The secretary will file the original and file-stamp and return one or more copies to you. In some states, an additional fee is

charged for submitting more than one copy of your articles for file-stamping. One copy should be sufficient—you can make copies of this file-stamped copy to send to financial institutions, grant agencies, and others when necessary as proof of your incorporation.

❸ Include a check for the total fees, made payable to the "Secretary of State" or another official title of the office that files articles in your state. Check your secretary of state instructions carefully to make sure your total fee payment is correct—otherwise, your articles may be returned to you unfiled.

❹ If you have reserved your corporate name, fill in the blanks here to show the certificate number and/or date your reservation was issued. In some states, the secretary simply sends you a file-stamped copy of your reservation letter; if so, just show the file-stamped date on the letter in the second blank.

Your next step is to wait when filing by mail. The secretary of state will make sure your corporate name is available for use and that your articles conform to law. If there are no problems, the secretary of state will mail you a certificate of incorporation (or file-stamped copy of your articles). If there are any problems with your articles, the secretary of state will usually return your articles, indicating the items that need correction. Often the problem is technical, not substantive, and easy to fix. If the problem is more complicated (such as an improper or insufficient corporate purpose clause), you may be able to solve the problem by rereading our examples and suggestions for completing the articles. If you get stuck, you will need to do a little research or obtain further help from a nonprofit lawyer with experience in drafting and filing nonprofit articles (see Chapter 11).

Customizing Your Articles

Although the standard articles discussed in this chapter and included in your secretary of state's form will be sufficient for most incorporators, some may wish to adopt special operating rules or provisions. Although it is preferable to include these special rules in the bylaws (which can be adopted and changed with relative ease), some special provisions must, under state law, be included in the articles to be effective. For example, the following types of provisions, if adopted by the corporation, must often be included in the articles:

- establishing different classes of membership (such as voting and nonvoting members)
- allowing specific members of the board to be designated by individuals rather than elected by the board or voting membership
- requiring a supermajority vote (such as two-thirds or three-fourths) of directors or members for the approval of certain matters, and
- providing for special indemnification or immunity for directors and officers.

Your state website instructions may list the special provisions you have to include in your articles.

It's also very important to realize that until you obtain your federal and state tax exemptions, your corporation is liable for the payment of state and federal income taxes. Furthermore, until you apply for and obtain your federal 501(c)(3) tax exemption and public charity status, your corporation will be unable to receive most public and private grant funds, and will be unable to assure donors that contributions made to the corporation are tax deductible. Therefore, make sure to follow through with the procedures contained in the succeeding chapters—doing so is vital to the success of your new corporation.

Sign Documents on Behalf of the Corporation

Congratulations! Once your articles are filed, your organization is a legally recognized nonprofit corporation. But before you rush out to pursue your nonprofit objectives, remember that your corporation is the one who is now doing business, not you as an individual. This means that signatures on any document, such as an agreement with a vendor, application for a grant, a lease, or another financial or legal form must clearly show that you're acting on behalf of the corporation (and not for yourself). Your signature should be a block of information (plus a signature), which looks like this:

Parents for a Better Society, Inc.

By: _____ [your signature] _____
[Your corporate title, such as
Director, President, or Secretary]

If you fail to sign documents on behalf of the corporation and in your capacity as a corporate director, officer, or employee, you are leaving yourself open to possible personal liability for corporate obligations. From now on, it is extremely important for you to maintain the distinction between the corporation that you've organized and yourself. As we've said, the corporation is a separate legal "person" and you want to make sure that other organizations, businesses, the IRS, and the courts respect this distinction.

Sample

Articles of Incorporation

Pursuant to the provision of the Nonprofit Corporation Act of this state, the undersigned incorporators hereby adopt the following Articles of Incorporation:

Article 1
The name of this corporation is: The Bluegrass Music Society of the Appalachians, Inc.

Article 2
The name and address of the registered agent and registered office of this corporation is:
 [*Name of one of the initial directors, address of corporation.*]

Article 3
This corporation is organized and operated exclusively for educational purposes within the meaning of 501(c)(3) of the Internal Revenue Code. [*This is a statement of tax-exempt purposes required under IRC Section 501(c)(3).*]

   The specific purposes for which this corporation is organized are: To establish a musical society open to the general public to foster an appreciation of American bluegrass music, through lectures, seminars, study groups, public and classroom performances, exhibits, and any and all other appropriate means. [*This is a statement of specific purposes.*]

Article 4
The number of initial directors of this corporation is three   and the names and addresses of the initial directors are as follows:
 [*Names and addresses of three initial directors*]

Article 5
The name and address of the incorporators of this corporation are:
 [*Name and address of one of the initial directors listed above*]

Article 6
The period of duration of this corporation is: perpetual.

Article 7

The classes, rights, privileges, qualifications, and obligations of members of this corporation are as follows:

As stated in the bylaws of this corporation.

Article 8

Additional provisions (attach separate page if necessary):

The property of this corporation is irrevocably dedicated to educational purposes. Upon the dissolution or winding up of the corporation, its assets remaining after payment, or provision for payment, of all debts and liabilities of this corporation shall be distributed to a nonprofit fund, foundation, or corporation that is organized and operated exclusively for educational purposes and that has established its tax-exempt status under Section 501(c)(3) of the Internal Revenue Code. [*This is the dedication of assets statement required under IRC Section 501(c)(3).*]

No substantial part of the activities of this corporation shall consist of carrying on propaganda, or otherwise attempting to influence legislation (except as otherwise provided by Section 501(h) of the Internal Revenue Code), and this corporation shall not participate in, or intervene in (including the publishing or distribution of statements), any political campaign on behalf of, or in opposition to, any candidate for public office. [*This is the optional limitation on political activities statement under IRC Section 501(c)(3).*]

No part of the net earnings of this corporation shall inure to the benefit of, or be distribut-able to, its members, directors, officers, or other private persons, except that this corporation shall be authorized and empowered to pay reasonable compensation for services rendered and to make payments and distributions in furtherance of the purposes set forth in these articles. [*This is the optional limitation on private inurement statement under IRC Section 501(c)(3).*]

Notwithstanding any other provision of these articles, this corporation shall not carry on any other activities not permitted to be carried on (1) by a corporation exempt from federal income tax under Section 501(c)(3) of the Internal Revenue Code or (2) by a corporation contributions to which are deductible under Section 170(c)(2) of the Internal Revenue Code. [*This is the optional general limitation on activities statement under IRC Section 501(c)(3).*]

The undersigned incorporators hereby declare under penalty of perjury that the statements made in the foregoing Articles of Incorporation are true.

Dated: _____

[*Signature of incorporator*]

Name and Address of Incorporator: _____

_____

_____

[*Normally, the incorporator(s) must sign the articles. Some states require initial directors, if named in articles, to sign instead. If notarization is required, the signature(s) must be given in the presence of a notary.*]

Articles Filing Letter

[Name and address of incorporator] ❶ _____

_____

_____

_____

[Date] _____

[Name and address of secretary of state office] _____

_____

_____

Re: Articles of Incorporation Filing

I enclose an original and _[number]_ ❷ copies of the proposed Articles of Incorporation of

[name of corporation] _____.

Please file the Articles of Incorporation and return a Certificate of Incorporation (or file-stamped copy of the original Articles) to me at the above address.

A check/money order in the amount of $_____❸_____, made payable to your office, for total filing and processing fees is enclosed.

The above corporate name was reserved for my use pursuant to Reservation # _____❹_____ issued on _____.

Sincerely,

[Signature of incorporator] ❶ _____

[Typed name] _____, Incorporator

Prepare Your Bylaws

Your next step is to prepare your bylaws. This document is, for all practical purposes, your corporation's internal affairs manual. It sets forth the rules and procedures for holding meetings, electing directors and officers, and taking care of other essential corporate formalities. Specifically, the bylaws:

- contain information central to the organization and operation of your particular corporation (for example, dates of meetings, quorum requirements)

- restate the most significant legal and tax provisions applicable to tax-exempt nonprofit corporations. This is useful for your own reference and necessary to assure the IRS and the state that you are eligible for these tax exemptions.

- provide a practical, yet formal, set of rules for the orderly operation of your corporation: to resolve disputes, provide certainty regarding procedures, and manage corporate operations.

Preparing bylaws for a nonprofit corporation is not difficult. It simply involves filling in blanks. Before you begin work on your bylaws, you'll need to decide whether your nonprofit will have members.

CAUTION

Don't think of your bylaws as meaningless fine print. On the contrary, bylaws are crucial to the functioning of your organization. Be sure to read through them carefully, making sure you understand the purpose and effect of the different provisions included.

Choose a Membership or Nonmembership Structure

Your first step in preparing bylaws is to decide whether you want your nonprofit corporation to be a membership or nonmembership corporation. There are significant differences between the two structures and significant legal consequences that will result from your decision.

RELATED TOPIC

See "Membership Nonprofits," in Chapter 2, for a discussion of the two different types of structures and the legal consequences of setting up a membership versus a nonmembership structure.

Most smaller groups will probably want to form a nonmembership corporation. Why? Because a nonmembership corporation is simpler to establish and operate. Nonmembership corporations are run by a board of directors, as opposed to membership corporations, where members have the right to vote on major corporate decisions. And you don't lose any significant advantages by not having members—most people who want to support your group aren't interested in having the technical legal rights given to members.

Some groups, however, will decide that the nature of their activities requires a membership structure. This is a reasonable decision in circumstances where membership participation in the affairs of the nonprofit corporation is essential or desirable (for example, to increase member involvement in the nonprofit's mission and program). Members of a nonprofit corporation are given specific legal rights under state law to participate in corporate affairs. Such membership rights typically include the right to:

- vote for the election of the board of directors

- approve changes to the articles or bylaws of the corporation

- vote for a dissolution of the corporation, and

- approve a sale of substantially all of the corporation's assets.

Some nonprofits may even decide to combine a legal, voting membership structure with a larger group of dues-paying supporters.

> **EXAMPLE:** A large botanical society may have one class of formal members who elect the board of directors and an informal group of dues-paying supporters who receive the society's magazine and attend special events sponsored by the society.

If you do decide to adopt a formal membership structure for your nonprofit corporation, we show you below how to add basic membership provisions to your bylaws.

Purpose and Scope of Your Bylaws

This book contains a bylaws form that is suitable for all types of 501(c)(3) nonprofits—nonmembership and membership groups alike. You can download a copy of the form from the Nolo website (see Appendix A for the link). The provisions contained in this document were drafted to serve the following purposes:

- They contain information central to the organization and operation of your corporation (time, place, date, call, notice, and quorum requirements for meetings).

- They restate the most significant provisions applicable to tax-exempt nonprofit corporations, useful for your own reference and necessary to assure the IRS that your corporation is eligible for its tax exemptions.

- They provide a practical, yet formal, set of rules for the orderly operation of your corporation—to resolve disputes, to provide certainty regarding legal procedures, and to ensure at least minimum control over corporate operations.

Why Not Having Members Makes Sense

Here are some reasons why most nonprofit incorporators prefer not to have members:

- Setting up a formal membership with voting rights dilutes directorship control over corporate operations.

- It isn't always easy to expel a member. State law may require that members only be expelled for good cause following a formal hearing.

- Nonmembership groups can still receive support from subscribers, sponsors, patrons, friends, benefactors, and so on. You can offer discounts or other benefits to outsiders who participate in the activities and programs of the corporation without giving them a legal right to participate in the management and other affairs of the corporation.

  In some states, you may even call these outside supporters "members" of the corporation without running the risk of entitling these persons to voting and other legal membership rights in the corporation. Nonetheless, to be safe and to avoid confusion and controversy later on, we suggest you use another term for persons who will not be legal members of your corporation but who will otherwise contribute to, or participate in, corporate affairs and activities.

- They contain provisions intended to help you get and keep your 501(c)(3) tax exemption. For example, we include conflict of interest and compensation approval provisions that the IRS recommends, as one way to comply with the IRS regulations. You'll see that the IRS asks you if you have these provisions in place when you complete your federal income tax exemption application and your annual federal 990 returns. Although these are optional provisions, including these and other IRS-recommended provisions in your bylaws can go a long way toward making your dealings with the IRS a lot easier, both now and in future years.

RESOURCE

For an excellent guide to the type of governance policies the IRS likes to see in an organization's bylaws, see the Panel on the Nonprofit Sector's *Principles for Good Governance and Ethical Practice,* available at www.independentsector.org.

RESOURCE

Should you consult a nonprofit professional? The primary practical reason to adopt the rules contained in the bylaws is to allow the incorporators to arrive at a good, workable consensus regarding the ground rules of the corporation. However, these may not meet all your needs or you may have questions about one or more of them. If so, check the provisions in our form against your state's nonprofit statutes or have them reviewed and customized by a lawyer with nonprofit experience.

Form 990—See What the IRS Looks for in Bylaws

By going through the IRS 990 annual nonprofit return and instructions, you'll see what the IRS asks about (and likes to see) in bylaws. Namely, you'll see that the IRS is interested in:

- the avoidance of excess benefit and conflict of interest transactions
- the contemporaneous recording of nonprofit minutes of meetings and written consents
- independent (noncompensated) board members
- the ability of nonprofit insiders to report wrongdoing (documented by a written whisteblowing policy)
- document retention and destruction (evidenced by a written document retention and destruction policy), and
- public disclosure of the organization's exemption application and annual tax returns on its website and/or on request by the public (through a written public disclosure policy).

Our bylaws help you meet the first two recommendations. We suggest you give thought to adding provisions to your bylaws that address one or more of the additional policies listed above. This will help you meet the other good governance policies and practices the IRS asks about.

What the IRS doesn't like to see authorized or allowed in bylaws is:

- a small board of directors composed of related people. (Even for a smaller nonprofit, four or five board members look better than just two or three.)
- board members who are paid or related to paid people. If all or most of the board is paid or related to paid people in your nonprofit, expect questions from the IRS (which will be trying to determine whether your nonprofit is set up to benefit the paid directors instead of the public).

How We Deal With State Law Differences

As you know, nonprofit corporation laws vary slightly from state to state. The provisions contained in our general purpose bylaws should conform to the statutory requirements of most states. In some areas where state legal rules do diverge somewhat, our bylaw provisions simply refer to the laws of your state. For example, the indemnification provisions in the bylaws state that your directors and officers are entitled to indemnification *to the fullest extent permissible under the law of this state.*

If a specific area of nonprofit law or procedure is particularly important to you or your legal adviser, you can easily replace the general purpose provisions in the bylaws with the exact provisions contained in your state's nonprofit corporation code. For a discussion about looking up the law yourself, see Chapter 11.

Making Modifications to the Bylaws

In the text, we discussed various reasons why some groups may wish to insert specific statutory rules from their state's nonprofit corporation law in their bylaws. There are many good reasons why groups may wish to customize their bylaws to add special language or provisions.

For example, if your nonprofit corporation plans to receive federal or other public grants or monies, some funding agencies may require that you include special provisions in your bylaws that state that no member of the board, officer, or other person exercising supervisory power in the corporation, or any of their close relatives can individually benefit from the receipt of grant funds. Generally, provisions of this sort are meant to prohibit board members, officers (president, vice president, secretary, and treasurer), and their families from being paid from, or directly benefited by, grant monies given to the organization.

Prepare Your Bylaws

You can download a copy of the bylaws from the Nolo website and complete them following the instructions below. (See Appendix A for information on how to access the bylaws form online.) Or, you can make a photocopy of the bylaws form contained in Appendix C and fill in the blanks on that form following the instructions below.

RESOURCE

If you prefer to create your bylaws through an online service, check out Nolo's Online Bylaws for Nonprofits (https://store.nolo.com/products/bylaws-for-nonprofit.html). After answering a few questions, you will have customized bylaws that you can amend at any time.

Don't Worry About References to Members in the Bylaws

There are certain provisions in the bylaws that refer to "the members, if any," of the corporation or use other language making certain provisions applicable to the corporation only if the corporation has members. These provisions have no effect for nonmembership corporations using these bylaws—they simply allow membership corporations to add membership provisions to the bylaws, as explained in "Prepare Membership Provisions," below.

Below we go over the sample bylaw provisions. An article number and heading identifies the subject matter of each provision, and explanatory text with examples or blanks, if applicable, follows.

Heading

Type the name of your corporation.

Article I, Section 1.
Principal Office

Type the name of the county and state where the corporation's principal office is located—this is the corporate office where you will keep a copy of your bylaws, records of meetings, and other formal corporate records mentioned in various bylaw provisions. Customarily, the principal office designated here will be the same as the legal office of the corporation (the address specified in the articles as the registered office of the corporation where legal papers must be served on the corporation).

CAUTION

Don't fill in the blanks for change of address at the end of Section 2. Use these blanks later, if necessary, to change the principal office of the corporation to another location within the same county, by showing the new address and date of the address change.

Article 2, Section 1.
IRC Section 501(c)(3) Purposes

This section contains a standard statement of 501(c)(3) tax-exempt purposes (similar to the tax-exempt purpose clause discussed earlier for the articles of incorporation). We include this statement in the bylaws to remind the IRS that your corporation is organized exclusively for a bona fide 501(c)(3) purpose.

Article 2, Section 2.
Specific Objectives and Purposes

Use the space provided here to state the specific tax-exempt objectives and purposes of your nonprofit corporation. If you included a statement of specific purposes in your articles of incorporation, it should have been brief. Here you can go into as much detail as you want in describing the specific purposes and activities of your corporation. We suggest you list your major purposes and activities, showing your nonprofit goals and the means by which you plan to achieve them. This will be useful not only as an exercise to help define and clarify your nonprofit objectives, but also as a way to give the IRS additional information regarding the tax-exempt purposes and activities of your corporation.

Dance Group. Here's an example of an expanded list of objectives and purposes that might be used by an educational purpose, nonprofit dance group. It is illustrative of the large number of 501(c)(3) nonprofit corporations that will derive tax-exempt revenue primarily from the performance of services related to their exempt purposes, rather than from grants and contributions:

Section 2. Specific Objectives and Purposes
The specific objectives and purposes of this corporation shall be:

(a) to provide instruction in dance forms such as jazz, ballet, tap, and modern dance;

(b) to provide instruction in body movement and relaxation art forms such as tumbling, tai-chi, and yoga;

(c) to give public performances in dance forms and creative dramatics;

(d) to sponsor special events involving the public performance of any or all of the above art forms as well as other performing arts by the corporation's performing troupe as well as by other community performing arts groups; and

(e) to directly engage in and to provide facilities for others to engage in the promotion of the arts, generally.

Nonprofit Book Festival. Here's a completed statement of specific objectives and purposes for a nonprofit educational purpose group that sponsors a book fair and promotes book reading and publishing in the local community:

Section 2. Specific Objectives and Purposes

The specific objectives and purposes of this corporation shall be:

(a) to sponsor an annual book fair with an emphasis on exhibiting books created and published in our community;

(b) to sponsor other informational events open to the public that focus on books;

(c) to educate the public concerning our community's contributions to book creation, publication, and distribution;

(d) generally, through educative and other efforts, to help make books and reading as inviting and accessible to as broad an audience as possible; and

(e) to engage in other activities related to educating the public about book writing, publishing, and distribution in our community.

Women's Health Information Resource Center. Here's a completed statement for a women's health group:

Section 2. Specific Objectives and Purposes

The specific objectives and purposes of this corporation shall be:

(a) to maintain a women's health library open to the public containing books, articles, and other material related to women's health issues;

(b) to maintain a physicians referral listing containing patient evaluations of physicians practicing in the community;

(c) to sponsor seminars and workshops open to the general public where ideas, opinions, and writings relating to women's health issues and health concerns may be expressed and shared with others;

(d) to publish a monthly newsletter containing articles informative of women's health issues; and

(e) to engage in other activities related to educating the public concerning women's health issues and health concerns.

Environmental Conservation and Protection Organization. Here's a sample for an environmental group:

Section 2. Specific Objectives and Purposes

The specific objectives and purposes of this corporation shall be:

(a) to educate the public concerning the necessity of preserving the nation's wetlands;

(b) to publish a newsletter that focuses on information related to wetlands preservation efforts and developments;

(c) to sponsor seminars and other educational events where community and environmental leaders, governmental and organizational representatives, and other concerned members of the public and government may meet to exchange ideas, suggest solutions, and implement strategies to protect the nation's wetlands;

(d) to meet with governmental representatives; to report to governmental committees, agencies, and boards; and generally to attempt to help local, state, and federal lawmakers establish enforceable legislation to help protect wetland areas; and

(e) to expand and redefine our educational and environmental program from time to time as necessary to meet the continuing challenge of protecting the nation's wetland resources.

Private College. Here's a completed statement for a private school:

Section 2. Specific Objectives and Purposes

The specific objectives and purposes of this corporation shall be:

(a) to establish a private university, licensed by the state and accredited by a recognized regional accreditation organization;

(b) to maintain a regularly enrolled student body, an established curriculum, and a full-time faculty;

(c) to participate in federal and state student loan and other student educational and financial incentive programs; and

(d) to have the normal functions, operations, programs, and pursuits incidental to a fully recognized and operational nonprofit center of learning and higher education.

 TIP

Be sure to authorize related activities. The last item in each of the above examples contains a clause that authorizes the corporation to engage in activities necessary or incidental to its main purposes and pursuits. We suggest you use similar language to allow your corporation to engage in activities related to its specific objectives and purposes.

Article 3, Section 1.
Number of Directors

Insert the total number of directors who will serve on your board. Make sure the number of directors you specify here is equal to or greater than the minimum number required in your state (see the instructions to your state's articles form; also see "How Many People Are Needed to Form a Nonprofit Corporation?" in Chapter 2). Also, consider how many directors you will need to efficiently run your nonprofit corporation. We discuss this point further in Chapter 2.

Often, the number shown here will be the same as the number of initial directors specified in your articles (if initial directors are listed in the articles). However, you may state a greater number at this time if you wish to allow additional directors to be elected to your board.

Article 3, Section 2.
Qualifications for Directors

Our bylaws provide that directors must be of the age of majority in your state. Although not a legal requirement in every state, we think this is a sensible provision to avoid legal problems that can occur if minors conduct or manage business.

We suggest that you not add qualifications to limit the makeup of your board to a particular group of individuals (for example, to educators or enrolled students of a school or to parents of children who attend a nonprofit day care center). The IRS likes to see various segments of the community represented on the board of a 501(c)(3) tax-exempt group, not just a select group with a singular nonprofit perspective or interest.

Instead of imposing a blanket qualification requirement on all board positions, it often makes sense to allocate a certain number of director positions to specific groups of individuals. This type of "selective diversity" is, in fact, encouraged by the IRS.

EXAMPLE: A nonprofit hospital wishes to set aside three board positions for physicians, three for health care administrators, and three for community representatives. This section of the bylaws is completed as follows:

Section 2. Qualifications
Directors shall be of the age of majority in this state. Other qualifications for directors of this corporation shall be as follows:
Three board positions shall be filled by licensed physicians in private practice in Jefferson County; three board positions shall be filled by health care administrators of nonprofit hospitals in Jefferson County; and three board positions shall be filled by representatives of the Jefferson County community who are not health care professionals.

Article 3, Section 5.
Term of Office of Directors

Indicate the length of the term of office for directors in this blank.

Most states specify an annual (one-year) term for directors. Many states allow you to provide for a longer term (subject to a maximum, typically of three to six years). We recommend you state a one-year term. This way you will meet your state's requirements, and you can reelect your directors to successive one-year terms each year if they are performing satisfactorily. If you want to specify a term of more than one year, check your state's nonprofit law to make sure you can do so.

Here is a sample bylaw for appointing directors for one year:

> Each director shall hold office for a period of one year and until his or her successor is elected and qualifies.

Customizing Director Provisions. Some nonprofits with larger boards or other special requirements may wish to draft their own term of office or board election provisions. For example, some may wish to provide for a staggered board, in which only a portion of the full board is elected each term to guarantee that there will always be a majority of experienced members. Or some may want to allow certain members of the board to be appointed by specified individuals or organizations (such as a city council, board of directors of a hospital, or committee of an environmental organization). There are other possibilities as well. For example, you may wish to provide that a director can only serve two or three consecutive terms so as to bring in new directors periodically.

CAUTION

Check before you use alternative bylaw provisions. In all cases, we suggest that you check your nonprofit corporation law to determine whether the alternate provisions are permitted by your state's statutes.

Are Staggered Boards Allowed in Your State?

The nonprofit laws of some states specifically allow staggered boards. Staggered boards are also allowed in a number of states whose nonprofit statutes are silent on this issue (for example, in states whose statutes only specify particular terms of office for directors). However, if your state law doesn't address this issue but requires that all directors must be elected at an annual (or other periodic) meeting for the election of directors, staggered boards may not be valid—the statutes can be read to require that all board members be elected at one time. Check with a nonprofit lawyer if you wish to authorize a staggered board and have a question regarding your state's statute on directors' terms of office.

Staggered Board Provision. Here's an example of a substitute bylaw that provides for the election of a staggered board. A corporation with a 12-person board, for instance, could use this provision to elect four directors each year:

> Each year, one-third [*or some other percentage or number*] of the authorized number of directors shall be elected to serve on the board of directors. Each director shall hold office until his or her successor is elected and qualifies.

The above provision can be used to elect a portion of the board each term. Of course, more complicated schemes are possible with different classes of directors serving for different lengths of time.

By the way, how do you tell which members of the initial board should first be selected to serve staggered terms? Here's one idea (simply a fancy way of saying that the corporate secretary can draw straws to make this selection):

> If, at a meeting for the election of directors, more than one group of initial board members is elected to serve for a first staggered term of office, then the secretary of the corporation shall assign each director to a numbered group and shall make a chance selection between or among the numbered groups (by selecting among numbered lots or by some other chance selection procedure). The group corresponding to the number so chosen shall be subject to election to a staggered term at the meeting.

Article 3, Section 6.
Director Compensation

As we've said, nonprofit directors customarily serve without compensation because the IRS will probably view substantial payments to directors for performing director duties as instances of prohibited private inurement. This is the wise approach. This bylaw section, however, does allow the corporation to pay directors a reasonable fee for attending meetings as well as reasonable advancement or reimbursement for expenses incurred in performing director duties. In practice, many nonprofits do not pay directors even these lesser amounts except to reimburse directors who must travel a long distance to attend board meetings. However, some nonprofits may authorize minimal payments as incentives to individuals for serving on the board.

Article 3, Section 8.
Regular Board Meetings

In the blanks in the first paragraph, specify the date(s) and time(s) when regular meetings of the board will be held. Many nonprofits with active agendas hold regular board meetings on a monthly or more frequent basis. Smaller or less active organizations may schedule a regular board meeting less frequently (quarterly, semiannually, or even annually) and call special meetings during the year to take care of specific items of business.

We recommend that you use this bylaw provision to schedule regular board meetings on at least a monthly basis. The majority of nonprofit corporations, whether large, mid-sized, or small, should keep their boards busy managing corporate projects and programs; setting up, supervising, and hearing back from a number of corporate committees; and just generally taking care of business on an ongoing basis. And remember, to help avoid personal liability for management decisions, each board member should be able to show that he or she is as fully informed of, and actively involved in, corporate business as possible. Corporate records showing director attendance at, and participation in, regular meetings of the board are an excellent way to show that your directors meet this standard of corporate conduct. Here is a sample bylaw calling for regular board meetings:

> Regular meetings of directors shall be held on the second Tuesday of each month at 7:30 p.m.

In the second paragraph of this section, nonmembership nonprofits should fill in the blank to indicate which one of the regular board meetings will be specified for election (or reelection) of corporate directors.

Membership Note: The provisions in the second paragraph of this section take effect only for nonmembership corporations—membership corporations can leave this item blank because they will add provisions to their bylaws that specify that the members, not the directors, elect directors of the corporation.

In a nonmembership corporation, the directors vote for their own reelection or replacement. The frequency of this regular meeting to elect directors depends upon their term of office. If the term is one year, then one regular meeting per year will be designated for election of the board. Likewise, if you have specified a three-year term for directors, then one regular meeting every third year will be designated as the meeting to elect directors. Under the terms of this bylaw, each director casts one vote for each candidate (up to the number of candidates to be elected), and the candidates receiving the highest number of votes are elected.

Directors Elected Annually. Here's an example of a bylaw for a nonmember corporation where the directors are to be elected annually:

> If this corporation makes no provision for members, then, at the regular meeting of directors held on January 1 of each year, directors shall be elected by the board of directors. Voting for the election of directors shall be by written ballot. Each director shall cast one vote per candidate, and may vote for as many candidates as the number of candidates to be elected to the board. The candidates receiving the highest number of votes up to the number of directors to be elected shall be elected to serve on the board.

EXAMPLE: Your nonprofit board consists of 15 members. The names of 20 candidates to the board are placed in nomination at the beginning of the regular meeting for election of the board. Pursuant to this bylaw provision, each director casts one vote for 15 (of the 20) candidates. The 15 candidates receiving the highest number of votes are elected to the board. Smaller nonmembership nonprofits commonly hold uncontested elections in which each director simply places him- or herself in nomination and the board votes itself in for another annual term.

RESOURCE

If you wish to add special nomination, balloting, or other director election procedures to your bylaws in place of this standard provision, check your state's nonprofit statutes before doing so (look for a section heading entitled "Election of Directors").

Article 3, Section 10. Notice of Board Meetings

Section (a) of this bylaw dispenses with notice of all regular meetings of directors (this includes the regular meeting for the election of directors). This is a standard provision codified in the nonprofit statutes of most states. It is assumed that directors will keep track of, and attend, regular meetings, once they have been given the schedule. As a practical matter, you may wish to call and remind less active directors of all upcoming meetings of the board.

Section (b) requires that the date, time, place, and purpose of special directors' meetings be communicated to each director at least one week in advance. Our bylaw specifies that notice may be given in person, or by mail, telephone, or fax machine. Since fax messages may go unnoticed or unread (or occasionally be eaten by the machine), they must be acknowledged by a return fax or telephone call within 24 hours.

Section (c) allows the corporation to obtain a written consent from a director prior to or after a meeting. Written consents and waivers of this sort are specifically authorized under the nonprofit statutes of many states and are a good way to ensure that a director is informed of the meeting. Also, this avoids having to worry about complying with any special statutory rules that may exist for calling, noticing, or holding the meeting. If a director consents in writing to the meeting, he or she cannot protest later that the corporation failed to comply with a formality contained in your nonprofit corporation code.

TIP

You may want to customize your notice provisions. We think these are reasonable notification provisions, which keep all directors informed of special business while eliminating premeeting preliminaries and delays for all regular meetings. You may wish to adopt provisions that match exactly any special requirements in your state or you may wish to customize these provisions to suit your own needs or circumstances. For example, you may wish to mail written notice and agendas of all regular and special board meetings to each director one week prior to the meeting date. Or, if allowed in your state, you may wish to allow email notice and acknowledgement of notice procedures.

Article 3, Section 11.
Quorum for Board Meetings

Indicate the percentage of the full board (or the number of directors) who must be present at a directors' meeting to constitute a quorum so that business can be conducted. We recommend a majority quorum as a sensible rule that will satisfy the director quorum requirements in most states. Some states let you lower the requirement to less than a majority, but check your state's nonprofit law if you want to do this.

Quorum Specified as Percentage of Full Board. Here is a sample bylaw, which defines a quorum as a percentage of the board:

> A quorum shall consist of a majority of the members of the board of directors.

Quorum Specified as Number of Directors. Here is a sample bylaw that qualifies a quorum as a specific number of members of the board:

> A quorum shall consist of three of the members of the board of directors.

Most corporations specify a majority of the board as the director quorum requirement, even if state law allows a smaller percentage or number

of directors to be specified. Of course, you can set a larger quorum requirement if you wish. Whatever you decide, you should realize that this section of the bylaws concerns a quorum, not a vote requirement. Under the provisions of the next section in the bylaws, normal board action can be taken by a majority of directors at a meeting at which a quorum is present.

EXAMPLE: If a six-director corporation requires a majority quorum and a meeting is held at which a minimum quorum (four) is present, action can be taken by the vote of three directors, a majority of those present at the meeting.

Article 3, Section 13.
Conduct of Board Meetings

Use this blank to specify the rules of order that will be used at directors' meetings. Some larger nonprofits use *Robert's Rules of Order* (major editions change every ten years or so), but you may indicate any set of procedures for proposing, approving, and tabling motions that you wish. *Robert's Rules of Order* has a procedural guide for holding meetings (see www.robertsrules.com). If you will have a small informal board, you may wish to leave this line blank if you see no need to specify formal procedures for introducing and discussing items of business at board meetings, or you may wish to specify "such procedures as may be approved from time to time by the board of directors" to allow your board to develop its own set of procedures for conducting meetings.

Article 4, Section 1.
Designation of Officers

This section provides for the four standard officer positions of president, vice president, secretary, and treasurer and allows the board to designate and fill other corporate officer positions as needed. In most nonprofits, directors are appointed to serve as the unpaid officers of the corporation. The officers, in turn, oversee the salaried staff. For a list of the formal duties and responsibilities associated with each officer position, see Sections 6 through 9 of this article in the form.

TIP
In some states, one person may not fill more than one corporate officer position. For example, the same person cannot serve as both the corporate president and corporate secretary. See your state's nonprofit law if you want to see any special rules that apply in your state (also see "How Many People Are Needed to Form a Nonprofit Corporation?" in Chapter 2).

Even if you set up a small nonprofit run by just a few individuals, it is customary to fill these four primary officer slots with different people. You will elect officers when you hold your first meeting of directors. Under this bylaw provision, your board may designate and fill other officer titles and positions whenever it wishes to do so.

Article 5, Section 1.
Executive Committee of the Board

This section allows the board to appoint an executive committee of directors to make management decisions for the corporation. If you wish to use this provision, insert the number of directors who will serve on this committee. Note that this provision requires that the designation of an executive committee be approved by a majority of directors.

Typically, under state law, a committee of the board can't approve major decisions, such as amendments to articles or bylaws or major

structural changes. See your state's nonprofit law for more information.

While we do not necessarily recommend that board authority be delegated, establishing an executive committee of directors may be advisable in certain nonprofits where action must routinely be taken in between formal board meetings or where distance, time, or other constraints sometimes make it difficult to achieve a quorum for board meetings. In all cases, the executive committee should keep minutes of its meetings and document all formal action. Regular and timely reports of executive committee actions should be presented to the full board.

CAUTION
Directors can be personally liable for board action. Under state law and court decisions, less active board members (those who sit on the full board and approve actions taken by the more active executive committee members) can be held personally accountable (and, in extreme cases, personally liable) for executive committee decisions. Mostly, such personal liability occurs if members of the full board are willfully or grossly negligent in carrying out their duties, which include reasonably monitoring executive committee action.

Article 7, Sections 3 and 4.
Director and Member Inspection Rights

These provisions give directors and members broad rights to inspect the corporation's properties and financial and corporate records. State law may impose additional inspection rights and obligations (or may allow you to restrict these rights). For the details of any additional inspection provisions that may apply in your state, see your nonprofit corporation law.

Article 7, Section 6.
Periodic Report Requirements

In most states, nonprofit corporations must file an annual or other periodic report form with the secretary of state, the attorney general's office, or some other state office or agency showing the names and addresses of the corporation's directors and officers and other information. Standard corporate financial statements and reports of charitable solicitation programs and finances may also be required.

TIP

Go online for your state's form. Your state's corporate filing office website should provide—or show you how to order—a copy of your state's corporate annual report form.

Special Membership Reports

Your state's nonprofit corporation act may also require you to furnish annual corporate financial statements to members. In addition, it may require you to make an annual written report to members detailing specific transactions, such as the making of loans or guarantees to directors or officers. Your state nonprofit law will contain any special membership reporting requirements that apply in your state.

Article 8. 501(c)(3) Tax Provisions

The various sections in this article contain language that will help show the IRS and, if applicable, your state revenue or tax department, that you qualify for tax-exempt status. These provisions also help you qualify to use the simpler 1023-EZ exemption application (as explained in Chapter 18).

- Section 1 contains specific and general limitations on your nonprofit activities. The first paragraph indicates that you will comply with the specific 501(c)(3) prohibitions against substantial lobbying activities and involvement with political campaigns for public candidates (the reference to IRC Section 501(h) is a reminder that you may elect to fall under the alternative political expenditures test available to 501(c)(3) public charities—see "Limitation on Political Activities" in Chapter 3). The second paragraph limits the activities of the corporation, generally, to those permitted to 501(c)(3) organizations and to organizations that qualify for tax deductible charitable contributions (under IRC § 170(c)(2)).

- Section 2 restates the 501(c)(3) prohibition against private inurement (benefiting individuals associated with the nonprofit organization). Payments made to individuals as reasonable compensation for services rendered and to further the tax-exempt purposes of the group are specifically authorized.

- Section 3 irrevocably dedicates the assets of the organization to another 501(c)(3) group or to a governmental office or agency for a public purpose. The last sentence is a reminder that such assets must be distributed in accordance with state law.

- Section 4 contains technical language restating the requirements applicable to 501(c)(3) organizations classified as private foundations. These provisions state that for any year the corporation is classified as a 501(c)(3) private foundation, it will operate in such a way as to avoid all private foundation excise taxes imposed under various sections of the Internal

Revenue Code. As you will not want to be classified as a private foundation (but, rather, as a public charity), why include these provisions in the bylaws? Simply to show the IRS that you mean business (in a nonprofit sense, of course) and will comply with any and all 501(c)(3) restrictions—whether your organization is classified as a public charity or as a private foundation.

Article 9. Conflict of Interest and Compensation Approval Policies

Article 9 of the bylaws included in this book contains rules and procedures for approving or avoiding conflict of interest transactions, including compensation arrangements, between your nonprofit and its directors, officers, employees, contractors, and others. This bylaw provision contains the conflict of interest language recommended by the IRS (included in the sample conflict of interest policy in Appendix A of the instructions to IRS Form 1023). It also contains language for the approval of compensation arrangements that attempts to comply with the safe harbor provisions of the excess benefit rules (see "Limitation on Profits and Benefits" in Chapter 3). You will need to become familiar with this provision, and make sure you are comfortable with its procedures for the approval and review of financial transactions with—and salary and other compensation paid to—your directors, officers, and others who are in a position to influence your nonprofit. If you decide to make changes to this provision, do so only after reading "Prepare Your Tax Exemption Application," in Chapter 8, instructions to Part V, where we refer to this bylaw provision when providing sample responses to questions on the application. If you

make any changes, you will need to create your own responses to some of the questions on the 501(c)(3) application.

Adoption of Bylaws

Use the Adoption of Bylaws page as the last page of your completed bylaws. In the blank, specify the number of preceding pages in your bylaws. Fill in the date and have each of the persons named as an initial director in your articles sign on a blank line below the first paragraph. If directors were not named in your articles, have each of your incorporators (the person or persons who signed your articles) sign here.

After you adopt your bylaws, make sure to keep a copy with your corporate records (so the organization can refer to them as needed in the future). You will also need to make a copy of your bylaws to attach to your federal tax exemption application, as explained in the next chapter.

Prepare Membership Provisions

This section shows how to add membership provisions to the bylaws prepared in the preceding section.

SKIP AHEAD

If you have decided to form a nonmembership corporation (as most nonprofits will), this section does not apply to you and you should skip ahead to Chapter 8.

To add membership provisions to your bylaws, follow the instructions below.

Customizing Your Membership Provisions

There are significant state law differences with respect to membership rules and procedures. In drafting the membership provisions, we have specified general membership rules that avoid significant state differences and provide a skeletal membership structure for your corporation to help you complete your bylaws and continue with your incorporation process (apply for your tax exemptions, and so on).

You may need to customize your membership rules—for example, to provide for different classes of membership, proxy voting, special director nomination or selection procedures, additional grounds and procedures for terminating memberships, and so on. Drafting extra membership provisions that comply with your state's rules will require legal research or a consultation with a nonprofit lawyer.

Heading

Type the name of your corporation in this blank.

Article 12. Membership Provisions

The membership provisions start with Article 12. You will include these membership provision pages at the end of the basic bylaw pages, as explained below.

Article 12, Section 2. Qualifications of Members

Use this blank to indicate any special qualifications required of members in your corporation. We suggest you do not limit or qualify membership in your corporation unless the qualification is of obvious utility (members must be of the age of majority) or is clearly related to the tax-exempt purposes or activities of your organization.

EXAMPLE 1: A nonprofit private college decides to limit membership to alumni because the founders wish to confer legal membership power only on those who have attended and completed the educational program. Because any person may enroll in the school, the IRS should have no objection.

EXAMPLE 2: A specialized philanthropic and fundraising newsletter only admits as members persons who can show a few years' prior experience working with or for nonprofit organizations. This selection criterion is intended to generate a membership that is involved in the organization's areas of interest and should be acceptable to the IRS.

No Specified Membership Qualification. If you do not wish to limit or qualify membership in your corporation, complete this blank as follows:

> The qualifications for membership in this corporation are as follows: Any person is qualified to become a member of this corporation.

CAUTION

Dues and fees go in Section 4, below. Do not use this blank to limit your membership to those who pay membership fees or dues; you will specify any initial and ongoing payments required of members in separate membership provisions, as explained below.

Article 12, Section 3. Admission of Members

Most smaller nonprofit corporations do not require formal application for membership in the corporation. A few, however, may do this to determine if prospective members meet the qualification requirements set forth in Article 12, Section 2, as discussed above. Others will use this bylaw to indicate that members must pay an admission fee and/or annual dues prior to acceptance as a member in the corporation.

Specified Membership Qualification. Here is a sample bylaw which provides for membership qualification, an application fee, and annual dues:

> Applicants shall be admitted to membership on making application therefore in writing and upon approval of the application by the membership committee of this corporation [*and/or*] upon payment of the application fee and first annual dues, as specified in the following sections of this bylaw.

The actual amounts paid by members will be specified in the following sections of this bylaw.

Article 12, Section 4.
Membership Fees and Dues

Use these blanks to authorize or specify any application fee or annual dues charged to members:

> (a) The following fee shall be charged for making application for membership in the corporation: [*state specific admission fee, leave to discretion of board (for example, "in such amount as may be specified from time to time by resolution of the Board of Directors charged for, and payable with, the application for membership"), or, if no fee, type "None"*].
>
> (b) The annual dues payable to the corporation by members shall be [*state amount of annual dues, leave to discretion of board (for example, "in such amount as may be determined from time to time by resolution of the Board of Directors"), or type "None"*].

Article 12, Section 9.
Termination of Membership

The termination of membership provisions here are basic ones. Membership can be terminated voluntarily by a member or by the corporation if the member fails to pay dues. The corporation may also terminate a member for cause if the member is provided written notice and an opportunity to be heard.

RESOURCE

The statutes and court decisions of your state may contain specific substantive and procedural rules for terminating membership in a nonprofit corporation. If you do need to expel a member, we suggest you do so only after checking the latest annotated nonprofit statutes in your state (look under Membership Provisions in your state's nonprofit corporation act).

Article 13, Section 2.
Regular Meetings of Members

In the blanks in the first paragraph of this section, indicate the date and time of the regular meeting of members held to elect the board of directors. Typically, membership nonprofits will specify an annual meeting to elect the board here. The frequency of this meeting will, of course, depend on the length of the term of office for your directors (see the instructions for Article 3, Section 5, above).

Directors Elected Annually. Here is a sample bylaw for electing directors annually:

> A regular meeting of members shall be held on January 2 of each year at 1 p.m. for the purpose of electing directors and transacting other business as may come before the meeting.

In the second paragraph, type the date and time of any *additional* regular meetings of members you wish to schedule. Although we encourage frequent membership meetings, some smaller membership nonprofits may not wish to provide for regular meetings (other than the regular meeting to elect directors as specified in the preceding paragraph of the bylaws) and will leave these items blank. Others with a more active membership will use these blanks to specify frequent or occasional (for example, monthly or semiannual) regular meetings of members.

TIP

Remember special meetings. Your nonprofit membership corporation can also call and hold special meetings of members during the year—see the discussion below.

Article 13, Section 3.
Special Meetings of Members

This provision allows the chairperson of the board or the president of the corporation to call special meetings of members—this represents standard practice (and the standard state rule) for most nonprofits. Your nonprofit corporation law may allow other special meetings to be called by a specified percentage of the membership of the corporation—see your nonprofit corporation law if you wish to allow members to call special meetings (look under "Special Meetings of Members").

Article 13, Section 4.
Notice of Members' Meetings

Our notice provisions for members' meetings are, for the most part, standard provisions found in state nonprofit statutes, requiring personal or mailed notice for regular and special membership meetings. If you wish to extend or shorten the notice period (ten to 50 days), dispense with notice for regular meetings, or make other changes, check that your language conforms to your state's nonprofit law before making your changes.

As with the director notice provisions, members can waive notice of a meeting in writing—this procedure can come in handy if you don't have time to give formal notice of a meeting to members.

TIP

You can use telephone and fax machine notice. Our bylaw permits personal notification by telephone or fax machine. Again, a fax notice must be personally acknowledged by a return fax message or telephone call within 24 hours. If you want to allow email notification and acknowledgement of notice, check your state nonprofit law to make sure doing so is allowed.

Article 13, Section 5.
Quorum for Members' Meetings

Most smaller nonprofits indicate a majority quorum rule here (a majority of the members must be present to hold a members' meeting). The nonprofit corporation laws of a number of states are flexible on this point and allow the corporation to set its own members' meeting quorum requirement. If you wish to provide for less than a majority membership quorum, check your state nonprofit law first to see any limits that apply to setting a quorum at less than a majority.

Specifying a Quorum as a Majority of Voting Members.

A quorum shall consist of a majority of the voting members of the corporation.

TIP

For membership approval at a meeting, the vote of a majority of those present is required. (See Article 13, Section 6, of the membership provisions.) For example, in a corporation with 50 members and a majority quorum rule for membership meetings, a quorum for meetings consists of 26 members. If 26 members attend a meeting, action can be approved at the meeting by 14 members, a majority of those present.

Article 13, Section 8.
Action by Written Ballot

To make membership provisions more applicable and realistic, we have included this written ballot procedure to allow members to elect directors and transact other membership business by mail. These are standard, workable provisions—but they may not cover all the technical requirements found in your state's nonprofit statutes. To be certain, check our provisions against the membership written consent or written ballot procedures in your nonprofit statute or check with a lawyer.

Many states authorize membership action by written consent but require follow-up notice of any action taken to any nonconsenting members. See your state's nonprofit law for specific information.

Article 13, Section 9.
Conduct of Members' Meetings

Indicate, if you wish, the set of rules that will govern the proposing and taking of action at your membership meetings. *Robert's Rules of Order* is the standard, of course, but you may specify another set of procedures if you wish or leave this item blank if you see no reason to adopt formal rules for conducting membership meetings.

Completion of Membership Bylaws

Assemble your membership bylaws by adding the completed membership provision pages to the end of your completed bylaw pages. Then use the Adoption of Bylaws page as the last page of your bylaws. This page is included as the last page of the bylaws form. Fill in this page according to the Adoption of Bylaws instructions, given earlier. ●

Apply for Your Federal 501(c)(3) Tax Exemption

Now that that you've filed your articles and prepared your bylaws, it's time to prepare your federal tax exemption application (IRS Form 1023). Obtaining your federal exemption is a critical step in forming your nonprofit organization because most of the real benefits of being a nonprofit flow from 501(c)(3) tax-exempt status. Most groups complete and submit their federal tax exemption application before obtaining their state tax exemption because state exemptions often are contingent on nonprofits obtaining their federal tax exemption first—see "Obtain State Corporate Income Tax Exemption" in Chapter 9. To make your tax exemption retroactive to the date of your incorporation, your 1023 application must be submitted within 27 months from the end of the month in which you filed your articles of incorporation.

There are two different 1023 applications: the standard Form 1023 and the Form 1023-EZ, a shorter streamlined form. Most groups that qualify for the 1023-EZ form will want to use it because it is easier to prepare and its $275 filing fee is lower than the $600 filing fee for the standard 1023 exemption application. Smaller nonprofits (those with gross receipts of $50,000 or less and assets of $250,000 or less) are eligible to use the Form 1023-EZ. Both the standard Form 1023 and Form 1023-EZ must be completed and submitted online.

Whichever form you use, following our line-by-line instructions in this chapter can help you accomplish the task in substantially less time than it would otherwise take. We provide a lot of handholding and suggestions for responses to make the task of filling in your tax exemption application easier and less time consuming. And remember: You will be well rewarded in the end for the time and effort you devote to this task.

CAUTION

Special purpose nonprofits may use a different IRS form. If yours is a special purpose nonprofit group (formed for other than religious, educational, charitable, scientific, or literary purposes), you're likely to be exempt under subsections of Section 501(c) other than Subsection (3). To apply for your federal tax exemption, you may need to use IRS Form 1024 instead of IRS Form 1023. Certain cooperative hospital service organizations and cooperative educational service organizations can use Form 1023. See the Instructions to Form 1023 and Form 1023-EZ for more information on the application process for special purpose groups.

Getting Started

Before diving into the task at hand, take a moment to read this section, which goes through some of the preliminary steps you need to take and things to consider before you get started. Think of this portion of the chapter as your orientation.

Register With Pay.gov

Starting January 1, 2020, all Form 1023 applications—the longer Form 1023 and the shorter Form 1023-EZ—must be submitted electronically through Pay.gov. To get started, go to Pay.gov and register for an account. Once you're registered, enter "1023" in the Pay.gov search box and select which Form 1023 you are going to use. You can preview the form or start completing it online. At any point, you can save your answers and pick up again later where you left off.

Public Inspection Rights

Keep in mind that members of the public, not just some anonymous IRS application examiner, can obtain access to the information you provide in your exemption application. So, don't include Social Security numbers, bank account information, home addresses, or other personal information that you do not wish to disclose to the public in your tax exemption application or the attachments. Your federal 1023 tax exemption application, any supplemental pages submitted with the application, and your tax exemption determination letter from the IRS must be made available by your organization for public inspection during regular business hours at your organization's principal office. However, any information that has been submitted to the IRS and approved by it as confidential is not required to be publicly disclosed (see "How to Keep Form 1023 Information Confidential," below), and you do not have to disclose the names and addresses of contributors if you qualify as a public charity—which we assume you will.

How to Keep Form 1023 Information Confidential

Any information submitted with your 1023 is open to public inspection. However, if an attachment or response to your application contains information regarding trade secrets, patents, or other information that would adversely affect your organization if released to the public, you can clearly state "NOT SUBJECT TO PUBLIC INSPECTION" next to the material and include your reasons for requesting secrecy. If the IRS agrees, the information will not be open to public inspection.

IRS Regulation 301.6104(a)-5 says that the IRS will agree if you convince it that "the disclosure of such information would adversely affect the organization."

If your organization regularly maintains one or more regional or district offices having three or more employees (defined as offices that have a payroll consisting of at least 120 paid hours per week), you must make copies of the documents available for public inspection at each of these offices. Copies of your organization's three most recent annual information returns must also be available for public inspection at your principal office (and, if applicable, your regional or district office).

Members of the public can also make a written request for copies of your organization's tax exemption application and its tax returns for the last three years. You must comply within 30 days and are allowed to charge only reasonable copying and postage costs. The public also can request copies or public inspection of your organization's exemption application or its annual returns by calling IRS Exempt Organizations Customer Account Services at 877-829-5500. These public inspection requirements apply to 501(c)(3) public charities, not to 501(c)(3) private foundations—again, we expect most incorporators to qualify as public charities.

It's important to comply with inspection requests. If you don't permit public inspection, you could face a $20-per-day penalty. The IRS will impose an automatic $5,000 additional penalty if your failure to comply is willful.

These penalties are not imposed on the organization—they are applied against "the person failing to meet (these) requirements." See IRS Publication 557 and IRC Sections 6104(e), 5562(c)(1)(C) and (D), and 6685 for further information on these rules.

Filing Deadline

You should file your Form 1023 within 27 months after the end of the month in which you filed your articles of incorporation. In our experience, the most common problem faced by nonprofits is failing to file their Form 1023 on time. What happens if you file late?

First, if you file on time (within 27 months of incorporating) and the IRS grants your exemption, the exemption takes effect on the date on which you filed your articles. The same is true if you can show "reasonable cause" for your delay (this means you have convinced the IRS that your tardiness was understandable and excusable). If you file late and don't have reasonable cause (or the IRS doesn't accept your explanation), your tax-exempt status will begin as of the submission date on your form. For more information, see "Prepare Your Tax Exemption Application," Part VII, below, including the instructions to Schedule E.

TIP

Use the 1023 form to show reasonable cause for filing late. If you file late and want to request relief from the 27-month deadline, you must submit the 1023 form. You cannot ask for relief from the deadline if you use the shorter 1023-EZ form.

TIP

Tax Technicality: If you submit your 1023 application after the 27-month deadline, but are one of the groups that did not need to apply during your pre-application period (see the next section, "Do You Need to File Form 1023"), instead of requesting your exemption application to be retroactive due to reasonable cause, you may be able rely on your "automatic" tax-exempt status during the pre-application period. If you find yourself in this situation, check with a nonprofit tax lawyer to be sure you can rely on being exempt during your pre-application period.

If your nonprofit has been organized for several years and you're just now getting around to filing your Form 1023, don't worry—you've got plenty of good company. The important point here is to persevere, complete your application, and mail it to the IRS as soon as possible.

Do All Nonprofits Need to File a Form 1023?

Almost all nonprofit groups that want 501(c)(3) tax-exempt status will file an application for a federal tax exemption (Form 1023 or Form 1023-EZ). Your application for recognition of exemption serves two important purposes:

- It is used by nonprofit organizations to apply for 501(c)(3) tax-exempt status.
- It serves as your notice to the IRS that your organization is a public charity, not a private foundation. Remember, as discussed earlier, the IRS will presume that your 501(c)(3) nonprofit group is a private foundation unless you notify the IRS that you qualify for public charity status.

This said, there are a few groups that are not required to file an application for a 501(c)(3) tax exemption—these groups will be considered automatically exempt if they meet the requirements of Section 501(c)(3). You aren't required to file if you are:

- a church or a group that qualifies for public charity status and normally has gross receipts of not more than $5,000. (The IRS uses a special formula to determine whether a group "normally" has annual gross receipts of not more than $5,000—for specifics, see IRS Publication 557, "Organizations Not Required to File Form 1023," "Gross Receipts Test.")

Note: Even if you are not required to apply for your tax exemption, you should still file 990-N postcard annually. Call the IRS Customer

Account Services at 877-829-5500 (a toll-free number) and ask that the organization be set up to allow filing of Form 990-N.

TIP

Something to keep in mind. You need to file an application for a 501(c)(3) tax exemption within 90 days of the date your organization no longer has annual gross receipts over $5,000 (using the special 3-year "normally" formula that tests gross receipts over a three-year period—again see IRS Publication 557, "Organizations Not Required to File Form 1023," "Gross Receipts Test"). If you think it likely that your organization will exceed this gross receipts threshold sometime in the near future, it's probably best to go ahead and apply for your 501(c)(3) income tax exemption now.

- a church (a church includes synagogues, temples, and mosques), interchurch organization, local unit of a church, convention, or association of churches, or an integrated auxiliary of a church, or

- a subordinate organization covered by a group exemption letter (but only if the parent organization timely submits a notice to the IRS covering the subordinate organization—see the group exemption letter requirements in IRS Publication 557).

Even if one of the above exceptions applies to you, we recommend that you file a tax exemption application anyway. Why? First, it's risky to second-guess the IRS. If you're wrong and the IRS denies your claim to 501(c)(3) tax status several years from now, your organization may have to pay substantial back taxes and penalties. Second, the only way, on a practical and legal level, to assure others that you are a bona fide 501(c)(3) group is to apply for an exemption. If the IRS agrees and grants your tax exemption, then, and only then, can you assure contributors, grant agencies, and others that you are a qualified 501(c)(3) tax-exempt, tax-deductible organization listed with the IRS.

Are You Eligible to Use Form 1023-EZ?

Before starting your federal tax exemption application, read the instructions to Form 1023-EZ, available on the IRS website, and go through the included Eligibility Worksheet to see if you qualify to use the EZ form. Most smaller new groups with modest expectations as to gross receipts ($50,000 in receipts annually before deducting expenses) and assets ($250,000 or less) that are not setting up an institutional nonprofit (such as a school, hospital, or church) should qualify. If you qualify and use Form 1023-EZ, you will be charged the lower $275 application fee and will not need to provide financial data or complete extra schedules.

If you use the longer online 1023 form, you will have more information to complete, including providing financial data and possibly preparing additional schedules. You will be charged a $600 fee to submit the standard 1023 form. The official instructions to Form 1023 and Form 1023-EZ and additional information on both forms are available on the IRS website.

TIP

A downside to using the 1023-EZ form. The 1023-EZ form asks you to select the public charity status that applies to you, while the standard 1023 form lets you hand off this decision to the IRS by checking a special box on the form. No worries, though—by referring to Chapter 4, you can make an informed decision as to the most appropriate public charity classification to select for your nonprofit on the 1023-EZ form.

Forms and Publications

You'll encounter several IRS forms as you make your way toward federal tax-exempt status. We go over these forms and provide information on how to complete them:

- IRS Form 1023-EZ, *Streamlined Application for Recognition of Exemption Under Section 501(c)(3) of the Internal Revenue Code*. This is a simple form that many small organizations can use to easily apply for their federal income tax exemption.

- IRS Form 1023, *Application for Recognition of Exemption*. This is the "long form" application that organizations that do not qualify for the streamlined 1023-EZ form must use instead.

- Form SS-4, *Application for Employer Identification Number*. Use the online form to apply for an EIN for your organization.

- Form 5768, *Election/Revocation of Election by an Eligible Section 501(c)(3) Organization to Make Expenditures to Influence Legislation*. This is a special form that only applies to certain politically active nonprofits.

For more background information, the following federal IRS tax publications are surprisingly readable and give a lot of practical information. They are available on the IRS website or by calling the IRS forms and publications request number, 800-TAX-FORM.

- Publication 557, *Tax-Exempt Status for Your Organization*
- Publication 4220, *Applying for 501(c)(3) Tax-Exempt Status*
- Publication 4221-PC, *Compliance Guide for 501(c)(3) Public Charities*
- Publication 4221-PF, *Compliance Guide for 501(c)(3) Private Foundations*
- Publication 1828, *Tax Guide for Churches and Religious Organizations*.

All groups should skim through Chapters 1, 2, and 3 of IRS Publication 557 and Publications 4220 and 4221-PC—the information there covers the basic requirements for obtaining a 501(c)(3) tax exemption. You should also be familiar the IRS Form 990 Annual Return and Instructions. This form, called *Return of Organization Exempt from Income Tax*, must be filed each year with the IRS by 501(c)(3) organizations. If your nonprofit has receipts of $50,000 or less, you may file Form 990-N (an e-Postcard), instead of the longer Form 990. Smaller nonprofits that don't qualify for the 990-N postcard may still qualify to file a simplified 990-EZ form. See the Form 990, 990-EZ, and 990-N instructions on the IRS website for more information. Churches and certain other types of nonprofits are exempt.

RESOURCE

You can find additional helpful information, including articles on special exempt organization issues, from the IRS website at www.irs.gov. Click the "Charities & Nonprofits" button on the irs.gov website. Also, see the IRS online workshops and minicourses at IRS Stay Exempt—Tax Basics for Exempt Organizations (www.stayexempt.irs.gov).

Form 1023-EZ: Step-By-Step Instructions

Below are instructions to help you complete the Form 1023-EZ application. Most nonprofits that qualify to use the 1023-EZ will choose to use it because it is so much shorter and easier than the standard 1023 application. Many of the questions are self-explanatory and easy to answer. We provide a few pointers to help you understand what the IRS is looking for. You will need to register for an account with Pay.gov and then follow the instructions for completing the form, paying the filing fee, and submitting the completed form online to the IRS. For additional guidance go to Pay.gov or check the official IRS instructions to Form 1023-EZ, available on the IRS website.

Top of Form

Check the box at the top of the form to confirm that you completed the 1023-EZ Eligibility Worksheet and are eligible to file the 1023-EZ. You should be able to check "No" to the gross receipts (more than $50,000) and assets (more than $250,000) questions to show that you qualify to use Form 1023-EZ.

Part I: Identification of Applicant

Line 1(a)–(f). Write the name of your corporation exactly as it appears in your articles of incorporation. Provide the mailing address of the corporation. If you do not have a street address, provide a post office box address. The IRS wants you to include the full nine-digit zip code in your address. Include it if you know it. (Zip code information can be obtained online at the U.S. Postal Service Zip Code lookup page.)

Line 2. You'll need a federal Employer Identification Number (EIN) for your nonprofit corporation. See Form 1023 instructions, below, Part I, Line 2, for information on how to get one.

Line 3. Insert the month your corporation's tax year ends. Use a two-digit month number for your response. See Form 1023 Instructions, below, Part I, Line 3, for more information.

Lines 4–6. State the name of a director or officer the IRS can contact regarding your application, the phone number where this person can be contacted during business hours, and a fax number. The fax number is optional—if you don't want to provide one, insert "not applicable."

Line 7. $275 is the user fee that you pay if you qualify to use Form 1023-EZ.

Line 8. List the names, titles, and mailing addresses of your officers, directors, or trustees. Only list five. If you have more than five, select the ones to be listed as explained in the official instructions to Form 1023-EZ. Most smaller nonprofits have a president (or CEO), treasurer (or CFO), secretary, and perhaps a vice president and/or chairman of the board.

If a person serves in more than one capacity, only list the person once and show the title of all positions held by that person. You can use the address of the corporation as the mailing address of your directors and officers.

Line 9 (a)–(b). If applicable, list the website address of your nonprofit, and its email address. Any website content should be consistent with your nonprofit purposes and program as described in your 1023 application. Insert "N/A" if either item is not applicable.

Part II: Organizational Structure

Line 1. Check the corporation box.

Line 2. Check this box to indicate that you have the required organizing document; namely, articles of incorporation that have been certified as having been filed with the state.

Line 3. Insert the date your articles were filed by the secretary of state in mm/dd/yyyy format.

Line 4. Insert your state of incorporation.

Lines 5–7. If you followed our instructions in Chapter 6 for preparing your articles, you should be able to check each of these three boxes to indicate that your articles of incorporation contain the required provisions with respect to 501(c)(3) purposes, limitation of activities, and dedication of assets.

Part III: Your Specific Activities

In this section, the IRS wants to get an idea of how your nonprofit will actually operate. In some cases, your response may result in follow-up questions from the IRS (for example, if you indicate that you will pay officers or directors or engage in legislative activity, the IRS may want to make sure that the compensation is reasonable or the political activities insubstantial before granting your exemption). It's best to be as honest as you can at the start, and dispose of any issues the IRS raises early on, to avoid any potential problems later. Before filling in this section, read the official 1023-EZ instructions for each of the questions in this section; these instructions provide or point you to more information on some of the issues, activities, and purposes listed in this section.

Line 1. Provide a brief description of your primary tax-exempt activities or goals. Try not to repeat verbatim the purpose clause language in your articles (Chapter 6). A summary or gloss of the purpose clause language from your bylaws (Chapter 7) may be used here if it describes your most important activities or mission.

Line 2. The list of three-character NTEE Codes is included at the end of the official 1023-EZ instructions (available on the IRS website at www.irs.gov/pub/irs-pdf/i1023ez.pdf).

Select the one that best matches your 501(c)(3) purposes and/or activities.

Line 3. Check the box(es) that match(es) the 501(c)(3) purpose(s) contained in your articles (see instructions in Chapter 6 to preparing Article 3, "Federal 501(c)(3) Tax-Exempt Purpose Clause").

Line 4. You should be able to check this box to show that you will abide by these 501(c)(3) operational requirements (see Chapter 3, "Other Requirements for 501(c)(3) Groups," for more information on these requirements).

Line 5. If you will attempt to influence legislation, check the "Yes" box. For the 501(c)(3) limits on this activity, and to consider whether you should make an election using Form 5768, see Chapter 3, "Limitation on Political Activities."

Line 6. If you will pay your officers or directors (or think you will), check the "Yes" box. We've already explained the basic 501(c)(3) prohibition against private inurement and the excess benefit rules that penalize nonprofits and their managers if they pay unreasonable compensation to insiders and outsiders (see the discussion on the

excess benefit rules in "Limitation on Profits and Benefits," in Chapter 3).

Lines 7–12. If you check "Yes" to any responses, the IRS may ask for additional details in follow-up questions to ensure that your nonprofit is operating within allowable 501(c)(3)limits. These are: no private inurement or special benefits to individuals (including directors and officers); only incidental—not substantial—unrelated business income; no support to restricted foreign entities; and no bingo or gaming activities. Here are some pointers for more information on some special issues associated with these items:

- **Unrelated Business Income.** If you anticipate that your organization will earn $1,000 or more in annual unrelated business income, the IRS may send you additional questions to determine, based on the description you provide of your proposed operations, that such business income will not be a primary activity of your nonprofit (see Chapter 3, "Unrelated Business Activities"). Also be prepared to file annual 990-T forms as explained in "Federal Corporate Tax Returns" in Chapter 10).

- **Bingo and gaming.** See IRS Publication 3079, *Tax-Exempt Organizations and Gaming.*

- **Foreign operations.** Special tax exemption and deductibility of contribution rules apply to nonprofits created or operated abroad. If you plan to operate or provide assistance abroad, you may wish to seek guidance from a nonprofit adviser who has experience in advising nonprofits that operate in the foreign countries where you plan to operate. Also see "Foreign Organizations in General" in the official standard Form1023 instructions for basic information on nonprofits formed abroad. Finally, realize that a big part of the IRS's energies is now devoted to scrutinizing the operations of foreign-based nonprofits as part of the service's participation in antiterrorism.

Here is an excerpt from the IRS 2005 EO (Exempt Organization) report:

> In FY 2005, EO will examine a sample of foreign grant making organizations; the primary focus of the examinations is to ensure that funds are used for their intended charitable purpose and not diverted for terrorist activity.
>
> The project will gather information about current practices, that is, the existence and effectiveness of controls put in place to monitor the distribution of overseas grants and other assistance. This committee will also address the need for possible guidance or other modifications to the laws in this area.

- **Disaster Relief.** The IRS may prioritize the processing of your application if your organization provides disaster relief. For more information, see IRS Publication 3833, *Disaster Relief: Providing Assistance Through Charitable Organizations.*

Part IV: Foundation Classification

This is a technical section, which seeks to determine whether your 501(c)(3) will be a public charity or a private foundation. To help you answer the questions in this section, reread Chapter 4, where we explain the importance of qualifying your 501(c)(3) tax-exempt organization as a public charity and explain the three basic ways your organization can qualify as a public charity. Also read the official 1023-EZ instructions for this section.

Line 1. Certain nonprofits that may qualify for public charity status (we call this category "Automatic Public Charity Status" in Chapter 4), including churches, schools, and hospitals, do not qualify to use Form 1023-EZ. These nonprofits have to check "Yes" for this question and must use online Form 1023 to apply for their tax exemption and public charity status.

Therefore, Form 1023-EZ and the remaining questions in this section of the 1023-EZ only apply to groups that can check "No" for this question and can seek to qualify as a public charity because of the types of public support or exempt purpose revenue they receive (they qualify as a public charity under either the "Public Support Test" or the "Exempt Activities Support Test" as described in Chapter 4).

Line 2. Check one of the boxes in this section to tell the IRS how you plan to qualify as a public charity. You can use the 1023-EZ instructions to calculate whether you meet either of these two tests:

- (a) Check this box if you calculate that you should qualify as a public charity under the "Public Support" test covered in Chapter 4.

- (b) Check this box if you calculate that you should qualify as a public charity under the "Exempt Activities Test" test covered in Chapter 4.

- (c) Certain organizations operated for the benefit of a governmental college or university (e.g., state school) qualify as public charities. We assume you are not forming this special type of nonprofit, but if you are, see a nonprofit specialist with experience with this sort of organization for guidance in forming your nonprofit and obtaining your tax exemption and qualifying as a public charity.

Line 3. We assume readers will check Box 2(a) or (b) to seek public charity status for their 501(c)(3) tax-exempt organization. If you do not calculate that you should qualify to check either the 2(a) or (b) box, and end up prepared to check Box 3, you should get the help of a nonprofit adviser to form a private foundation and obtain its 501(c)(3) tax exemption (see Chapter 4, "Private Foundations" for more information).

Part V: Reinstatement After Automatic Revocation

You can ignore this section. It is used by nonprofits that have already obtained and lost their 501(c)(3) exemption due to a failure to file their annual IRS Form 990 informational tax form. (Read the official 1023-EZ instructions to this section for more information). It's good to know that Form 1023-EZ can be used for this purpose, but by staying on top of your ongoing nonprofit tax filing responsibilities after you obtain your tax exemption (see Chapter 10), you will never need to do so.

The Standard Form 1023: Step-by-Step Instructions

If you do not qualify to use the 1023-EZ online application, you will need to apply for your tax exemption by completing the longer Form 1023 application. Starting January 1, 2020, you must submit the longer Form 1023 application electronically through Pay.gov. To get started, go to Pay.gov, register for an account,

and enter "1023" in the search box. Select the longer Form 1023 and then follow the instructions for completing the form, paying the filing fee, and submitting the completed form online to the IRS.

> **TIP**
>
> **Read the online help provided with the form.** When filling in the 1023 application, read the help tips associated with each line item (click the "?" icon). These tips provide essential information that will help you complete the form.

Adding Supplemental Pages

If you complete the standard Form 1023, you should be able to provide all responses in the predefined response boxes. However, you may need to continue some of your longer responses on supplemental pages. Any supplemental pages must be included with your articles of incorporation and bylaws and assembled into a PDF file that you will upload to the Pay.gov site after completing the online 1023 application.

Sample Supplemental Page

Attachment to Form 1023, Page 1

GoodWorks, Inc.

EIN # XXXXXXXX

Part IV, Narrative Description of Activities: The nonprofit organization also will engage in the following activities: …

_____

Part V, Line 1a, Names, titles, mailing addresses, and compensation of officers, directors, and trustees (continuation):

Name	Title	Mailing Address	Compensation (actual or proposed)

_____

_____

When preparing supplemental pages, add the following information at the top of each page:

- the name and EIN (Employer Identification Number) of your corporation
- for each response, state the part and line number to which the response relates.

You do not need to have a separate supplemental page for each continuation response—just list your responses one after the other on your supplemental pages (as shown on the sample above).

When including copies of your articles and bylaws in your PDF file, each page should have a heading to identify the document, such as "Articles of [name of your corporation]" or "Bylaws of [name of your corporation]." Each page should also show the page number in the header or footer.

Part I: Identification of Applicant

Line 1(a). Write the name of your corporation exactly as it appears in your articles of incorporation.

Line 1(b). If you have designated one person in your organization to receive return mail from the IRS regarding your 1023 application, such as one of the founders, list this person's name as the "c/o name." Otherwise, insert "not applicable."

Line 1(c)-1(i). Provide the mailing address of the corporation. If you do not have a street address, provide a post office box address. The IRS wants you to include the full nine-digit zip code in your address. Include it if you know it. (Zip code information can be obtained online at the U.S. Postal Service zip code lookup page.) If your nonprofit has an address in a foreign country, consult a nonprofit specialist to help you apply for an exemption.

Line 2. All nonprofit corporations (whether or not they have employees) must obtain a federal Employer Identification Number (EIN) prior to applying for 501(c)(3) tax exemption. You will insert this number here on your 1023 form and use this identification number on all your future nonprofit federal information, income, and employee tax returns. Even if your organization held an EIN prior to incorporation, you must obtain a new one for the nonprofit corporate entity. If your nonprofit corporation has not yet obtained an EIN, it should do so now.

The easiest and quickest (and IRS-preferred) way to get an EIN is to apply online from the IRS website. Go to www.irs.gov and type "EIN" in the upper search box and select the link to the online EIN application. Then complete and file your IRS Form SS-4, *Application for Employer Identification Number*, online and receive your EIN immediately. You also can apply for an EIN by phone, fax, or mail. See the IRS website for instructions.

Follow the instructions, below, when completing the SS-4 form:

- **Name and SSN of officer.** You will need to specify the name and Social Security number of one of your principal officers. Normally the chief financial officer or treasurer will provide a name and SSN here.

- **Type of entity.** Check "church or church-controlled organization" if you are forming one; if not, check "other nonprofit organization" and specify its 501(c)(3) purpose (educational, charitable, and so on).

- **GEN number.** Most groups will ignore this item—it applies only to a group exemption application request. Members of an affiliated group of nonprofits can specify a previously assigned Group Exemption Number.

- **Reason for applying.** Check "started new business," then specify "formed nonprofit corporation" in the blank. If you are converting an existing unincorporated association (that has previously filed any appropriate tax returns for its association tax years with the IRS) to a nonprofit corporation, you can check "changed type of organization" instead and then insert "incorporation" in the blank.

- **Date Business Started.** The date you started your business is the date your articles were filed with the state filing office. Use the file-stamped date on the copy of your articles returned by the state office.

- **Employees.** You can enter zeros in the next item that asks the number of employees you expect to have in the next 12 months.

Line 3. Select the month your accounting period will end.

The accounting period must be the same as your corporation's tax year. Most nonprofits use a calendar year as their accounting period and tax year. If you choose to do the same, select "December."

If you anticipate special seasonal cycles for your activities or noncalendar-year record keeping or grant accountability procedures, you may wish to select a noncalendar accounting period for your corporation. For example, a federally funded school may specify June, which reflects an accounting period of July 1 to June 30.

If you have any questions regarding the best accounting period and tax year for your group, check with your (probable) funding sources and consult your accountant or bookkeeper for further guidance.

Lines 4–6. State the name of a director or an officer the IRS can contact regarding your application, the phone number where this person can be contacted during business hours, and a fax number. The fax number is optional. We suggest you list the name and telephone number of the director or officer who is preparing and will sign your tax exemption application. Don't expect the IRS to call to ask questions. If the IRS has questions about your application, it will usually contact you by mail.

Line 7. $600 is the user fee you pay for your online application.

Line 8. Insert the URL for your nonprofit's website, if you have one. Any website content should be consistent with your nonprofit purposes and program as described in your 1023 application. If your organization doesn't have a website, insert "not applicable" in the blank.

Line 9. Provide the names, titles, and mailing addresses of the initial directors named in your articles and your initial officers. You can ignore the instructions concerning trustees—your directors are the trustees of your nonprofit corporation. List your initial directors and your top-tier officer team, if you know who will fill these officer positions (such as president or chief executive officer, vice president, secretary, and treasurer or chief financial officer, or any other title used in your organization). For director or officer mailing addresses, you can state the mailing address of the corporation.

Part II: Organizational Structure

Line 1. Most tax-exempt nonprofits are formed as nonprofit corporate entities, and we expect you to follow the standard practice of forming a corporation too. Check "Corporation" to indicate that your group is a corporation. At the end of the online form, upload a copy of your articles. The copy should be a certified copy you received from the state filing office. It should show a file-date stamp on the first page or include a certification statement or page that states it was filed with the state and is a correct copy of the original filed document.

Other Nonprofit Entities

Very few nonprofits are formed as limited liability companies. If this is what you are attempting to do, you should consult with a lawyer.

An unincorporated association requires special paperwork (association charter or articles and association operating agreement), and it leaves the members potentially personally liable for the debts of and claims made against the association. If you are applying for a tax exemption for an unincorporated association, you should check with a lawyer before applying for your tax exemption.

If you are interested in establishing a tax-exempt trust, see an expert.

Line 2. Insert the date your articles were filed by the secretary of state in mm/dd/yyyy format, such as 01/05/2021. This is the date your nonprofit corporation was formed unless you requested a delayed effective date for your articles—if you did request a delayed effective date for your articles, show the delayed date instead.

Line 3. Select your state of formation. If you are seeking an IRS 501(c)(3) tax exemption for a corporation formed abroad, select "Foreign Country," and seek additional help from an adviser who can assist you through your more complicated tax exemption application process.

Line 4. Check "Yes." At the end of the online form, upload a copy of the bylaws you have prepared as part of Chapter 7. Make sure you have filled in all the blanks in your printed bylaws and include a completed Adoption of Bylaws page at the end of your bylaws. The adoption page should show the date of adoption and include the signatures of your initial directors.

Line 5. Most groups will check "No" to this question. However, if you are a successor to an incorporated or a preexisting organization (such as an unincorporated association), mark "yes."

Successor has a special technical meaning, which is explained in the official IRS instructions to this item. Basically, you are most likely to be a successor organization if your nonprofit corporation has:

- taken over the activities of a prior organization—this is presumably the case if your nonprofit corporation has appointed initial directors or officers who are the same people who served as the directors or officers of the prior association, and your nonprofit has the same purposes as the prior association

- taken over 25% or more of the assets of a preexisting nonprofit, or

- been legally converted from the previous association to a nonprofit—typically by filing special articles of incorporation to state the name of the prior association and a declaration by the prior officers of the association that the conversion to a nonprofit corporation was properly approved by the association, or by filing articles of conversion to convert a profit-making entity to your new nonprofit corporation.

We assume most readers will be starting new nonprofits, not inheriting the assets, people, and activities of a preexisting formal nonprofit association. We also assume most readers have not adopted special articles to legally convert a prior association or profit-making entity to a nonprofit corporation. In the real world, this formal conversion of a prior association to a nonprofit corporation only occurs if the prior group was a highly organized and visible entity with a solid support base that it wants to leverage by formally converting the association to a nonprofit corporation.

However, in most cases, a small nonprofit that existed previously as an informal nonprofit group with few assets, little support, and hardly any formal infrastructure normally starts out fresh with a newly formed corporation that is not a successor to the prior group. If you think your nonprofit corporation is a "successor" organization, we suggest you get help from a nonprofit expert to complete Schedule G and make sure all the paperwork for your new nonprofit as well as the prior group is in order.

Part III: Required Provisions in Your Organizing Document

Line 1 and 1(a). Your articles, which you will upload at the end of the online application must contain a 501(c)(3) tax-exempt purpose clause (see "Federal 501(c)(3) Tax-Exempt Purpose Clause" in "Complete Your Articles" in Chapter 6). Check the 'Yes" box, and on Line 1(a) insert the article, and paragraph where the 501(c)(3) purpose clause appears. Make sure you reference the 501(c)(3) purpose clause, not any state-required lawful purpose or specific purpose clause also included in your articles. For example, the following articles contain both a 501(c)(3) tax-exempt purpose clause and a state-required specific purpose clause:

> Article 3. The purposes for which this corporation is organized are:
>
> This corporation is organized and operated exclusively for educational purposes within the meaning of 501(c)(3) of the Internal Revenue Code. The specific purposes for which this corporation is organized are to educate the general public in dance and other art forms. The means of providing such education includes, but is not limited to, maintaining facilities for instruction and public performances of dance and other art forms.

The group would check the "Yes" box in Line 1, and then, Line 1(a), insert "Article 3, Paragraph 1"—because the 501(c)(3) tax-exempt purpose clause appears in the first paragraph of Article 3 of the articles.

This group specified only one 501(c)(3) purpose—educational—in its 501(c)(3) exempt purpose clause. You can choose to use a more general statement that specifies one or more or all of the allowable 501(c)(3) exempt purposes (see "Sample Completed Articles" in Chapter 6).

Line 2 and 2(a). Check the Line 2 "Yes" box to indicate that your articles contain a 501(c)(3) asset dedication clause (we assume your articles will contain a dedication clause as explained below), and fill in the blank in 2(a) to state the article and paragraph where the dissolution clause appears in your articles.

To recap: A requirement for 501(c)(3) tax-exempt status is that any assets of a nonprofit that remain after the entity dissolves be distributed to another 501(c)(3) tax-exempt nonprofit —or to a federal, state, or local government for a public purpose (see "Limitation on Profits and Benefits" in Chapter 3), and "Additional Federal Tax Exemption Language" in "Complete Your Articles" in Chapter 6). You can meet this irrevocable dedication of assets requirement by including an explicit dedication clause in your articles of incorporation or by relying on state law, if you live in a state that has adopted a 501(c)(3) default dedication clause. Some states have laws requiring all 501(c)(3)s formed in the state to dedicate their remaining assets upon dissolution to another 501(c)(3). We believe that, even if you live in a state that has a default dedication provision, you should always include an explicit dedication clause in your articles. It's best to state any major restrictions on assets and operations explicitly in your articles as a cautionary reminder to your directors, officers, members, and others. And you won't have to research your state law to find out if you have an applicable default provision, or be at risk of your state law changing or the IRS deciding that your state's dissolution clause is not sufficient to meet the 501(c)(3) dedication of assets requirement.

For example, assume a nonprofit has the following asset dedication clause on Page 3 of its articles:

Article 8. Additional Provisions

The property of this corporation is irrevocably dedicated to [*state one or more of your actual tax-exempt purposes , such as "charitable," "religious," "educational," "literary," and/or "scientific"*] purposes and no part of the net income or assets of this corporation shall inure to the benefit of any director, officer, or member thereof or to the benefit of any private person. Upon the dissolution or winding up of the corporation, its assets remaining after payment, or provision for payment, of all debts and liabilities of this corporation shall be distributed to a nonprofit fund, foundation, or corporation that is organized and operated exclusively for [*repeat the same purpose or purposes stated in the first blank*] purposes and that has established its tax-exempt status under Section 501(c)(3) of the Internal Revenue Code.

No substantial part of the activities of this corporation shall consist of carrying on propaganda, or otherwise attempting to influence legislation (except as otherwise provided by Section 501(h) of the Internal Revenue Code), and this corporation shall not participate in, or intervene in (including the publishing or distribution of statements), any political campaign on behalf of, or in opposition to, any candidate for public office.

No part of the net earnings of this corporation shall inure to the benefit of, or be distributable to, its members, directors, officers, or other private persons, except that this corporation shall be authorized and empowered to pay reasonable compensation for services rendered and to make payments and distributions in furtherance of the purposes set forth in these articles.

Notwithstanding any other provision of these articles, this corporation shall not carry on any other activities not permitted to be carried on (1) by a corporation exempt from federal income tax under Section 501(c)(3) of the Internal Revenue Code or (2) by a corporation contributions to which are deductible under Section 170(c)(2) of the Internal Revenue Code.

This nonprofit would check the "Yes" Line 2 box, and insert the following on the Line 2(b): "Article 8, first paragraph." This article provision (which is taken from "Complete Your Articles," in Chapter 6, Article 8 instructions) contains additional optional 501(c)(3) compliance language that we recommend all groups include in their articles (see "Optional 501(c)(3) Tax Exemption Language" under "Complete Your Articles" in Chapter 6).

Part IV: Your Activities

You should be familiar with the material in Chapter 3 concerning the basic requirements for obtaining a 501(c)(3) tax exemption before providing the information requested in this part of the form. We will refer to earlier explanations as we go along, but you may want to look over Chapter 3 now before you proceed.

TIP

Tell it like it is. When you describe your proposed activities, don't limit your narrative to only those activities that fit neatly within the 501(c)(3) framework if you're simply "gilding the lily" to gain IRS approval. Sure, you'll probably get your tax exemption, but you may not keep it. The IRS can always decide later, after examining your actual sources of support, that your activities go beyond the scope of the activities disclosed in your application. In short, it's a lot more painful and expensive to shut down your nonprofit if it loses its tax exemption than to decide at the outset not to apply for 501(c)(3) status because your proposed mission does not qualify for tax-exempt status.

Line 1. In the space provided on the online form, provide a detailed description of all of your organization's activities—past, present, and future—in their order of importance (that is, in order of the amount of time and resources devoted to each activity). For each activity, explain in detail:

- the activity itself, how it furthers an exempt purpose(s) of your organization, and the percentage of time your group will devote to it

- when it was begun (or, if it hasn't yet begun, when it will begin)

- where and by whom it will be conducted, and

- how it will be funded (the financial information or projections you provide later in your application should be consistent with the funding methods or mechanisms you mention here). For example, if your application shows you will be obtaining the bulk of your tax-exempt revenue from providing program-related services, such as tuition or admission fees, and/or from grant funds, you will want to mention these sources of support here (see additional instructions on describing your financial support below).

Many new groups will be describing proposed activities that are not yet operational, but you must still provide very thorough information.

If you plan to conduct any unrelated business (business that doesn't directly further your non-profit goals), describe it here. Most nonprofits will not have planned unrelated business activities at this point. If you have, you will not want to stress the importance or scope of these incidental unrelated activities (for an explanation of the tricky issues surrounding unrelated business activities, see Chapter 3).

Tempting though it might be, resist copying the language that already appears in the purpose clause in your articles—the IRS wants a narrative, not an abbreviated, legal description of your proposed activities. You may include a reference to, or repeat the language of, the longer statement of specific objectives and purposes included in Article 2, Section 2, of your bylaws. However, unless your bylaw language includes a detailed narrative of both your activities and purposes, we suggest you use it only as a starting point for a fuller response here. Generally, we recommend starting over with a fresh, straightforward statement of your group's nonprofit activities.

EXAMPLE 1: A response by an environmental organization might read in part as follows:

The organization's activities will consist primarily of educating the public on environmental issues with an emphasis on energy conservation. Since January 20XX, the organization has published brochures promoting solar energy heating systems as an alternative to traditional energy sources. The price for the brochures is slightly above cost—see copies of educational material enclosed, Attachments A–D. The brochures are published in-house at [*address of principal office*].

Both paid and volunteer staff contribute to the research, writing, editing, and production process. This work constitutes approximately 80% of the group's activities. In addition to publishing, the organization's other activities include the following [*list in order of importance other current, past, or planned activities and percentage of time devoted to each, where performed, etc.*].

EXAMPLE 2: A nonprofit organization plans to sponsor activities for the purpose of supporting other nonprofit charities. It should describe both the activities in which it will engage to obtain revenue at special events and the manner in which this money will be spent to support other groups. Percentages of time and resources devoted to each should be given.

If you are forming an organization that automatically qualifies for public charity status (a church, school, hospital, or medical research organization) or has special tax exemption requirements, you will want to show that your organization meets the criteria that apply to your type of organization. See "Automatic Public Charity Status," in Chapter 4, for a discussion of each of these special types of nonprofits. The 1023 form contains schedules that apply to each type of special group (for example, Schedule A for churches, Schedule B for schools, and Schedule C for hospitals).

Your description should indicate your organization's anticipated sources of financial support—preferably in the order of magnitude (most money to least money). Here are a few tips to help you address this portion of your response:

- Your sources of support should be related to your exempt purposes—particularly if you plan to be classified as a public

charity under the support test described in "Exempt Activities Support Test," in Chapter 4, where the group's primary support is derived from the performance of tax-exempt activities.

- If you plan to qualify as a publicly supported public charity (described in "Public Support Test," in Chapter 4), your responses here should show significant support from various governmental grants, private agency funding, or individual contributions.

- If you expect your principal sources of support to fluctuate substantially, describe anticipated changes.

Your description should show how you will fund your activities. For example, if you will give classes, state how you will recruit instructors and attract students. If you will rely on grants, state your likely sources of grant support—for example, the particular or general categories of grant agencies you plan to approach. If your nonprofit expects to obtain funds through grant solicitations or other fundraising efforts—that is, by soliciting contributions from donors either directly or through paid fundraising—make sure you provide a narrative description of these efforts here. In Part VI of your online application you will provide additional information on your fundraising activities.

Fundraising activities include unrelated business activities that will bring cash into your nonprofit. If you have concrete plans to engage in unrelated activities (which, of course, you should be able to clearly describe as an insubstantial part of your overall activities), include the details if you have not done so already in your response.

If your organization has or plans to have a website, provide information on the existing site (including its URL) or the planned site. The existing or proposed website content and any revenue it generates should be related to and further the exempt purposes of the group. If your website is used to solicit contributions or generate other revenue, explain how this is or will be done.

Finally, if your group intends to operate under a fictitious business name (an aka—"also known as"—or dba—"doing business as"—name) that differs from your formal corporate name as stated in your articles (see "File Fictitious or Assumed Business Name Statement" in Chapter 9), make sure to mention the alternate name here, and state why you want to use an alternate name.

Line 2. Look at the list of 3-character NTEE Codes in Appendix D of the Instructions for Form 1023 (available online at the IRS website at www.irs.gov/pub/irs-pdf/i1023.pdf).

Enter the code that best matches your 501(c)(3) purposes and/or activities or check the box to let the IRS select a code for your organization.

Line 3. Most groups will answer "No" to this question because the IRS frowns on groups that limit benefits, services, or funds to a specific individual or group of individuals. However, if the group of people benefited by the nonprofit is broad (not limited to specific individuals) and related to the exempt purposes of the nonprofit group, the IRS should have no objection. If you answer "yes," provide an explanation.

> **EXAMPLE:** A nonprofit musical heritage organization plans to provide programs and benefits to needy musicians residing in the community. If the overall tax-exempt purpose of the organization is allowed, the IRS will permit this limitation of benefits to a segment of the community.

Line 4. In this question, the IRS is looking for prohibited self-inurement—in this case, whether your nonprofit is set up primarily or directly to provide goods, services, or funds to individuals who have a family or business relationship with your directors, officers, or highest-paid employees or contractors. Most groups will answer "No" here. However, if you think someone who fits in one of these categories may receive goods, products, or services incidentally from your nonprofit as a member of the public, check "Yes" and explain how these related people will have access to your nonprofit's benefits. If your response makes it clear that these related people are not the focus of your nonprofit programs, but as members of the general public only coincidentally qualify, you should be okay.

Line 5. A 501(c)(3) nonprofit organization may not participate in political campaigns (although some voter education drives and political debate activities are permitted—see "Limitation on Political Activities" in Chapter 3). The IRS may deny or revoke your tax-exempt status if you participate in or donate to a campaign. Most groups should answer "No" here.

If you think you should answer "Yes" to this question, check with a nonprofit lawyer or tax consultant—a "Yes" response means you do not qualify for a 501(c)(3) tax exemption. However, you may qualify for a 501(c)(4) tax exemption.

Line 6. This question concerns your group's plans, if any, to affect legislation. Most groups will answer "No" to Question 6 and move on to Line 7. If you plan to engage in efforts to influence legislation, check "Yes" to line 6 and answer 6(a).

If you plan to elect to fall under the alternate political expenditures test discussed in "Limitation on Political Activities," in Chapter 3, check "Yes" to Line 6(a), and upload a completed IRS Form 5768, *Election/Revocation of Election by an Eligible Section 501(c)(3) Organization To Make Expenditures To Influence Legislation* at the end your online application. The political expenditures test is complicated, and you'll probably need the help of an experienced nonprofit adviser to decide whether you will be able to meet the requirements and gain a benefit from electing this special test for political legislative activities.

If you check "Yes" to Line 6 but will not make the Form 5768 election, check "No" to Line 6(a) and describe the extent and percentage of time and money you expect to devote to your legislative activities compared to your total activities. Be as specific as you can about the political activities you expect to promote and how you will promote them. If possible (and accurate), make it clear that your legislative activities will make up an "insubstantial" part of your overall nonprofit programs and activities. If the IRS feels that your political program will be substantial, it will deny your 501(c)(3) tax exemption.

Line 7. This question asks if your nonprofit plans to publish, own, or have rights in intellectual property, such as art, books, patents, trademarks, and the like (see the 1023 instructions for definitions). If you answer "Yes," provide the information about ownership of the intellectual property, if and how you will derive revenue from the property, and generally how the property will be used as part of your nonprofit activities. In essence, the IRS wants to know whether your nonprofit plans to acquire and exploit copyrights, patents, and other forms of intellectual property and, if so, how. Examples of groups that would answer "Yes" include a visual arts exhibit studio, an educational book publisher, a scientific research center that engages in original (patentable) research, and any group that plans to market its trade name (a name used by the nonprofit

and associated with its activities), trademark, or service mark (logos, words, and images used by the nonprofit to market its goods and services).

501(c)(3) nonprofits that conduct scientific research in the public interest are expected to make their patents, copyrights, processes, or formulae available to the public, not simply develop and exploit results of their research for their own use (see "Scientific Purposes" in Chapter 3). There is nothing wrong or underhanded, however, about a nonprofit owning and exploiting intellectual property related to its exempt purpose—for example, a qualified literary or education nonprofit's owning and obtaining royalty revenue from the sale of its published educational works, or a nonprofit's selling donated art to raise funds for its exempt purpose. Be careful, though: If a nonprofit deals in intellectual property as a routine method of raising operating revenue— for example, if a nonprofit licenses its trade name to obtain revenue—the IRS is likely to consider this income unrelated business income. If this unrelated income is clearly more than a small portion of the group's overall revenue, the IRS will likely question or deny the group's 501(c)(3) tax exemption.

The issue of copyright ownership sometimes is key to this issue. Remember: If copyrights in published works are owned by a 501(c)(3) nonprofit, this means that the copyrights, like all other assets owned by the nonprofit, are irrevocably dedicated to tax-exempt purposes and must be distributed (transferred) to another tax-exempt nonprofit when the organization dissolves. Hence, the IRS is apt to look more favorably on an educational nonprofit that holds copyrights in its published works.

Conversely, if a nonprofit education group does not own the copyright to its published works, but instead publishes the works owned by others under the terms of standard commercial royalty contracts, the IRS may feel that the group is simply a commercial publisher that is not entitled to a 501(c)(3) educational tax exemption. However, if the group publishes education material written by volunteers or its employees or under "work for hire" contracts with outside authors, copyrights in the works are owned by the nonprofit, not by the authors. Publication of this material is clearly in the public interest and contains content related to the educational purpose of the nonprofit. Thus, the IRS is more likely to agree that the group is entitled to a tax exemption.

The sale of art by nonprofits often piques the interest of IRS examiners. For example, if an educational nonprofit exhibits artwork owned by artists and collects a commission on each sale, the IRS may conclude that the organization runs a commercial art gallery that is not entitled to a tax exemption. There is no bright-line test for groups that deal in art or sell goods and services. The IRS looks at all the facts and circumstances related to a group's activities and operations to determine if the group's primary purpose is a charitable, educational, or another 501(c)(3) purpose or, instead, represents a commercial enterprise. For examples of when the IRS has reached different conclusions after examining the activities of groups that sell art as part of their activities, see the summaries of selected IRS revenue rulings below:

TIP

How to read IRS rulings. Each IRS revenue ruling is referenced with a two- or four-digit year prefix followed by a number—for example, revenue ruling 2004-98 is a 2004 ruling and revenue ruling 80-106 is a 1980 ruling. The rulings are distinguished from other rulings during the year by the second number.

- Rev. Rul. 80-106. Thrift shop; consignment sales. An organization operated a thrift shop that sold items that were either donated or received on consignment. Substantially all of the work in operating the thrift shop was performed without compensation, all transactions were at arm's length, and all profits were distributed to Section 501(c)(3) organizations. The organization qualified for exemption as an organization operated for charitable purposes.

- Rev. Rul. 76-152. Art gallery. A nonprofit educational organization, formed by art patrons to promote community understanding of modern art trends by selecting for exhibit, exhibiting, and selling artworks of local artists, and which retained a commission on sales that was less than customary commercial charges and was not sufficient to cover the cost of operating the gallery, did not qualify for exemption under Section 501(c)(3). The following statement in the ruling provides perhaps the best clue as to why the IRS rejected the group's application: "Since ninety percent of all sales proceeds are turned over to the individual artists, such direct benefits are substantial by any measure and the organization's provision of them cannot be dismissed as being merely incidental to its other purposes and activities."

- Rev. Rul. 71-395. Art selling. A cooperative art gallery, which was formed and operated by a group of artists for the purpose of exhibiting and selling their works, did not charge admission but received a commission from sales and rental of art sufficient to cover the cost of operating the gallery. It did not qualify for exemption under Section 501(c)(3) as an educational organization.

- Rev. Rul. 66-178. Art exhibits. A nonprofit organization was created to foster and develop the arts by sponsoring a public art exhibit at which the works of unknown but promising artists were selected by a panel of qualified judges for display. Artists eligible to have their works displayed were those who were not affiliated with art galleries and who had no medium for exhibiting their creations. The organization did not charge the artists any fees, nor did the organization sell or offer the displayed works for sale.

  For the exhibit, the organization prepared a catalog that listed each work displayed, the name of its creator, and the artist's home or studio address. The catalog was sold for a small fee to the public. The organization also received income from nominal admission fees to the exhibit and from contributions. Funds were paid out for renting the exhibition hall, printing the catalogs, and administrative expenses. The organization qualified for a 501(c)(3) tax exemption.

If nothing else, the above rulings reinforce one fundamental fact about seeking and obtaining a tax exemption: The IRS looks at the full context of a nonprofit's operations—including its sources and uses of revenue—when deciding whether a group qualifies for 501(c)(3) tax exemption. Normally, no one fact is fatal or determinative. The more a group demonstrates that its operations are public rather than private or commercial, the better its chances of obtaining a tax exemption. And on a more subjective note, the above rulings also hint at the importance of couching your nonprofit activities in the most acceptable (least commercial) terms—for example, it may sound and look better to the IRS if your group collects admission or consignment fees rather than commissions, since the latter term typically connotes overt commercial activity.

Below are two revenue rulings related to educational nonprofits that involve the publication of books and music. The first repeats the theme that the more a group looks and acts like a regular commercial venture, the less its chances of qualifying for 501(c)(3) tax-exempt status. The second shows that nonprofits that cater to a small, traditionally noncommercial segment of public education stand a better chance of obtaining a tax exemption, at least partially because the nonprofit activity is, in fact, less likely to reap significant profits.

The two rulings provide as follows:

- Rev. Rul. 66-104. Educational publishing. An education organization was created to meet the need for more satisfactory teaching materials and textbooks in economics and related fields. The organization contracted with commercial publishing firms for the publication of these materials, which were used primarily by colleges and universities. The organization did not hold the copyright in its published material. The contracts between the organization and the publishers provided that the publishers pay all publication costs and a royalty to the organization on sales of the publication.

  In return, the publisher received the copyright, publishing, and selling rights. The agreement between the organization and the editors and authors provided that the royalty income would first be applied to pay for the costs of preparing the materials for publication, including funds to authors and editors. The remaining royalty was divided into specific percentages between the organization and the editors and authors. The IRS concluded that: "Although educational interests are served by the publication of better teaching materials, the facts in this case show only an enterprise conducted in an essentially commercial manner, in which all the participants expect to receive a monetary return." The IRS denied the organization's 501(c)(3) tax exemption.

- Rev. Rul. 79-369. Musical recording. The organization was created to stimulate, promote, encourage, and sustain interest in and appreciation of contemporary symphonic and chamber music. The organization recorded the new works of unrecognized composers as well as the neglected works of more established composers. The music selected for recording had a limited commercial market and was not generally produced by the commercial music publishing and recording industry for sale to the public. The organization sold its recordings primarily to libraries and educational institutions. Some records were provided free to radio stations operated by educational institutions. The organization also made sales to individuals. The records were not made available for sale through commercial record dealers except in a few specialty shops, but were sold through mail orders. The organization did not engage in any advertising, but relied upon those who were interested in this type of music to communicate the availability of the records. All sales were facilitated by the use of a catalog published by the organization. The catalog contents included information about the compositions and the composers. This information was retained in the catalog so that the catalog served as an archive with respect to these compositions and recordings. Copies of all recordings were maintained for availability in the future. The liner notes on the album covers contained a biography of the composer and a description of the composition by its composer. Composers received royalties from the sale of recordings as required by federal law. Due to the limited commercial market for this type of music, the royalties received by the composers were not significant. The group qualified for a 501(c)(3) tax exemption.

Line 8. If your nonprofit answers "Yes" to this question, will provide consumer credit or other financial counseling, see the 1023 instructions to this line and consult a nonprofit adviser to get help with your application. The provisions of Internal Revenue Code 501(q) may apply to your organization (search "501(q)" on IRS.gov for information on these requirements and whether they apply to you).

Line 9. If your nonprofit will make grants or loans to other organizations or receive and disburse funds (for example, as a fiscal agent) for other organizations, answer "Yes" to Line 9 then provide the requested information in Line 9 and (a) through 9(i) (some items in this section may not appear depending on your responses). If you answer "No" to Line 9, move on to Line 10.

Most smaller nonprofits do not make grants or loans to other nonprofits, but may receive grant money as fiscal agents for other nonprofits. If your group does plan to make grants, loans or other distributions to other organizations, your responses should show that the groups you sponsor promote activities that are related to your tax-exempt purposes and that you exercise oversight in making sure the funds are accounted for and used properly by the groups you sponsor. If your responses demonstrate or imply that you disburse funds as a "feeder" group to promote regular commercial or nonexempt activities, the IRS will deny your exemption. The questions listed here should give you an indication of what the IRS is looking for—formal applications, grant proposals, fiscal reporting controls, and other procedures that you will use to select, monitor, and assess the groups that you sponsor.

If you will make grants, loans, or distributions to foreign organizations, the questions seek to determine if your organization applies extra scrutiny to any foreign groups you sponsor (see the antiterrorism note in the 1023 instructions for Lines 9g-i; it is one of the drivers for this extra IRS scrutiny of groups that sponsor or assist foreign organizations).

Line 10. If your nonprofit plans to operate in one or more foreign countries, answer "Yes" to Line 10 and provide the information requested in 10(a) through 10(c). Special tax-exemption and deductibility of contribution rules apply to nonprofits created or operated abroad. If you answer "Yes," see a nonprofit adviser who has experience in advising nonprofits that operate in the foreign countries where you plan to operate for help in completing your 1023 application. Also see the 1023 instructions for this line. Finally, realize that a big part of the IRS's energy is now devoted to scrutinizing the operations of foreign-based nonprofits as part of the service's participation in antiterrorism. Here is an excerpt from the IRS 2005 *EO* (*Exempt Organization*) *Report*:

> In FY 2005, EO will examine a sample of foreign grant making organizations; the primary focus of the examinations is to ensure that funds are used for their intended charitable purpose and not diverted for terrorist activity. The project will gather information about current practices, that is, the existence and effectiveness of controls put in place to monitor the distribution of overseas grants and other assistance. This committee will also address the need for possible guidance or other modifications to the laws in this area.

Line 11. See the 1023 instructions for this line—it concerns the special practice of soliciting and using "donor-advised" or "donor-directed" funds. Most nonprofits will not have plans to use this practice, but if you do, answer "Yes" and provide the information requested. The IRS will want to make sure that your organization does not use funds to meet the private needs of donors, but instead will use donor-directed funds for purposes that are consistent with the tax-exempt purposes of the nonprofit.

Here is a statement from the 2005 IRS *Exempt Organization (EO) Report* that explains why the IRS is concerned about donor-advised funds, and indicates that it will be keeping an eye out for abuse in this area:

> Donor-advised funds allow private donors to provide input as to how their charitable contributions will be spent. A number of organizations have come to light through examinations, referrals from other parts of the IRS, and public scrutiny which appear to have abused the basic concepts underlying donor-advised funds. These organizations, while promoted as legitimate donor-advised funds, appear to be established for the purpose of generating questionable charitable deductions, providing impermissible economic benefits to the donors and their families (including tax-sheltered investment income for the donors), and providing management fees for the promoters.
> EO Examinations will identify organizations with a high potential for abuse in this area and commence examinations during FY 2005.

Line 12. As explained in the 1023 instructions to this line, a school is defined as an educational organization that has the primary function of presenting formal instruction, normally maintains a regular faculty and curriculum, normally has a regularly enrolled body of students, and has a place where its educational activities are carried on (for example, private primary or secondary schools and colleges (see the section on "Schools" in "Automatic Public Charity Status," in Chapter 4). Check the "Yes" box and fill in Schedule B if one of your purposes, whether primary or otherwise, is operating a nonprofit school.

Schedule B. Schools, Colleges, and Universities

See the 1023 instructions to Schedule B for help in completing this schedule. Your responses to this schedule should show that your operations are nondiscriminatory and in accordance with a nondiscrimination statement included in your bylaws or adopted by resolution of your board and published in the community in which you serve. For information on drafting and publishing this statement of nondiscrimination, see "Educational Purposes" in Chapter 3. Also see the 1023 instructions and IRS Publication 557, under "Private Schools."

Line 13. If your nonprofit is setting up a hospital or medical care facility, including a medical research facility (see the definitions in the 1023 instructions and "Hospitals and Medical Research Organizations" in "Automatic Public Charity Status," in Chapter 4), answer "Yes" and complete Schedule C.

Schedule C. Hospitals and Medical Research Organizations

If you are applying for an exemption for a hospital, generally this schedule seeks to determine two things:

- whether the hospital is charitable in nature and qualifies for 501(c)(3) tax-exempt status, and

- whether the hospital or medical research organization qualifies for automatic public charity status (see the Schedule C instructions in the official 1023 instructions and IRS Publication 557, under "Hospitals and Medical Research Organizations").

A 501(c)(3) charitable hospital normally has many of the following characteristics:

- staff doctors selected from the community at large

- a community-oriented board of directors (directors come from the community served by the hospital)

- emergency room facilities open to the public

- a policy of allowing at least some patients to be treated without charge (on a charity basis)

- a nondiscrimination policy with respect to patient admissions (it doesn't pick and choose its patient population) and particularly does not discriminate against Medicare or Medicaid patients, and

- a medical training and research program that benefits the community.

Hospitals need to be careful when it comes to renting space to physicians who are members of the board—and carrying out a private practice that's unrelated to the community service programs of the hospital. The IRS will be particularly suspicious if such physicians are prior tenants and their rent is below fair market value. Section 1, Question 7, of Schedule C addresses this issue.

Part V of the 1023 instructions suggests that hospitals adopt a suitable conflict of interest policy in their bylaws. Article 9 of the bylaws included with this book contains most of the provisions in the sample conflict of interest policy provided in Appendix A of the official 1023 instructions. However, it does not include the special bracketed provisions that apply specifically to hospitals. There are two, which are clearly marked in Appendix A of the 1023 instructions with the words "[*Hospital Insert— for hospitals that complete Schedule C ...*]." Make sure you insert these additional bracketed provisions to the provisions in Article 9 of the bylaws included with this book.

The Affordable Care Act (ACA) added new requirements for charitable hospitals. (See Notice 2010-39 and Notice 2011-52 and ask your tax adviser for more information.)

Line 14. If you are forming a nonprofit to provide low-income housing, check "Yes" and complete Schedule F.

Schedule F. Low-Income Housing

See the 1023 instructions for help in filling out this schedule. In part, this schedule attempts to determine whether housing facilities are made available to low-income members of the public or the community and whether facilities are adequate to house a sufficient number of low-income residents.

Line 15. Refer to the 1023 instructions for definitions of related terms before answering this question. If your nonprofit, whether it is a school or otherwise, will provide scholarships or other education or education-related financial aid or assistance to individuals, check "Yes" and fill in Schedule H – Section I.

Schedule H. Organizations Providing Scholarships, Educational Loans, or Other Educational Grants

Schedule H is used by the IRS to determine whether your nonprofit will provide financial aid on a nondiscriminatory basis. The IRS wants to know that financial aid funds will not be set aside specifically to help put family and friends of people associated with your nonprofit and that the providing of funds in general will promote your group's tax-exempt public purposes, which typically will be charitable and/or educational. For further information on IRS guidelines, see IRS Publication 557, under "Charitable Organization Supporting Education" and "Organization Providing Loans."

Section II of this schedule, if it displayed during your online application session, can be used to get IRS approval of an organization's grant-making procedure if it is expecting to be classified as a private foundation (not as a public charity) If you are forming a private foundation, consult your tax adviser to help you complete Section II.

Line 16. Read the official instructions to this line to learn the definition of fundraising and some of the different ways it may be conducted. If your nonprofit will be obtaining revenue and operating funds only from the performance of its exempt functions— that is, by providing services or goods related to your exempt purpose—you can check "We will not engage in fundraising activities." If you expect your nonprofit to do any type of fundraising, such as soliciting government grants, attracting private and public donations or contributions, or going whole hog and hiring a professional fundraiser, check each box that applies to your organization, and, if applicable, also check the "Other" box and describe any additional fundraising activities.

Line 17. If your nonprofit will do fundraising for other organizations, click "Yes" and provide the information requested. Most nonprofit organizers using this book will not raise funds for other organizations even if they plan to raise funds for themselves, and will select "No."

Part V: Compensation and Financial Arrangements

The IRS has expanded this part of the application to try and prevent people from creating and operating nonprofits simply to benefit one or more of the nonprofit's founders, insiders, or major contributors (called "disqualified persons"). We've already explained the basic 501(c)(3) prohibition against private inurement and the excess benefit rules that penalize nonprofits and their managers if they pay unreasonable compensation to insiders and outsiders (see "Limitation on Profits and Benefits" in Chapter 3). In this part of the application, the IRS tries to find out if your nonprofit runs the risk of violating any of these rules. So if you have compensation or other financial arrangements with any of your founders, directors, officers, employees, contractors, contributors, and others, now is the time to disclose this information. It's better to find out ahead of time that the IRS objects to your proposed financial arrangements rather than pay hefty excess benefit taxes later and run the risk of losing your tax exemption.

TIP
Who is a "disqualified person"? The excess benefit rules apply to "disqualified persons," as defined under the Internal Revenue Code, Section 4958. For these purposes, a disqualified person means anyone who exercises substantial influence over the nonprofit, such as founders, directors, officers, and substantial contributors. People who fall within the definition of disqualified persons are not prohibited from being paid by your nonprofit. Instead, their salaries and benefits are subject to scrutiny under the excess benefit rules.

Also, don't get confused or concerned if you run up against different definitions of "disqualified persons" that apply to nonprofits. For example, a different definition of disqualified person (under IRC § 4946) is used to determine permitted sources of public support for 501(c)(3) public charity support tests and when applying the excise tax restrictions that apply to private foundations (see Chapter 4).

Line 1. Before answering Line 1, read the 1023 instructions for this part. Note that "highest compensated" employees or independent contractors are persons to whom you pay over $100,000 of compensation, including compensation from related organizations. (Note: There is nothing special or suspect about paying an employee more than $100,000. If you are interested in the highest compensated category and how it fits within the excess benefit rules, see IRS Regulation 53.4958-3(d)(3)(i) and IRC Section 414(q)(1)(B)(i).) At this stage in the organization of your nonprofit, you may not be absolutely certain whether or what you will pay your initial directors and officers. Respond according to your current plans and

expectations. In the sample bylaws included in this book, we say that directors will not be paid a salary but may be paid a per-meeting fee and reimbursed expenses (see Article 3, Section 6). Officer salaries must be reasonable and in return for services rendered the corporation (Bylaws Article 4, Section 10). If you answer "No" to Line 1, move on to Line 2.

Line 1a-1f. If you use the bylaws in this book, you can check "Yes" to each of these items (see Article 9, Section 5 of the bylaws).

Line 1g: If you will use other practices to set reasonable compensation, check "Yes" and provide the details. It is best if you also describe these additional practices in your bylaws and refer to the bylaw in your response.

Line 2. If you use the bylaws in this book, you should be able to check "Yes." The policy set out in Article 9 of the bylaws is based on the sample conflict of interest policy contained in Appendix A of the 1023 instructions, and also includes additional provisions contained in IRS Regulation 53.4958-6 that provide a "safe-harbor" rule for smaller organizations to obtain salary comparability data. Note for hospitals: The bylaws do not contain additional provisions that should be inserted for hospitals (see Appendix A of the IRS 1023 instructions). If you check "No," describe your custom conflict of interest provisions. Note: Adoption of a conflict of interest policy isn't required to obtain tax-exempt status, but it should help the IRS look favorably on your application, and of course, it will help keep your nonprofit make honest, arms-length decisions.

Line 3. The IRS instructions to Form 1023 explain what the terms "fixed payment" and "nonfixed payment" mean. Essentially, this question asks if your organization will pay its directors, officers, highly paid employees, or highly paid contractors any discretionary amounts (such as bonuses) or amounts based on your organization's revenues (such as a salary kicker or bonus computed as a percentage of annual contributions received by your nonprofit). Obviously, it looks best if your nonprofit's principals and employees do not receive these types of revenue-driven incentives, which are more typical in a business, not a nonprofit, setting. We assume most small nonprofits will be able to answer "No" to this question. If, however, you have an overriding need to pay directors, officers, and employees discretionary bonuses or provide them with revenue- or performance-based compensation or commissions, you need to provide the information requested. Your response should show that these nonfixed payments will be fairly and reasonably paid as incentives to promote the nonprofit purposes of your organization (this may not be easy to show), and that it won't be used simply to pay out revenues to your principals. Remember—private inurement is a nonprofit no-no—so siphoning over revenue to nonprofit principals is not allowed, even in the guise of bonus or performance-based employee incentives.

Line 4. Most nonprofits will be able to answer "No" to this question because they will want to stay clear of insider sales and purchase transactions, simply to avoid the appearance (if not the actuality) of self-dealing. That said, it's also a fact of life that some smaller nonprofits have to look to their directors, officers, and principal employees or contractors to buy or sell goods or services: These may be the only people willing to do business with the nonprofit at the start of its operations. Even more typically, a small nonprofit may want to buy goods at a special discount offered by a director or an officer. If you answer "Yes" to this question, provide the requested information in your response. Your response should make clear that any such purchases or sales will be at arm's

length (see the official 1023 instruction to this line for an explanation of this standard)—that is, your nonprofit will pay no more and sell at no less than the commercially competitive, fair market value price for the goods, services, or assets. If you plan to buy goods, services, or assets at a discount from a director, an officer, an employee, or a contractor, make sure to say so, since this sort of bargain purchase is better than an arm's-length deal from the perspective of the nonprofit.

The official instructions for this line indicate that you can ignore purchases and sales of goods and services in the normal course of operations that are available to the general public under similar terms or conditions. In other words, if you buy normal inventory items from an insider at standard terms paid by the general public for these inventory items, you do not have to mark "Yes." Frankly, if your organization plans to purchase any type of goods or services from a director, an officer, or an employee, we think it should be disclosed in your application, since a deal of this sort may have the appearance of a self-dealing transaction. In such a case, you can check "Yes," then make it clear in your response that your organization will pay the same price for the inventory or other standard items purchased from a director, an officer, or an employee as the price paid by the general public (the current commercially competitive fair market value price).

If you answer "Yes" and have adopted the bylaws included with this book, you can add in your response that "Article 9, Section 3, of the organization's bylaws requires the approval of transactions or arrangements between the organization in which one of its directors, officers, or any other 'disqualified person' as defined in Section 4958(f)(1) of the Internal Revenue Code and as amplified by Section 53.4958-3 of the IRS Regulations has a direct or indirect financial interest by the vote of a majority of disinterested directors or members of a board committee, only after a finding that a more advantageous transaction or arrangement is not available to the organization and that the proposed transaction or arrangement is in the organization's best interest, is for its own benefit, and is fair and reasonable."

Line 5. To avoid the appearance if not the actuality of self-dealing, it's best not to deal with nonprofit insiders when leasing property or contracting for goods, services, or making other business arrangements. Most nonprofits will shy away from doing this, and will answer "No."

However, newly formed nonprofits sometimes find it most practical (and economical) to lease or rent property owned by a founder, a director, or an officer, or may otherwise have to enter into a contract or an arrangement with one of these people. There is nothing absolutely forbidden about doing so, but you will want to make sure that any lease, contract, or agreement between your nonprofit and one of these people reflects fair market value terms or better. For example, it looks best if a director leases property owned by the director to the nonprofit at a lower-than-market-value rate (best of all, of course, is when the director lets the nonprofit use the lease premises rent free).

If you answer "Yes," provide the information requested. If possible, upload a copy of any lease, rental, or other agreement at the end of your application and refer to this agreement in your response. For a discussion of leases together with a sample assignment of lease, see "Prepare Assignments of Leases and Deeds" in Chapter 9. If you answer "Yes" and have adopted the bylaws included with this book, you can add in your response that "Article 9, Section 3, of the organization's bylaws requires the approval of transactions or arrangements

between the organization in which one of its directors, officers, or any other 'disqualified person' as defined in Section 4958(f)(1) of the Internal Revenue Code and as amplified by Section 53.4958-3 of the IRS Regulations has a direct or indirect financial interest by the vote of a majority of disinterested directors or members of a board committee, only after a finding that a more advantageous transaction or arrangement is not available to the organization and that the proposed transaction or arrange-ment is in the organization's best interest, is for its own benefit, and is fair and reasonable."

Line 6. See the official instructions for definitions of key terms, such as "develop." If you plan to work with another organization to develop, build, market, or finance facilities, answer "Yes" and provide the information requested. Mostly, the IRS wants to make sure that your nonprofit is not planning to make any "sweetheart" development deals that benefit people associated with your nonprofit. If you answer "Yes" and have adopted the bylaws included with this book, you can add in your response that "Article 9, Section 3, of the organization's bylaws requires the approval of transactions or arrangements between the organization in which one of its directors, officers, or any other 'disqualified person' as defined in Section 4958(f)(1) of the Internal Revenue Code and as amplified by Section 53.4958-3 of the IRS Regulations has a direct or indirect financial interest by the vote of a majority of disinterested directors or members of a board committee, only after a finding that a more advantageous transaction or arrangement is not available to the organization and that the proposed transaction or arrangement is in the organization's best interest, is for its own benefit, and is fair and reasonable."

Line 7. See the official 1023 instructions for definitions of key terms, such as "manage." If your nonprofit will maintain facilities, such as a building or an office space or another physical address, and plans to use anyone other than employees or volunteers to manage the facilities—for example, if it plans to hire a management company to manage property—check "Yes" and provide the information requested. Again, the IRS wants you to show that the managers are not getting special breaks or excess payments because they are family members or business associates of the nonprofit's directors or officers. If you answer "Yes" and have adopted the bylaws included with this book, you can add in your response that "Article 9, Section 3, of the organization's bylaws requires the approval of transactions or arrangements between the organization in which one of its directors, officers, or any other 'disqualified person' as defined in Section 4958(f)(1) of the Internal Revenue Code and as amplified by Section 53.4958-3 of the IRS Regulations has a direct or indirect financial interest by the vote of a majority of disinterested directors or members of a board committee, only after a finding that a more advantageous transaction or arrangement is not available to the organization and that the proposed transaction or arrangement is in the organization's best interest, is for its own benefit, and is fair and reasonable."

Line 8. See the official 1023 instructions for definitions of key terms, such as "joint venture." If your nonprofit plans to enter into joint ventures (business deals) with individuals or other nonprofits or commercial business entities, see a legal adviser before providing the information requested and completing your 1023 tax exemption application. Nonprofit organization joint ventures raise complex issues that require expert help to make sure they are structured properly to meet the requirements of the 501(c)(3) tax exemption.

Part VI: Financial Data

All groups should complete the Statement of Revenues and Expenses Balance Sheet. Start by reading the official 1023 instructions for this part. Also, click the help ("?") tips for each item to understand the types of financial data to provide on each line.

The financial data supplied with the 1023 application is used to show that the nonprofit can reasonably be expected to receive support over its first five years that qualifies it for the public charity status it is seeking (you will choose a public charity classification in Part VII). At the end of the five-year period, the IRS will look at groups' annual Form 990 or 990-EZ returns for the prior five years (the current year plus the prior four years) to see if the group continues to qualify as a public charity. If the group fails the five-year test for two years, it will lose its public charity status and will be reclassified as a private foundation. See Chapter 10 for more on Form 990s. For information on the five-year support test for public charity status, see "Advance Ruling Process Elimination-Public Support Test," on the IRS website at www.irs.gov/charities-non-profits/charitable-organizations/advance-ruling-process-elimination-public-support-test.

Line 1. Select the statement that applies to your organization. Most new groups will select that they have completed less than one tax year.

New groups with less than one tax year. If your nonprofit is newly formed, it probably has not been in existence for a full tax year. Put projected numbers for the current year, and projections for the next two years for a total of three years.

EXAMPLE: You are a new nonprofit formed on February 15 of the current year, with a tax year that goes from January 1 to December 31, and you are applying for your tax exemption in June of the corporation's first tax year. The beginning "from" date of the period shown at the top of the current tax year column is the date you filed your articles—February 15 of the current year. The "to" date for this period should be December 31, the end of the current tax year. Use the next two columns to show projected figures for your next two tax years, going from January 1 to December 31 of each of the next two years. Many new groups will repeat much of the information from their first tax year for the next two proposed tax years, unless they anticipate a major change in operations or sources of support.

Don't expect to fill in all the items. The IRS knows you've just commenced operations and that you are estimating possible sources of revenue and items of expense, and it expects to see a few blank lines. Also realize that some of your projected revenues and expenses may not neatly fit the categories shown in the printed revenue and expense table. You can use Revenue Item 7 (revenue not otherwise listed) and Expense Item 23 (expenses not otherwise classified) to list totals for these items, and in Line 25 list and describe these additional items of revenue and expense. The IRS does not like to see large lump sum amounts, so break down these additional items of revenue and expense as much as possible.

Groups with prior tax years.

Less than five tax years: If your nonprofit has been in existence more than one full tax year, but less than five tax years, you must show projected financial information for your current tax year, then show figures for your prior completed tax year(s) in one or more columns. You also may

need to show projected revenue and expense information in other columns for future tax years depending on how many years you have been in existence. Here is how it works.

If your group has been in existence one full prior tax year, show projected figures for the full current tax year in the current tax year column and your prior completed tax year in the next column. Then show projected figures for the next two years' revenues and expenses (the two tax years after the current tax year) in the next columns. This information represents four full tax years' worth of information—one completed tax year and three projected tax years.

If your group has been in existence two full prior tax years, show projected figures for the full current tax year in the current tax year column, your most recent completed tax year in the next column, and your first completed tax year in the next column. Then show projected figures for the next year's (the year after the current year) revenues and expenses in the next column. This information represents four full tax years' worth of information—two completed tax years and two projected tax years.

Line 12 of the revenue and expense statement asks you to list any "unusual grant" revenue. This term is explained in the instructions for this line in the official 1023 instructions, and we explain it in more detail in "Public Support Test" and "Exempt Activities Support Test," in Chapter 4, as it applies to the different public charity support tests. Also see the specific rules on unusual grants contained in IRS Publication 557.

Basically, unusual grants are permitted grants which can throw a kink in your public charity support computations because they come from one source, as opposed to several smaller grants from different sources. Remember, 501(c)(3) public support revenue is supposed to be spread out and come from a number of public sources, not just one or two. It is unlikely that you expect to receive an unusual grant this early in your nonprofit life—unusual grants normally happen only as a result of a sustained and successful outreach program that attracts one or two large grants that surprise the modest expectations of a small nonprofit. In effect, an unusual grant represents both good and bad news. The good news is the unusually large amount of the grant; the bad news is its potential damage to the group's ability to meet the technical public support requirements that apply to 501(c)(3) public charities. If you have received or expect to receive one or more unusual grants, insert the total number here on Line 12 in the appropriate column (past, present, or future tax year), and in Line 25 provide a description of each grant (what the grant was for, whether it was restricted to a specific use, and other terms of the grant), together with the donor's name, date, and amount of each unusual grant. If a large grant qualifies as an unusual grant, it will be disregarded by the IRS when it computes whether your support qualifies under the technical public charity support test rules.

Five or more tax years: If your nonprofit has been in existence for five or more prior tax years, show actual revenue and expense amounts for your last five completed tax years in the five columns. Note that the current year column will be used to show data from your last completed tax year, not the partially completed current tax year. You will be supplying figures for five completed tax years, and no projected information.

Balance Sheet

Prepare the balance sheet to show assets and liabilities of your corporation as of your last completed tax year, if any, or the current tax year if you have not yet completed one full tax year.

EXAMPLE: You have organized a new nonprofit corporation, formed on April 1. You are preparing your 1023 application in November of the same year. Your tax year goes from January 1 to December 31. The current tax year period covered by the first column of your Statement of Revenue and Expenses is from April 1 to December 31. Your balance sheet ending date will be the same ending date, December 31, the eventual ending date of your first tax year. This is the "Year End" date of your balance sheet information.

Even though this is a future end date, you should base your statement of assets and liabilities on current information—that is on your organization's current assets and liabilities at the time of the preparation of your exemption application. See the official instruction to this section of the application. If you have difficulty preparing the balance sheet, get the help of a tax or legal adviser.

It's not uncommon for a small starting nonprofit without liabilities and accounts receivable to simply show a little cash as its only reportable balance sheet item. Other common items reported are Line 8 depreciable assets— equipment owned by the corporation and used to conduct its exempt activities.

Line 17 of the balance sheet asks for fund balance or net asset information. Typically, this is the amount by which your assets exceed your liabilities—in other words, the net value of your assets. Again, see a financial advisor if you need help providing this technical financial information.

Part VII: Foundation Classification

You should be familiar with the material in Chapter 4 and the official 1023 instructions to Part VII in order to answer the questions in this part of the form. This is where terms such as "public charity" and "private foundation" become important. We will refer to earlier explanations as we go along, but you may want to look over Chapter 4 and the 1023 instructions now before you proceed. The questions in this part relate to whether you are seeking to be classified as a 501(c)(3) public charity or as a 501(c)(3) private foundation.

As you know by now, we assume you want your nonprofit to qualify as a 501(c)(3) public charity, not as a 501(c)(3) private foundation.

In Chapter 4, we discussed the distinction between the public charity and private foundation classifications and the reasons that you should try to meet one of the three primary tests for being classified as a public charity. The official 1023 instructions provide a list of groups that qualify for public charity status, which lumps all publicly supported groups together ("groups that have broad financial support"). We use a different classification scheme in Chapter 4, which puts public charities into one of three categories:

(1) **Automatic Public Charity Status:** Groups that are set up for a specific purpose or special function, such as churches, schools, hospitals, and public safety organizations, qualify as public charities (we say they "automatically" qualify because these groups, unlike the other two types of public charities listed below, do not have to meet public support tests).

(2) **Public Support Test Groups:** These are groups that are supported by contributions and grants and that meet the one-third or one-tenth public support tests described in "Public Support Test" in Chapter 4.

(3) **Exempt Activities Support Test Groups:** These are groups that obtain support through the performance of their exempt purposes, such as admissions, tuition, seminar fees, and receipts

from goods and services related to the group's exempt purposes, as described in "Exempt Activities Support Test" in Chapter 4.

We assume your nonprofit will either be setting up one of the special public charities that automatically qualify under (1), above, or a nonprofit that has or can reasonably expect to receive the type of support listed in (2) or (3), above.

Line 1. Check one box to select your expected foundation classification: Let's look at each of the categories below.

☐ **You are described in 509(a)(1) and 170(b)(1)(A)(vi) as an organization that receives a substantial part of its financial support in the form of contributions from publicly supported organizations, from a governmental unit, or from the general public.**

This box is for organizations that receive a substantial part of their support from government agencies or from the general public. These are the public support test groups discussed in Chapter 4. If you believe this is the public charity best suited to your organization's sources of support, check this box. As discussed in "Public Support Test," in Chapter 4, many groups will not want to fall under this public charity test because it does not allow your receipts from the performance of services related to the corporation's exempt purposes to be included as "qualified public support." If you are unsure whether this is the best support test to use for your group, you may wish to let the IRS make this decision for you as explained below.

If your nonprofit has not been in existence for more than five years, you can ignore Line 2 and continue to Part VIII. Line 2 (i) & (ii): These questions apply to your organization if it is applying as a public support test group **and it has been in existence for more than 5 years** (and is submitting five years of past financial information in Part VI).

- **Line 2 (i).** If your organization received more than 2% (0.02) of the total of all five years shown in Part VI-A (Statement of Revenues and Expenses), Line 8, check "Yes" and provide the requested information. Otherwise, click "No." Why does the IRS want this information? For public support test charities, the IRS generally does not count amounts that exceed 2% of the group's total support over the five-year period as qualified public support (for more on the 2% rule and its exceptions, see "Public Support Test" in Chapter 4 and IRS Publication 557, "Support from the General Public").

- **Line 2 (ii).** This question asks a group that has been in existence for more than five years to calculate whether it received at least one-third from public sources or at least ten percent and meets the attraction of public support test. Again, see Chapter 4, "Public Support Test" and the 1023 instructions for more information. Groups in existence for five years or more will be expected to respond "Yes" to qualify under this public support test as a public charity.

EXAMPLE: The Workshop for Social Change, an educational group that plans to receive support from public and private grant funds and from individual and corporate contributions, checks this box to request public charity status as a publicly supported organization.

☐ **You are described in 509(a)(2) as an organization that normally receives not more than one-third of its financial support from gross investment income and receives more than one-third of its financial support from contributions, membership fees, and gross receipts from activities related to its exempt functions (subject to certain exceptions).**

This box is for organizations that normally receive one-third of their support from contributions, membership fees, and gross receipts from activities related to the exempt functions of the organization (subject to certain exceptions) but not more than one-third from unrelated trades and businesses or gross investment income. This exempt activities support test is discussed in Chapter 4. This is the most common and often the easiest way to qualify a new nonprofit organization as a public charity. So reread the requirements of this test and the definition of terms associated with it in Chapter 4. If you believe this public charity test best suits your expected sources of support, check this box. If you are unsure, let the IRS make this decision for you as explained below.

If your nonprofit has not been in existence for more than five years, you can ignore Line 2a and continue to Part VIII. Complete Line 2a if your organization has been in existence for five years or more.

Line 2a (i) - (iii). These questions apply to your organization if it is applying as an exempt activities support test group and it has been in existence for more than five years (and is submitting five years of past financial information in Part VI-A). These questions disclose sources of support that the IRS does not consider qualified public support for groups that are seeking public charity status under the exempt activities support test (the groups covered in "Exempt Activities Support Test" in Chapter 4 that rely on support received primarily from their exempt purpose activities). We're talking here about contributions from disqualified persons or gross receipts from other individuals that exceed the larger of 1% of the organization's total support or $5,000 in any tax year.

- **Line 2a (i).** For a definition of disqualified persons, including a "substantial contributor," see the online help ("?") to this question. We provide a somewhat friendlier set of definitions of these terms in "Who Are Disqualified Persons?" If a disqualified person provided gifts, grants, or contributions, membership fees, or payments for admissions, or other exempt purpose services or products (these are the categories listed in Part VI, Statement of Revenues and Expenses) during any of the completed five tax years shown in Part VI, click "Yes" and provide the requested information.

- **Line 2a (ii).** If any person (other than a disqualified person) has paid more than the larger of either $5,000 or 1% of the amount shown in Line 10 of Part VI-A, Statement of Revenues and Expenses, during any of the completed five tax years shown in Part VI-A, provide the requested information. The list should be broken down year by year.

- **Line 2a (iii).** This question asks groups that have been in existence for more than five years to calculate whether it received more than one-third from permitted sources under the exempt activities support test and not more than one-third from investment income and unrelated business taxable income. See Chapter 4, "Exempt Activities Support Test" and the 1023 instructions for more information. Groups in existence for five years or more will be expected to respond "Yes" to qualify under this test as a public charity.

EXAMPLE: Everybody's Dance Studio and Dinner Theater, a group that expects to derive most of its operating revenue from student tuitions, special workshops, and ticket sales (as well as from other exempt purpose activities), checks this box to qualify as a public charity under the exempt activities support test.

☐ **You are described in 509(a)(1) and 170(b)(1)(A)(i) as a church or a convention or association of churches. Complete Schedule A.**

Check this box if you seek to qualify automatically for public charity status as a church. You will need to complete Schedule A. See the separate instructions to Schedule A in the official 1023 instructions, and the requirements for churches in "Automatic Public Charity Status," in Chapter 4 for help in filling out this schedule. The questions seek to determine whether your organization possesses conventional institutional church attributes—the more the better as far as the IRS is concerned.

EXAMPLE: The First Fellowship Church, a religious organization that plans to maintain a space to provide weekly religious services to its congregation, checks this box to request public charity status as a church.

☐ **You are described in 509(a)(1) and 170(b)(1)(A) (ii) as a school. Complete Schedule B.**

Check this box if you seek to qualify automatically for public charity status as a formal school and complete Schedule B. See the 1023 instructions to Schedule B and "Automatic Public Charity Status," in Chapter 4 (see the "Schools" section). Your responses to this schedule should show that your operations are nondiscriminatory and in accordance with a nondiscrimination statement included in your bylaws or adopted by your board and published in the community in which you serve. For information on drafting and publishing this statement of nondiscrimination, see "Educational Purposes" in Chapter 3. Also see IRS Publication 557, under "Private Schools."

Who Are Disqualified Persons?

People who are disqualified in the eyes of the IRS are not necessarily prohibited from participating in the operation of the 501(c)(3) nonprofit corporation. Instead, their contributions to the nonprofit may not count when figuring the public support received by public charities.

(Note that the definitions of disqualified persons discussed here are different from the definitions of disqualified persons under IRC § 4958—see the instructions to Part V, above, for information on this separate set of definitions.) If the corporation is classified as a 501(c)(3) private foundation, the corporation and the disqualified individual can be held liable for certain private foundation excise taxes. Disqualified persons for purposes of meeting the public charity support tests include:

1. Substantial contributors. These are donors who give more than $5,000, if the amount they contributed is more than 2% of the total contributions and bequests received by the organization. For example, suppose Ms. X makes a gift of $20,000 to your nonprofit corporation. If this gift exceeds 2% of all contributions and bequests made to your organization from the time it was created until the end of the corporate tax year in which Ms. X made the contribution, Ms. X is a substantial contributor.

For purposes of determining whether a substantial donor is a disqualified person, gifts and bequests made by that individual include all contributions and bequests made by the individual's spouse. Once a person is classified as a substantial contributor, he or she generally remains classified as one (regardless of future contributions made, or not made, by the individual or future support received by the organization). However, if other conditions are met, a person will lose his or her status as a substantial contributor if he or she makes no contribution to the organization for ten years.

2. All foundation managers. Directors, trustees, and officers (or people with similar powers or responsibilities), or any employee with final authority to act on a matter, are disqualified as foundation managers—this means the bigwigs in a nonprofit who exercise executive control. Officers include persons specifically designated as "officers" in the articles, bylaws, or minutes, and persons who regularly make administrative and policy decisions. Officers do not include independent contractors, such as accountants, lawyers, financial and investment advisers, and managers. Generally, any person who simply makes recommendations for action but cannot implement these recommendations will not qualify as an officer.

3. Owners and substantial players in entities that contribute. An owner of more than 20% of the total combined voting power of a corporation, the profits of a partnership, or the beneficial interest of a trust or an unincorporated enterprise are all disqualified, if any of these entities is a substantial contributor.

4. Family members. A member of the family—including ancestors, spouse, and lineal descendants, such as children and grandchildren, but not brothers and sisters—of any of the individuals described in 1, 2, or 3 above, is disqualified.

5. Other business entities. Corporations, partnerships, trusts, and so on in which the persons described in 1 through 4 above have at least a 35% ownership interest.

For more information on disqualified persons, type "private foundations and disqualified person" in the search box of the IRS website at www.irs.gov.

If you will set up and operate a school, but operating the school is not your primary purpose, do not check this box—you will need to qualify as a public charity by checking one of the other boxes. However, you must complete Schedule B if you plan to operate a school, even if operating the school is not your primary purpose and the basis for your claim to public charity status—see the online help ("?") instruction to this box.

> **EXAMPLE:** The School for Alternative Social Studies, an accredited private postgraduate school with a formal curriculum, full-time faculty, and regularly enrolled student body, checks this box to request public charity status as a formal private school.

☐ **You are described in 509(a)(1) and 170(b)(1)(A)(iii) as a hospital, a cooperative hospital service organization, or a medical research organization operated in conjunction with a hospital. Complete Schedule C.**

☐ **You are described in 509(a)(1) and 170(b)(1)(A)(iv) as an organization operated for the benefit of a college or university that is owned or operated by a governmental unit.**

☐ **You are described in 509(a)(1) and 170(b)(1)(A)(ix) as an agricultural research organization directly engaged in the continuous active conduct of agricultural research in conjunction with a college or university.**

☐ **You are described in 509(a)(3) as an organization supporting either one or more organizations described in 509(a)(1) or 509(a)(2) or a publicly supported section 501(c)(4), (5), or (6) organization. Complete Schedule D.**

☐ **You are described in 509(a)(4) as an organization organized and operated exclusively for testing for public safety.**

We list several of the remaining boxes together above. Few groups will choose one of these boxes —each applies to a special type of organization, such as a hospital, supporting organization, public safety organization, government agency for the benefit of a college or university, or an agricultural research organization affiliated with a college or university.

- Hospitals and medical research groups will need to complete Schedule C— see "Schedule C. Hospitals and Medical Research Organizations," above.

- Supporting organizations are a special type of nonprofit set up to support other public charities. They are operated solely for the benefit of, or in connection with, any of the other public charity organizations (except one testing for public safety). A supporting organization must complete Schedule D. This information helps the IRS determine whether this type of organization supports other qualified public charities.

> **TIP**
>
> **Get help when applying for an exemption for a special type of nonprofit.** If you check one of these boxes, the lawyer, accountant, or other adviser who is helping you organize one of these special corporations should help you with your application and any additional schedules you have to prepare and include with your application.

☐ **You are a publicly supported organization and would like the IRS to decide your correct classification.**

If you feel that your group may qualify as a public charity either under the "Public Support Test" or "Exempt Activities Support Test" (see Chapter 4 for descriptions of both of these public charity tests), but you aren't sure which to choose, you can check this box. The IRS will decide which of these two public charity classifications best suits your organization based upon the financial data and your responses to Questions 2 and 2a (see the instructions to Items 2 and 2a, above)

> **EXAMPLE:** The Elder Citizens' Collective and Information Exchange, which plans to derive support from contributions and grants as well as subscriptions to its weekly newsletter (and other exempt purpose services and products made available to members and the public at large), checks this box to have the IRS decide whether the group qualifies as public charity under the public support or exempt activities support test.

☐ **You are a private foundation.**

We assume you expect to qualify as a public charity and will not check this box. If you check this box, you are applying for recognition as a 501(c)(3) private foundation and must complete additional Lines 1a – 1d to help classify the private foundation into special subcategories—private operating and private nonoperating foundation categories. If your private foundation will provide scholarships, fellowships, educational loans, or other educational grants to individuals, including grants for travel, study, or other similar purposes, it must complete Schedule H. We assume you will get the help of an experienced legal or tax person who works with private foundations before completing these lines and submitting your exemption application.

Part VIII: Effective Date

Line 1. Most new groups will be able to check "Yes" here because they will be submitting their exemption application within 27 months after the end of month when their nonprofit corporation was formed. The date of formation is the date the corporation's articles

of incorporation were filed by the secretary of state and became effective. For example, if you filed your articles on January 12, 2021, you have until the end of April 2023 to submit (postmark) your exemption application. If you submit your application on time (within 27 months of incorporating) and the IRS grants your exemption, the exemption takes effect on the date on which you filed your articles

If you are submitting your exemption application after this 27-month deadline, check "No" and fill in and submit Schedule E with your 1023 exemption application.

Schedule E. Effective Date

Before filling in Schedule E, read the IRS 1023 instructions to Schedule E:

- **Line 1 – 1a:** These lines are used by groups that have had a previously granted exemption application revoked for failure to file required annual forms to the IRS for three years and are now reapplying to have their exemption reinstated. We assume you are using this book to apply for an initial tax exemption and will check "No" to Line 1.

- **Line 2.** Check the first box if you agree that your tax exemption, if granted, will be effective on the date of submission of the application. Check the second box if you wish to show reasonable cause for your late filing and ask the IRS to have your late-filed exemption effective on a date prior to the date of submitting your application (hopefully, on the date of the formation of your nonprofit corporation).

- **Line 2a:** Provide an explanation for your late filing. The 1023 instructions to Schedule E list reasons that can help you establish that you acted reasonably and in good faith and the grant of relief will not prejudice the interests of the government.

Part IX: Annual Filing Requirements

Line 1. Most nonprofits, except those listed if you check "Yes," must submit an annual reporting form to the IRS (Form 990, 990-EZ, or an e-postcard, 990-N). Generally, unless your organization is a church or a school or mission society associated with a church, you will check "No." See the 1023 instructions for more information on annual filing requirements and Chapter 10 for a summary of annual federal and state filing requirements.

Part X: Signature

One of the officers, directors (or trustees) listed in Part I, Line 9, must declare that the information in the 1023 application is correct by checking the box and typing his or her name.

You can satisfy the electronic signature requirement for Form 1023 if you include in the PDF file that you upload and submit as part of your application, a copy of the handwritten signature of the person whose name is typed as the authorized signer. You can submit either a copy of Part X of the completed application with the signer's signature above the typewritten name or you can create a separate document that includes the same information that is in in Part X (name of signer, title or authority of signer, date, and penalties of perjury statement as set out in Part X).

Preview and Print Your Completed Application

From any page of your completed 1023 application, click PDF Preview. If it is complete and correct, print the PDF to keep as your file copy.

Upload Your PDF file

See the 1023 instructions before checking these boxes and uploading your PDF file. Check the boxes to indicate the forms that you are including in your PDF file. We expect nonprofits using this book to check the "Organizing document" (Articles) and "Bylaws" boxes, and to include these documents in their PDF file. If you needed to add more information in response to application questions, check the "Supplemental responses" box, and include them in your PDF file, making sure to label the part and line number of the question associated with each response. Put the name of your organization and your EIN at the top of each supplemental page. Remember to include a copy of the authorized signor's written signature (see Part X).

Some nonprofits will decide to complete and include Form 8821 in their PDF to authorize someone in their organization to talk to the IRS about their application's status in case a follow-up discussion is necessary.

Including Form 2848, *Power of Attorney and Declaration of Representative*, should not apply to many readers of this book who are forming their own nonprofit corporation. However, if you are being helped by a lawyer, an accountant, or another professional representative, and you want that person to speak and act on your behalf with the IRS in any future communications, check this box and include IRS Form 2848 in your PDF. Note that the representative cannot sign your 1023 application unless they are an authorized director, officer, or other official of your nonprofit.

If you think you have a compelling reason to request expedited review (see "Requesting Expedited Review" in the 1023 instructions), check the "Expedited handling request" and explain your reasons on a supplemental page included in your PDF file.

You can only submit one PDF file with your 1023 online application and it cannot exceed the size limit stated in the 1023 instructions.

If it does exceed the limit and you can't trim it down to the required size (perhaps by editing supplemental responses), remove items to bring the file size to the required size, add a notation in the PDF that you removed the items that will be submitted later after contacting IRS customer services, and call IRS Customer Accounts Services at 877-829-5500 for guidance on how to submit the removed items after you submit your online application and truncated PDF file.

TIP

Creating a PDF file. You can add articles and bylaws included with this book, along with any supplemental responses, to a Microsoft *Word* file, then save it as a PDF file.

Final Steps

Complete the final online steps by paying the $600 application fee, then reviewing and submitting your application and PDF file.

Your next step is to wait. The IRS processing time can be three to six months or longer. For current processing timetables, search for "Where's My Application for Tax-Exempt Status?" on the IRS website (www.irs.gov). If you haven't been contacted within 180 days after submitting your application, you can call the IRS at 877-829-5500 to check on its status.

You can request expedited filing of your 1023 application by submitting a written request. The IRS may approve the request and speed up the processing of your application if your reason for the request is an impending grant deadline, if your nonprofit provides disaster relief, or if an IRS error has caused delays in review of the application. See "Requesting Expedited Review" in the 1023 instructions.

CAUTION

You must file annual federal and state information returns for your organization while your federal tax exemption application is pending (see "Annual Filing Requirements" in the 1023 instructions and Chapter 10). Indicate on your annual returns that your federal 1023 application is pending approval by the IRS.

If your application is pending and your nonprofit is eligible to file a 990-N postcard instead of Form 990 or 990-EZ, call Customer Account Services at 877-829-5500 (a toll-free number) and ask that the organization be set up to allow filing of Form 990-N.

What to Expect From the IRS

After reviewing your application, the IRS will do one of three things:

- grant your federal tax exemption
- request further information, or
- issue a proposed adverse determination (a denial of tax exemption that becomes effective 30 days from the date of issuance).

If the IRS asks for more information and you are not sure what they want from you—or you just feel that you are in over your head—consult a nonprofit attorney or tax adviser. If you receive a proposed denial and you wish to appeal, see a lawyer immediately. For further information on appeal procedures, see IRS Publication 557, *Tax-Exempt Status for Your Organization*. You can also go to the IRS website and type "Appeal Procedures" in the Search box for links to other appeals procedure information.

The Federal Determination Letter

The fortunate among you—and we trust it will be most of you—will get good news from the IRS. It will come in the form of a favorable determination letter, telling you that you are exempt from federal corporate income taxes under Section 501(c)(3) of the Internal Revenue Code, as a public charity. Unless you filed your application late and were not entitled to an extension, your tax exemption and public charity status will be effective retroactively to the date when your articles were filed with the secretary of state.

> ! **CAUTION**
>
> **If your determination letter tells you that you are exempt as a private foundation, see a tax or legal adviser immediately.** Most nonprofits will not want to maintain a nonprofit private foundation, and often either contest the determination or decide to dissolve their nonprofit corporation immediately.

Resist the natural temptation to file the letter without reading past the first sentences. The letter contains important information regarding the basis for your exemption and the requirements for maintaining it. Here's what to look for:

- **Are you properly classified?** Check to make sure that the public charity section listed by the IRS corresponds to the kind of public charity status you asked for. (You will find the various public charity code sections listed in Part VII, Foundation Classification, of your copy of the online 1023 PDF form.) Some groups will have checked the box in Part VII that asks the IRS to determine the proper public charity support test category support test for the organization.

- **Must you file a federal tax return?** The determination letter will tell you whether you must file a federal annual information return, IRS Form 990, Form 990-EZ, or the 990-N postcard. Most 501(c)(3) groups must file a 990 return (as explained in Chapter 10).

- **Are you liable for excise taxes?** The determination letter also should state that you are not liable for excise taxes under Chapter 42 of the Internal Revenue Code. These are the taxes applicable to private foundations.

  The letter will also refer to other excise taxes for which you may be liable. These are the regular excise taxes applicable to all businesses that engage in certain activities, such as the sale of liquor, the manufacturing of certain products, and so on. For further information, see IRS Publication 510, *Excise Taxes*.

- **Information on deductions for donors.** Your letter will include information on the deductibility of charitable contributions made to your organization and will refer to Internal Revenue Code sections that cover the deductibility of such donations.

- **Must you pay FUTA taxes?** Most groups will be told in their letter that they are exempt from federal unemployment (FUTA) taxes. You are, however, subject to filing nonprofit unrelated business income tax returns (Form 990-T). Nonprofits and their employees, however, are subject to Social Security (FICA) taxes—see "Federal and State Corporate Employment Taxes" in Chapter 10.

Congratulations! You've just finished the most complicated, and indeed most crucial, part of your nonprofit incorporation process. The remaining formal incorporation steps are explained in the next chapter. ●

Final Steps in Organizing Your Nonprofit Corporation

Most of the hard work is over, but there are still a few important details to attend to. Don't be overwhelmed by the number of steps that follow—many will not apply to your nonprofit corporation and others are very simple.

To chart your way through the tasks that follow, we recommend you use the Incorporation Checklist, included in Appendix C and on the Nolo website; see Appendix A for the link.

Obtain State Corporate Income Tax Exemption

Most states impose an annual corporate income, franchise, or other tax based on the net earnings of a corporation. In these states, your corporation must obtain an exemption from payment of these corporate taxes. In many cases, obtaining this state tax exemption is a formality—you will generally receive it once you file nonprofit articles in your state and obtain a federal 501(c)(3) tax exemption.

We suggest you browse your state corporate tax agency website now and request all information and forms necessary for you to apply for your state exemption from corporate taxes.

The state tax exemption application process will be simple and self-explanatory in most cases. In the few instances where you must answer detailed questions or submit separate financial data, the responses to your federal 1023 package should serve as sufficient responses on the state form.

Make sure to take care of your state tax exemption in a timely fashion (usually by the end of your first tax year). As with the federal form, if you reach the deadline date for your annual state tax return and your state tax exemption is pending, make sure to file your required annual state return, indicating that the state tax exemption application is pending.

Remember, like the IRS, state tax departments can impose fines and penalties for failing to file required tax returns, whether or not your corporation is subject to, or liable for, any corporate taxes.

Set Up a Corporate Records Book

Now take a few minutes to set up or order a corporate records book—this is an important part of your incorporation process.

Corporate Records Book

You will need a corporate records book to keep all your papers in an orderly fashion. These documents include articles of incorporation, bylaws, minutes of your first board meeting and ongoing director and shareholder meetings, tax exemption applications and determination letters, membership certificates (for those nonprofits with formal members), and any other related documents. You should keep your corporate records book at the principal office of your corporation at all times to make sure you always know where to find it.

To set up a corporate records book, you can simply place all your incorporation documents in a three-ring binder. If you prefer, however, you can order a custom-designed corporate records book.

Corporate Kits

You can order a nonprofit corporate kit through a legal stationery store. These nonprofit corporate kits typically include:

- a corporate records book with minutes paper and index dividers for charter (articles of incorporation), bylaws, minutes, and membership certificates

- a metal corporate seal (a circular stamp with the name of your corporation, the state's name, and year of incorporation), which you can use on important corporate documents, and

- membership certificates, printed with the name of your corporation.

Corporate Seals

Placing a corporate seal on a document is a formal way of showing that the document is the authorized act of the corporation. Nonprofits don't normally use a seal on everyday business papers (such as invoices and purchase orders), but they do use them for more formal documents, such as leases, membership certificates, deeds of trust, and certifications of board resolutions. A corporation is not legally required to have or use a corporate seal, but many find it convenient to do so.

A customized metal seal is usually included as part of a corporate kit you can order from a legal stationery store.

Corporate Membership Certificates

If you have decided to adopt a formal membership structure with members entitled to vote for the board of directors, you may want to use membership certificates. Unlike stock certificates used in profit corporations, membership certificates in nonprofit 501(c)(3) corporations do not represent ownership interests in the assets of the corporation. They serve only as a formal reminder of membership status.

The certificates that you issue should be numbered sequentially. Type the certificate number at the top of the form. Type the name of the corporation in the heading and the name of the member in the blank in the first paragraph. Have the certificate signed by your president and secretary, then place an impression of the seal of the corporation at the bottom. You should also record the name and address of the member and the number of the issued membership certificate in the membership list in your corporate records.

Prepare the Minutes of Your First Board of Directors' Meeting

Your next step is to prepare minutes of your first board of directors' meeting. The initial board of directors named in your articles of incorporation attends this meeting. If you did not name an initial board in your articles, see "If You Have Not Named Initial Directors in Your Articles," below, for instructions on having your incorporator(s) appoint the initial board. The purpose of this meeting is to transact the initial business of the corporation (elect officers, fix the legal address of the corporation, and so on) and to authorize the newly elected officers to take actions necessary to get your nonprofit corporation going (set up bank accounts, admit members if appropriate, and so on). Your directors should also discuss any other steps necessary at this point to get your nonprofit activities and operations started.

Prepare the minutes by filling in the blanks on the Minutes of First Meeting of Board of Directors available on the Nolo website (see Appendix A for the link) or in hard copy in Appendix C.

TIP
We have flagged optional resolutions in the special instructions below. If an optional resolution does not apply to you, do not include the optional resolution page in your final minutes.

Here are some instructions to help you prepare your minutes.

Waiver of Notice form. You can find this Waiver of Notice form preceding the minutes in Appendix C; a copy is also available on the Nolo website (see Appendix A for the link). The purpose of this form is to obtain the prior written consent of each initial director to hold your first board meeting. Under the statutes of many states, if the directors consent in writing, the corporation may dispense with special notice procedures that would otherwise apply to this first unscheduled meeting of the board. Even if this written consent procedure does not apply in your state, you can use this form to notify each of your directors of the upcoming first meeting of the board.

Fill in this form showing the name and address of your corporation and the date, time, and place of the meeting. Date the form and have each initial director sign.

Preamble to minutes. The first page of the minutes contains several standard paragraphs reciting facts necessary to hold a meeting of directors. Type the name of your corporation, the date and time of the meeting, and the address of the corporation, in the first few blanks. Next, list the names of the initial directors present at and, if applicable, absent from, the meeting. Remember, a quorum of the board, as specified in the bylaws, must be in attendance to carry out corporate business. Name one of the directors as chairperson and another as secretary of the meeting. You will elect permanent officers later in the meeting.

Articles of incorporation. Indicate the name of the state corporate filings office (usually the secretary of state) where the articles were filed and the date of this filing.

Bylaws. This resolution shows that your directors accept the contents of the bylaws.

Corporate tax exemptions. This resolution shows that your organization has obtained a favorable IRS determination of its 501(c)(3) tax-exempt status and is exempt from any applicable state corporate income taxes as well. Put the date of your federal determination letter in the blank in the first paragraph.

Election of officers. Type the names of the persons that the directors elect as officers of your corporation. Most nonprofits will wish to fill each of the four officer positions listed in this resolution. In many cases, particularly in larger nonprofits, officers are selected from among the board of directors.

If You Have Not Named Initial Directors in Your Articles

In some states, initial directors need not be named in the articles. If this is the case, then the incorporators (the person or persons who signed the articles) must appoint the initial board of directors. To do this, type the following form, fill in the name of the persons appointed to the board, and have each incorporator sign the form. Then prepare the minutes of your first board meeting as explained in the text. Make sure to place a copy of this form in your corporate minutes.

Meeting of Incorporators

On _____, 20_____, at _____ o'clock, a meeting of the incorporator(s) of [*name of corporation*] was held to elect the initial members of the board of directors. After nomination and discussion, the following persons were unanimously voted to serve on the board of directors of this corporation until their successors shall be elected and qualified:

_____

_____

_____

There being no further business, the meeting was adjourned.

Dated: _____

[*Signature(s) of incorporator(s)*]

RELATED TOPIC

Most states require a nonprofit to have a president, treasurer, and secretary, and allow one person to fill more than one or all of the officer positions. See your state's nonprofit law and check, "How Many People Are Needed to Form a Nonprofit Corporation?" in Chapter 2.

Principal office. Article 1, Section 1, of the bylaws indicates the county of the principal office of your corporation. Here you should provide the street address and city of this office. You should not list a post office box.

Bank account. You must keep corporate funds separate from any personal funds by depositing corporate funds into, and writing corporate checks out of, at least one corporate checking account. Indicate the bank and branch office where you will maintain corporate accounts in the first blank. In the second blank, indicate the number of persons (one or more) who must cosign corporate checks. In the remaining blanks, list the names of individuals allowed to cosign checks. Many corporations list the president and treasurer, among others.

Optional compensation of officers. Indicate any salaries to be paid to the officers in the blanks in this resolution. Type a zero to show unpaid officers' compensations. Most nonprofits do not compensate officers, or do so only minimally. If you do provide for real officer salaries, make sure they are reasonable and are related to what other people in the nonprofit sector make for providing similar services.

Optional corporate seal. If you've ordered a corporate seal, impress the seal in the space at the right of this resolution.

Optional corporate certificates. This is an optional resolution. Include this page in your final minutes if you have ordered director, sponsor, membership, or other certificates for your corporation and attach a sample of each certificate to your completed minutes.

Secretary certification page. Your secretary should date and sign the blanks on the last page of the minutes.

Place Minutes and Attachments in Corporate Records Book

You are now through preparing your minutes. Place your minutes and all attachments in your corporate records book. Your attachments may include the following forms or documents:

- Waiver of Notice and Consent to Holding of First Meeting of Board of Directors
- a copy of your articles, or certificate of incorporation, file-stamped or certified by the secretary of state
- a copy of your bylaws
- your federal 501(c)(3) tax exemption determination letter
- a copy of your state tax exemption application determination letter or other correspondence, and
- sample director, sponsor, or membership certificates.

Remember, you should continue to place an original or a copy of all formal corporate documents in your corporate records book (including minutes of directors', committee, and membership meetings) and keep this book at your principal office.

Issue Membership Certificates

If you have set up a membership corporation and have membership certificates, you will want to issue them to members after they have applied for membership in the corporation and paid any fees required by the membership provisions in your bylaws. The corporate president and secretary should sign each certificate before giving it to the member.

If you have ordered membership materials, record each member's name and address, together with the number of the certificate, in the membership register in your corporate records book. When you prepare your membership certificates, complete each certificate by typing the number of the certificate, the name of the corporation, and the name of the member on the certificate. Then execute the certificate by filling in the date and having the president and secretary sign at the bottom (if you have a seal, impress it at the bottom of each certificate). Give the certificate to the member, then record the member's name, address, certificate number, and date of issuance on a separate page in your corporate records book. The information on these pages, kept in the corporate records book, constitutes the membership book of the corporation.

File Fictitious or Assumed Business Name Statement

If your nonprofit corporation will engage in activities (raise funds, apply for grants, advertise, sell goods or services, and so on) under a name other than the exact corporate name given in your articles of incorporation, you will need to file an assumed or fictitious business name statement with your secretary of state and/or county clerk's office.

EXAMPLE: If the name stated in your articles is "THE ART WORKS, INC.," and the corporation plans to continue using the name of the preexisting organization that was incorporated as "THE ART STUDIO" (or chooses another name different from the one set out in the articles), you should file an assumed corporate name statement.

Your secretary of state website should contain information on assumed corporate name statements. If not, call or email your secretary of state or other corporate filings office and ask if this filing is made at the state or county level (or both). Order the form from the appropriate office and prepare and file the statement. In most cases, a small fee is charged for this filing. Also, the statement may need to be published locally in a legal newspaper and a proof of publication filed with your county clerk. Check the instructions to the form for the requirements in your state.

Filing an assumed or fictitious business name statement does not authorize you to use a name that another business is already using as a trademark, trade name, or service mark. Before you settle on a fictitious name, make sure the name is not already in use (just as you did with your corporate name—see "Choose a Corporate Name," in Chapter 6, for details).

Apply for a Federal Nonprofit Mailing Permit

Most 501(c)(3) tax-exempt nonprofit corporations will qualify for and want to obtain a third-class nonprofit mailing permit from the U.S. Postal Service. This permit entitles you to lower rates on mailings, an important advantage for many groups since the nonprofit rate is considerably lower than the regular third-class rate.

To obtain your permit, bring to your local or main postal service branch:

- a file-stamped or certified copy of your articles
- a copy of your bylaws
- a copy of your federal and state tax exemption determination letters, and
- copies of program literature, newsletters, bulletins, and any other promotional materials.

The postal service clerk will ask you to fill out a short application and take your papers. If your local postal service branch doesn't handle this, the clerk will send you to a classifications office at the main postal service office. You'll pay a one-time fee and an annual permit fee. The clerk will forward your papers to the classification office at the regional postal service office for a determination. In a week or so, you will receive notice of the USPS's determination.

Once you have your permit, you can mail letters and parcels at the reduced rate by affixing stamps to your mail; taking the mail to your USPS office and filling out a special mailing form; or by stamping your mail with an imprint stamp (made by a stampmaker) or leasing a mail stamping machine that shows your imprint information. Ask the classifications clerk for further information.

Apply for Property Tax Exemptions

We've already discussed state tax exemptions for real and personal property taxes in Chapter 5. Now is the time to apply for any property tax exemptions available to your group. Remember:

- Apply for an exemption from local personal property taxes if real property is owned or leased by the corporation.

- If you establish an exemption on leased premises, your landlord should give you a corresponding reduction in rent payments.

- Even if your federal tax exemption is pending, you may want to submit your application for a property tax exemption as soon as possible. When you get your federal tax exemption, forward a copy to the taxing agency. This way, you may be able to obtain at least a partial exemption for the current property tax year.

The procedure for applying for an exemption from local personal and real property taxes varies. Often you will need to submit a completed application form, copies of your articles and bylaws, and current and projected financial statements. You can copy the initial financial statements from, or base them on, the financial statement information you submitted with your federal 1023 form.

Call your county tax assessor or collector to find out what property tax exemptions are available for your tax-exempt 501(c)(3) nonprofit corporation and the procedures for applying. In some cases, you must apply to an office in the state capital; in others, the county office will process the papers locally. There may be multiple exemption categories to choose from. For example, a religious group may qualify for a church property tax exemption and for a separate property exemption available to 501(c)(3) nonprofit organizations. The county office should be able to advise you as to the most appropriate property exemption available to your group.

File an Initial Corporate Report Form

In most states you must file a periodic nonprofit corporate report form or statement with the secretary of state's office. Most states require you to file this form annually.

RESOURCE
Your state corporate filing office website should contain information on any periodic corporate report requirements and provide a downloadable form you can use.

While the nature and extent of the information required in each state varies, most states require certain basic organizational information, such as the address of your principal office, the names and addresses of your directors and officers, your registered agent and office, and so on. In some cases, you must also submit financial information, such as directors' and officers' salaries, supervisory staff compensation, fundraising receipts, and so on. Usually, the secretary of state makes this information available to the public.

Because failing to file a periodic report may lead to a fine or, for repeated failures, a suspension or forfeiture of corporate powers, make sure to file your corporate reports on time.

Register With the Attorney General

In some states, 501(c)(3) nonprofit corporations must register and report to the state attorney general's office. The attorney general scrutinizes nonprofit activities to make sure that the assets of the 501(c)(3) organization are being used for valid charitable or public purposes, not for private purposes.

The information sought on attorney general reporting forms varies. Most commonly, the financial reporting requirements seek to determine whether funds solicited from the public are being used for their stated purpose and whether any of the principals of the nonprofit (directors, officers, or staff) are benefiting unduly from nonprofit funds or programs.

In some states, you must file an initial registration form, with a periodic report required each succeeding year or so. We suggest you check with the attorney general's office by calling the main office in your state capital (the website of your state filing office may provide a link to the state attorney general's office). Ask if your 501(c)(3) tax-exempt nonprofit corporation must register or report to this office. In many states, this reporting function is handled by the charitable trusts division or department. Ask if your state has a similar division or department in the attorney general's office.

Check Local Ordinances

If you plan to solicit contributions locally (for example, as part of a door-to-door fundraising drive), make sure to comply with all local solicitation ordinances and regulations. Some counties and cities enforce local registration and reporting requirements. Other localities require you to furnish specific statements and disclose information to persons solicited by the nonprofit corporation.

Comply With Political Reporting Requirements

If your nonprofit corporation plans to lobby for legislation, hire a lobbyist, or otherwise be politically active (for example, by supporting or opposing state, county, or city measures to be voted on by the public), we suggest you check to see if your state imposes political registration or reporting requirements. (See "Limitation on Political Activities," in Chapter 3, for more on political activities and 501(c)(3) nonprofits.) Often, a fair political practices commission or similar body in the state capital oversees and administers these requirements. Another politically active nonprofit organization in your community should have experience with these requirements and should be able to direct you to the proper state office.

If you are active in campaigns for candidates to federal political office, also check whether you are subject to the registration and reporting rules under the Federal Election Campaign Act. For information on FECA and the rules and regulations administered under this act by the Federal Election Commission, go to www.fec.gov.

SKIP AHEAD

The final three steps of this chapter apply only to groups that have incorporated a preexisting organization.

Prepare Assignments of Leases and Deeds

If you have transferred a prior business or organization to your corporation, the prior owners or nonprofit organization may want to prepare assignments of leases or deeds if they are transferring real property interests to the corporation. Under an assignment, you step into the shoes of the old tenant—the terms and conditions of the lease don't change.

Here is a basic Assignment of Lease form you can use, or modify for use.

TIP

Renegotiate rental agreements or leases. Of course, assignments can be dispensed with if rental agreements or leases are simply renegotiated between the landlord and the new corporation. Even if you do prepare an assignment, the terms of the lease itself will normally require you to get the landlord's consent (the sample assignment of lease form below includes a clause showing the lessor's consent to the assignment). It is particularly important to communicate with the landlord

if the nonprofit corporation expects to obtain an exemption from local real property taxes on the leased premises (see "Apply for Property Tax Exemptions," above). A nonprofit group in this situation will want to insert a clause in its new lease allowing it a credit against rent payments for the amount of the decrease in the landlord's property tax bill as a result of its obtaining a real property tax exemption.

Assignment of Lease

[*Name of original lessee, for example, the unincorporated nonprofit organization*], Lessee of those premises commonly known as [*address of leased property*], hereby assigns the attached Lease relating to the above premises, executed [*date original lease was signed*], and all rights, liabilities, and obligations thereunder, to a proposed corporation, [*name of corporation*].

Dated: _____

[*Name of lessee*]

By: [*Signature of lessee representative*]
    [*Typed name of representative*]

The undersigned Lessor of the above premises hereby assents to this Assignment of Lease.

Dated: _____

By: [*Signature of lessor*]
    [*Typed name of lessor*], Lessor

A real estate broker or agent can help you obtain and prepare new leases and deeds. If a mortgage or deed of trust is involved, you may need the permission of the lender.

File Final Papers for Prior Organization

If you have incorporated a preexisting group, you may need to file final sales tax, employment tax, and other returns for the prior organization. You will also want to cancel any permits or licenses issued to the prior organization or its principals, obtaining new licenses in the name of the nonprofit corporation.

Notify Others of Your Incorporation

If a preexisting group has been incorporated, notify creditors and other interested parties, in writing, of the termination and dissolution of the prior organization and of its transfer to the new corporation. This is advisable as a legal precaution and as a courtesy to those who have dealt with the prior organization.

To notify past creditors, suppliers, organizations, and businesses of your incorporation, send a friendly letter that shows the date of your incorporation, your corporate name, and its principal office address. Retain a copy of each letter for inclusion in your corporate records book.

TIP

If the prior group was organized as a partnership (not a common situation), some states require the publication of a Notice of Dissolution of Partnership in the county or judicial district where the partnership office or property was located. To do this, call a local legal newspaper and ask if this notice form is published by the paper. If so, the newspaper will charge a small fee to publish the statement the required number of times and send you a proof of publication form for your files. If required, the newspaper should also file the proof of publication with the county clerk, the county recorder, or other appropriate county office.

After Your Corporation Is Organized

You have now incorporated your nonprofit and have handled many initial organizational details. But before you close this book, read just a little more. After incorporating, you need to become familiar with the formalities of corporate life, such as filing tax returns, paying employment taxes, and preparing minutes of formal corporate meetings. In this chapter, we look at some tax and other routine filings required by federal, state, and local governmental agencies. At the end, we give you an overview of what's involved in dissolving a nonprofit corporation.

The information presented here won't tell you everything you will need to know about these subjects, but will provide some of the basics and indicate some of the major areas that you (or your tax adviser) will need to go over in more detail.

Piercing the Corporate Veil —If You Want to Be Treated Like a Corporation, It's Best to Act Like One

After you've set up a corporation of any kind, your organization should act like one. Although filing your articles of incorporation with the secretary of state brings the corporation into existence as a legal entity, this is not enough to ensure that a court or the IRS will treat your organization as a corporation. What we are referring to here is not simply maintaining your various tax exemptions or even your nonprofit status with the state—we are talking about being treated as a valid corporate entity in court and for tax purposes. Remember, it is your legal corporate status that allows your organization to be treated as an entity apart from its directors, officers, and employees and allows it to be taxed (or not taxed), sue, or be sued, on its own. It is the corporate entity that

insulates the people behind the corporation from taxes and lawsuits.

Courts and the IRS do, on occasion, scrutinize the organization and operation of a corporation, particularly if it is directed and operated by a small number of people who wear more than one hat (such as those who fill both director and officer positions). If you don't take care to treat your corporation as a separate legal entity, a court may decide to disregard the corporation and hold the principals (directors and officers) personally liable for corporate debts. This might happen if the corporation doesn't have adequate money to start with, making it likely that creditors or people who have claims against the corporation won't be able to be paid; if corporate and personal funds are commingled; if the corporation doesn't keep adequate corporate records (such as minutes of meetings); or generally doesn't pay much attention to the theory and practice of corporate life. Also, the IRS may assess taxes and penalties personally against those connected with managing the affairs of the corporation if it concludes that the corporation is not a valid legal or tax entity. In legal jargon, holding individuals responsible for corporate deeds or misdeeds is called piercing the corporate veil.

To avoid problems of this type, be careful to operate your corporation as a separate legal entity. Hold regular and special meetings of your board and membership as required by your bylaws and as necessary to take formal corporate action. It is critical that you document formal corporate meetings with neat and thorough minutes. Also, it is wise to have enough money in your corporate account to pay foreseeable debts and liabilities that may arise in the course of carrying out your activities—even nonprofits should start with a small cash reserve. Above all, keep corporate funds separate from the personal funds of the individuals who manage or work for the corporation.

Federal Corporate Tax Returns

In this section, we list and briefly discuss the main IRS tax paperwork you can expect to face as a 501(c)(3) nonprofit corporation.

Your 990 and 990-T (unrelated business income return) forms must be made available for public inspection (go to the IRS website, at www.irs.gov, for more information).

CAUTION

Make sure your tax forms are current. IRS forms, instructions, fees, and penalties are subject to constant change. Be sure to get the most current information (on return deadlines, tax rates, penalties, and so on) when you file. To download the federal tax forms discussed in this section, go to "Forms & Instructions" on the IRS website, then "List All Current Forms & Instructions," and type in the form number.

Public Charities: Annual Exempt Organization Return

Nonprofit corporations exempt from federal corporate income tax under Section 501(c)(3) and treated or classified as public charities must file IRS Form 990, *Return of Organization Exempt From Income Tax* (together with Form 990, Schedule A). The filing deadline is on or before the 15th day of the fifth month (within four and a half months) following the close of their accounting period (tax year). You should file this even if your 1023 federal application for exemption is still pending. If your application is pending and your nonprofit is eligible to file a 990-N postcard instead of Form 990 or 990-EZ, call Customer Account Services at 877-829-5500 (a toll-free number) and ask that the organization be set up to allow filing of Form 990-N.

Depending on their annual gross receipts and total assets, some groups may be eligible to file a simplified IRS Form 990-EZ or may be required to file a 990-N (postcard) instead of Form 990 or Form 990-EZ. Also, some types of nonprofits, such as churches, are exempt from annual 990 filing requirements. See the instructions to these 990 forms on the IRS website, www.irs.gov, for more information. Section 501(c)(3) public charities that file Form 990 or 990-EZ must also complete and submit Form 990, Schedule A (with additional schedules if required), with their return. This form is used to test whether the publicly supported charity meets the applicable support test for the year (see Chapter 4).

CAUTION

Watch out for short deadlines. Your first 990 return deadline may come up sooner than you expect if your first tax year is a "short year"—a tax year of fewer than 12 months.

EXAMPLE: If your accounting period as specified in your bylaws runs from January 1 to December 31 and your articles were filed on December 1, your first tax year consists of one month, from December 1 to December 31. In this situation, your first Form 990 would have to be filed within four and a half months of December 31 (by May 15 of the following year), only five and a half months after your articles were filed. It is likely that your federal tax exemption application would still be pending at this time.

Your federal exemption determination letter should state whether you must file Form 990.

If your nonprofit corporation makes the political expenditures election by filing Federal Election Form 5768 (discussed in "Limitation on Political Activities" in Chapter 3), indicate on Form 990, Schedule A, that you made this election and fill in the appropriate part of the schedule showing your actual lobbying expenditures during the year.

CAUTION

IRS e-Postcard, Form 990-N, annual filing requirement for small nonprofits. Small tax-exempt organizations may be eligible to file IRS Form 990-N, *Electronic Notice (e-Postcard) for Tax-Exempt Organizations Not Required to File Form 990 or 990-EZ.* Organizations that do not file the e-Postcard or an information return Form 990 or 990-EZ for three consecutive years will have their tax-exempt status revoked.

For more information and to file a 990-N online, visit the IRS website, at www.irs.gov (type "990-N" in the search box).

Private Foundations: Annual Exempt Organization Return

Very few 501(c)(3) nonprofits will be classified as private foundations. If you are one, however, you must file a federal annual *Return of Private Foundation or Section 4947(a)(1) Nonexempt Charitable Trust Treated as a Private Foundation,* Form 990-PF, within four and one-half months of the close of your tax year. You file this Form 990-PF instead of Form 990 discussed above. You'll provide information on receipts and expenditures, assets and liabilities, and other information that will help the IRS determine whether you are liable for private foundation excise taxes. You should receive the form and separate instructions for completing it close to the end of your accounting period. Again, watch out for a short first year and an early deadline for filing your Form 990-PF.

The foundation manager(s) must publish a notice telling the public that they may see the annual report. Do so in a local county newspaper before the filing deadline for the 990-PF. The notice must state that the annual report is available for public inspection, at the principal office of the corporation, within 180 days after the publication of the inspection notice. A copy of the published notice must be attached to the 990-PF.

Unrelated Business Income: Annual Exempt Organization Tax Return

With a few minor exceptions, Section 501(c)(3) federal tax-exempt corporations that have gross incomes of $1,000 or more during the year from an unrelated trade or business must file an *Exempt Organization Business Income Tax Return* (Form 990-T). The form is due within two and a half months after the close of their tax year. For a definition and discussion of unrelated trades and businesses, see "Federal Unrelated Business Income Tax," in Chapter 5, and obtain IRS Publication 598, *Tax on Unrelated Business Income of Exempt Organizations.* Use this booklet and the separate instructions to Form 990-T to prepare this form.

More Information on Taxes

We suggest all nonprofits obtain IRS Publication 509, *Tax Calendars,* prior to the beginning of each year. This pamphlet contains tax calendars showing the dates for corporate and employer filings during the year.

Information on withholding, depositing, reporting, and paying federal employment taxes can be found in IRS Publication 15 (Circular E) *Employer's Tax Guide,* and the Publication 15-A and 15-B Supplements.

Other helpful IRS publications are Publication 542, *Corporations,* and Publication 334, *Tax Guide for Small Business.*

Helpful information on accounting methods and bookkeeping procedures is contained in IRS Publication 538, *Accounting Periods and Methods,* and Publication 583, *Starting a Business and Keeping Records.*

You can get IRS publications online, at www.irs.gov. You can also pick them up at your local IRS office (or order them by phone— call your local IRS office or try the toll-free IRS forms and publications request telephone number, 800-TAX-FORM).

The taxes imposed on unrelated business income are the same rates applied to normal federal corporate income. Remember that too much unrelated business income may indicate to the IRS that you are engaging in nonexempt activities to a "substantial" degree and may jeopardize your tax exemption.

File Your Returns on Time

The IRS and states are notoriously efficient in assessing and collecting late filing and other penalties. So, while it may be true that your nonprofit corporation does not have to worry about paying income taxes (because of its federal and state income exemptions), you should worry a bit about filing your annual information returns on time (including your employment tax returns and payments). Too many nonprofit corporations have had to liquidate when forced to pay late filing penalties (which add up quickly) for a few years' worth of simple informational returns that they inadvertently forgot to file.

Another important aspect of late filing penalties and delinquent employment taxes is that the IRS (and states) can, and often do, try to collect these often substantial amounts from individuals associated with the corporation if the corporation doesn't have sufficient cash to pay them. Remember, one of the exceptions to the concept of limited liability is liability for unpaid taxes and tax penalties. The IRS and states can go after the person (or persons) associated with the corporation who are determined to be responsible for reporting and/or paying taxes.

RESOURCE

For guidance on the Form 990 and other information on how to avoid IRS problems and retain your tax-exempt status, see *Every Nonprofit's Tax Guide*, by Stephen Fishman (Nolo).

State Corporate Tax Returns and Reports

Make sure to file your state corporate tax returns on time. In many states, the state forms are based on or follow the federal nonprofit corporate tax returns discussed above and are due on the same date. You can obtain state tax corporate forms online at your state tax office website. Or you can make a call to your state department of taxation and revenue (or similar state tax agency or department) to order annual nonprofit corporation tax forms, schedules, and instructions.

Federal and State Corporate Employment Taxes

You must withhold and pay federal and state employment (payroll) taxes on behalf of the people who work for your nonprofit corporation. Directors, with certain exceptions, are not considered employees if they are paid only for attending board meetings. However, if they are paid for other services or as salaried employees of the corporation, the IRS will consider them employees whose wages are subject to employment taxes. Check with the IRS and your local state employment tax office for further information.

501(c)(3)s are exempt from paying federal unemployment insurance (FUTA) taxes but must collect, withhold, report, and pay federal Social Security (FICA) and individual income taxes on employees' salaries. Your tax-exempt nonprofit may be exempt from having to pay some state employment taxes as well.

For information and help in computing your federal withholding and employer contribution payments, obtain the IRS publications listed in "More Information on Taxes," above. To register as an employer in your state and for information on meeting state payroll tax requirements, call the state employment tax office in your vicinity (or go to the employer registration office online—your state tax office website may provide a link).

Generally, independent contractors, such as consultants, who are not subject to the control of the corporation—both as to what shall be done and how the work is to be performed—are not considered employees. Wages paid to these people are not subject to payroll tax withholding or payment by the nonprofit corporation.

CAUTION
Be careful when classifying people as independent contractors. The law in this area is fuzzy, and the IRS (as well as the state employment tax office) is obstinate about trying to prove that outsiders really work for the corporation (and must be covered by payroll taxes). For more information, see IRS Publication 1779. An excellent legal guide to the ins and outs of independent contractor status is *Working for Yourself: Law & Taxes for Independent Contractors, Freelancers & Gig Workers of All Types*, by Stephen Fishman (Nolo).

Employee Income Tax Returns

Corporate staff and other compensated corporate personnel must report and pay taxes on employment compensation on their individual annual federal income tax returns (IRS Form 1040). If your state imposes a personal income tax, state income taxes are computed and paid with the employee's state personal income tax return.

Sales Tax Forms and Exemption From Sales Tax

Your corporation may be required to charge and collect state, county, and city sales, use, transit, excise, and other state taxes from customers or clients. In some cases, nonprofit exemptions from one or more of these state taxes may be available to your 501(c)(3) nonprofit corporation. Contact your state department of revenue, taxation, or similar state agency to register your corporation for sales tax and obtain any exemptions to which you may be entitled.

Licenses and Permits

Many businesses, whether operating as profit or nonprofit corporations, partnerships, or sole proprietorships, are required to obtain state licenses and permits before commencing business. So, while you may not be subject to the usual kind of red tape applicable to strictly profit-making enterprises (such as contractors, real estate brokers, or engineers), you should check with your state department of consumer affairs (or similar state licensing agency or department) for information concerning any state licensing requirements for your activities or type of organization. Many nonprofit institutions, such as schools or hospitals, will need to comply with a number of registration and reporting requirements administered by the state and, possibly, county government. A local business license or permit may also be required for your activities—check with your city business license department.

Workers' Compensation

Workers' compensation insurance coverage compensates workers for losses caused by work-related injuries and protects the corporation from lawsuits brought to recover these amounts. In some states, this coverage is mandatory; in others it is optional. Specific exemptions from coverage may be available to directors and officers in some instances. Make sure to check with your insurance agent or broker, or call your state compensation insurance commission, for names of carriers, rates, and extent of required coverage.

Private Insurance Coverage

Nonprofit corporations, like other organizations, should carry the usual types of commercial insurance to prevent undue loss in the event of an accident, fire, theft, and so on. Although the corporate form may insulate directors, officers, and members from personal loss, it won't prevent corporate assets from being jeopardized by such eventualities. Examine coverage for general liability, product liability, and fire and theft. You should also consider liability insurance for directors and officers, particularly if your nonprofit corporation wants to reassure any passive directors on the board that they will be protected from personal liability in the event of a lawsuit.

Dissolving a Nonprofit Corporation

A corporation may be dissolved either voluntarily or involuntarily. Voluntary dissolution occurs when a corporation decides to wind up its affairs by a vote of the board of directors, or a vote of the board in conjunction with the formal membership. The corporation might decide to dissolve because it runs out of program or administrative funds, because of an internal dispute within the nonprofit, or simply because the nonprofit program has accomplished its purposes or done as much as is reasonably possible in its area of endeavor.

A corporation dissolves voluntarily by filing articles of dissolution (or a similar document) with the secretary of state and, in some cases, obtaining a tax clearance from the state department of taxation or revenue. (Your secretary of state's website should contain forms and instructions to dissolve a nonprofit corporation in your state.)

Involuntary dissolution may occur if the corporation has failed to file its required annual financial report or pay state taxes for which it is liable for a given number of years. In such instances, the secretary of state or the attorney general will initiate the dissolution, depending on which department has jurisdiction over the misfeasance. The nonprofit corporation itself may petition the court to involuntarily dissolve it if its board is deadlocked, if it has been inactive for a number of years, or for other reasons specified under state statutes.

After a board decision to dissolve, the corporation must cease transacting business except to the extent necessary to wind up its affairs. All corporate debts and liabilities, to the extent of the corporation's remaining assets, must be paid or provided for. If any corporate assets are left after paying corporate debts, a 501(c)(3) tax-exempt nonprofit corporation must distribute them to another 501(c)(3) group. ●

Lawyers and Accountants

While we believe you can take care of the bulk of the work required to organize and operate your nonprofit corporation, you may need to consult a lawyer or an accountant on complicated or special issues. It also makes sense to have a lawyer or an accountant experienced in forming nonprofits and preparing tax exemption applications look over your papers. Reviewing your incorporation papers with an attorney or accountant is a sensible way to ensure that all of your papers are up to date and meet your needs. Besides, making contact with a legal and tax person early in your corporate life is often a sensible step. As your group grows and its programs expand, you'll be able to consult these professionals for help with ongoing legal and tax questions.

The professionals you contact should have experience in nonprofit incorporations and tax exemption applications. They should also be prepared to help you help yourself—to answer your questions and review, not rewrite, the forms you have prepared.

The next sections provide a few general suggestions on how to find the right lawyer or tax adviser and, if you wish to do your own legal research, how to find the law.

Lawyers

Finding the right lawyer is not always easy. Obviously, the best lawyer to choose is someone you personally know and trust, who has lots of experience advising smaller nonprofits. Of course, this may be a tall order. The next best is a nonprofit adviser whom a friend, another nonprofit incorporator, or someone in your nonprofit network recommends. A local nonprofit resource center, for example, may

be able to steer you to one or more lawyers who maintain active nonprofit practices. With patience and persistence (and enough phone calls), this second word-of-mouth approach almost always brings positive results.

Another approach is to locate a local non-profit legal referral panel. Local bar associations or another nonprofit organization typically run panels of this sort. A referral panel in your area may be able to give you the names of lawyers who are experienced in nonprofit law and practice and who offer a discount or free consultation as part of the referral panel program. Ask about (and try to avoid) referral services that are operated on a strict rotating basis. With this system, you'll get the name of the next lawyer on the list, not necessarily one with nonprofit experience.

You can check Nolo's Lawyer Directory at www.nolo.com/lawyers for nonprofit lawyers in your area. The Nolo Directory offers comprehensive profiles of the lawyers who advertise, including each attorney's education, background, areas of expertise, fees, and practice philosophy. It also states whether the lawyer is willing to review documents or coach clients who are doing their own legal work.

What About Low-Cost Law Clinics?

Law clinics advertise their services regularly on TV and radio. Can they help you form a nonprofit organization? Perhaps, but usually at a rate well above their initial low consultation rate. Because the lawyer turnover rate at these clinics is high and the degree of familiarity with nonprofit legal and tax issues is usually low, we recommend you spend your money more wisely by finding a reasonably priced nonprofit lawyer elsewhere.

When you call a prospective lawyer, speak with the lawyer personally, not just the reception desk. You can probably get a good idea of how the person operates by paying close attention to the way your call is handled. Is the lawyer available, or is your call returned promptly? Is the lawyer willing to spend at least a few minutes talking to you to determine if he or she is really the best person for the job? Does the lawyer seem sympathetic to, and compatible with, the nonprofit goals of your group? Do you get a good personal feeling from your conversation? Oh, and one more thing: Be sure to get the hourly rate the lawyer will charge set in advance. If you are using this book, you will probably want to eliminate lawyers who charge top dollar to support an office on top of the tallest building in town.

Legal Research

Many incorporators may want to research legal information on their own. You can browse most state nonprofit laws online. And in most states, county law libraries are open to the public (you need not be a lawyer to use them) and are not difficult to use once you understand how the information is categorized and stored. They are an invaluable source of corporate and general business forms, federal and state corporate tax procedures, and other information. Research librarians will usually go out of their way to help you find the right statute, form, or background reading on any corporate or tax issue.

Whether you are leafing through your own copy of your state's nonprofit corporation law or browsing corporate statutes online or at your local county law library, finding a particular corporate provision is usually a straightforward process. First define and, if necessary, narrow down the subject matter of your search to essential key words associated with your area of interest. For example, if one of the directors on your board resigns and you want to determine whether your state has any statutory rules for filling vacancies on the board, you will define and restrict your search to the key areas of "directors" and "vacancies." Look for these headings in your state's nonprofit corporation law.

Legal Shorthand and Definitions

A number of the rules contained in the corporate statutes are often given in legal shorthand—in short legal catchwords and phrases that are defined elsewhere in the code. For example, a common requirement contained in corporate statutes is that a matter or transaction be "approved by the board" or "approved by a majority of the board." Each of these phrases is defined in a separate section of the corporations code. (By the way, the first phrase usually means approval by a majority of directors present at a meeting at which a quorum of directors is present; the second usually means approval by a majority of the full board.) Special definitions of this sort are usually listed at the beginning of the state's nonprofit corporation law—read this starting definition section first to understand any special rules and legal shorthand used throughout your nonprofit corporation statutes.

At the beginning of your state's corporation law, a main table of contents will show headings for the major topics covered in the corporation law. One of these major topics will probably be labeled "Directors," followed by a range of code sections devoted to this subject area. Just before the first of these code sections in the corporation code, a subsidiary table of contents should be included showing individual headings for each code section in this range. In this mini table of contents for the "Directors" code sections, one heading may be listed for a code section devoted to "Vacancies."

Another search strategy is to simply start at the beginning of the corporation law and leaf through all the major and minor headings. Eventually—usually after just a few minutes or so—you will hit upon your area of interest or will satisfy yourself that the area in question is not covered by your corporate statutes. By the way, after going through your nonprofit law this way once or twice, you should become acquainted with most of its major headings. This will help you locate specific nonprofit subject areas and statutes quickly when searching this material in the future.

When you look up a nonprofit statute, whether online or in a book, you might want to use an "annotated" version of the codes. Annotated codes include not only the text of the statutes themselves, but also brief summaries of court cases that mention and interpret each statute. After you find a relevant statute, you may want to scan these case summaries—and perhaps even read some of the cases—to get an idea of how courts have interpreted the language of the statute.

RESOURCE

If you are interested in doing your own legal research, an excellent source of information is *Legal Research: How to Find & Understand the Law,* by Stephen Elias and the Editors of Nolo (Nolo).

Accountants and Tax Advice

As you already know, organizing and operating a nonprofit corporation involves a significant amount of financial and tax work. While much of it is easy, some of it requires a nitpicking attention to definitions, cross-references, formulas, and other elusive or downright boring details, particularly when preparing the federal long-form 1023 tax exemption application. As we often suggest in the book, you may find it sensible to seek advice or help from an accountant or other tax adviser when organizing your nonprofit corporation.

For example, you may need help preparing the income statements, balance sheets, and other financial and tax information submitted with your IRS tax exemption application. Also, if your organization will handle any significant amount of money, you will need an accountant or a bookkeeper to set up your double-entry accounting books (cash receipts and disbursement journals, general ledger, and so on). Double-entry accounting techniques are particularly important to nonprofits that receive federal or private grant or program funds—accounting for these "restricted funds" usually requires setting up a separate set of books for each fund (and the assistance of a professional).

Nonprofit corporation account books should be designed to allow for easy transfer of financial data to state and federal nonprofit corporate tax returns and disclosure statements. It should be easy to use the books to determine, at any time, whether receipts and expenditures fall into the categories proper for maintaining your 501(c)(3) tax exemption, public charity status, and grant or program eligibility. You will also want to know whether your operations are likely to subject you to an unrelated business income tax under federal and state rules.

Once your corporation is organized and your books are set up, corporate personnel with experience in bookkeeping and nonprofit tax matters can do the ongoing work of keeping the books and filing tax forms. Whatever your arrangement, make sure to at least obtain the tax publications listed in "More Information on Taxes," in Chapter 10. These pamphlets contain essential information on preparing and filing IRS corporation and employment tax returns.

When you select an accountant or a bookkeeper, the same considerations apply as when selecting a lawyer. Choose someone you know or whom a friend or nonprofit contact recommends. Be as specific as you can regarding the services you want performed. Make sure the adviser has had experience with nonprofit taxation and tax exemption applications, as well as regular payroll, tax, and accounting procedures. Many nonprofit bookkeepers work part-time for several nonprofit organizations. Again, calling people in your nonprofit network is often the best way to find this type of person.

Using the Downloadable Forms and Other Online Material

This book comes with interactive files that you can access online at:

www.nolo.com/back-of-book/NNP.html

To use the files, your computer must have specific software programs installed. You can open, edit, print, and save RTF form files with most word processing programs such as Microsoft *Word*, Windows *WordPad*, and recent versions of *WordPerfect*.

Editing RTFs

Here are some general instructions about editing RTF forms in your word processing program. Refer to the book's instructions and sample agreements for help about what should go in each blank. Editing features include:

- **Underlines.** Underlines indicate where to enter information. After filling in the needed text, delete the underline. In most word processing programs you can do this by highlighting the underlined portion and typing CTRL-U.

- **Bracketed and italicized text.** Bracketed and italicized text indicates instructions. Be sure to remove all instructional text before you finalize your document.

- **Signature lines.** Signature lines should appear on a page with at least some text from the document itself.

Every word processing program uses different commands to open, format, save, and print documents, so refer to your software's help documents for help using your program. Nolo cannot provide technical support for questions about how to use your computer or your software.

CAUTION

In accordance with U.S. copyright laws, the forms provided by this book are for your personal use only.

List of Forms

The following files are in rich text format (RTF) and are available for download at:

www.nolo.com/back-of-book/NNP.html

Form/Document Title	File Name
Incorporation Checklist	CHECKLIST.RTF
Application for Reservation of Corporate Name	RESERVE.RTF
Articles of Incorporation	ARTICLES.RTF
Articles Filing Letter	FILING.RTF
Bylaws (including Membership Provisions and Adoption of Bylaws)	BYLAWS.RTF
Waiver of Notice and Consent to Holding of First Meeting of Board of Directors	WAIVER.RTF
Minutes of First Meeting of Board of Directors	MINUTES.RTF

How to Locate Incorporation Resources Online

This appendix explains how you can locate your state's websites that have the legal and tax rules for forming and operating your nonprofit corporation. We show you methods for locating corporate offices and information online using other websites that automate the process of locating links for these websites, instead of asking you to manually type in often complicated webpage addresses in your browser's address bar. Another advantage of using these online links is that they are maintained and updated on a regular basis and are less likely to go out of date than links that are listed in an appendix and manually updated only with each edition of this book.

How to Find Your State's Corporate Filing Office Website

The corporate filing office is where you file articles (or a similar document) to form a corporation. You can go to this site (or call the office at the telephone number listed on the site) to check the availability of your proposed corporate name and to reserve your name if you wish to do so. State filing office websites typically provide downloadable articles, name reservation request forms, and the latest corporate filing fee information. Many websites allow you to reserve your name and form your corporation online from the website, without having to prepare, print, and mail paper forms for filing to the state corporate filing office.

To find your state's corporate filing office website, go to www.statelocalgov.net and follow your State Government link to find the link for your secretary of state.

How to Find Your State's Tax Office Website

The state tax office website provides state nonprofit tax exemption forms and in formation, as well as other corporate and individual tax forms and information. To find your state's tax office website, go to the Federation of Tax Administrators website at www.taxadmin.org. Select "Taxpayers & Preparers," then "State Tax Agencies," and then select the tax agency link for your state.

How to Find Your State's Corporation Law Lookup Website

To find your state's Nonprofit Corporation Act or similarly titled law, visit the state law legal research area of Nolo's website. This will bring you to your state's statutory lookup webpage. You will see either a list of state law headings with title and chapter numbers and the name of each state law, or a search box that asks for a statute number. Just look for a Nonprofit Corporations heading. If you don't see one, look for a Business Entities or Corporations heading, then drill down to find the Nonprofit Corporation law heading.

If you are browsing through your state's nonprofit law for a general subject, select the heading from the heading list in your law that seems most appropriate for the subject. For example, open the "Directors" heading to look for statutes about directors or directors meeting requirements, then select the particular statute of interest listed under the heading. Nonprofit corporation laws normally are not extremely long, so it should not be difficult to search through heading or statute lists to find the subject areas you're seeking. With practice, you'll soon get to know how your nonprofit corporation law is organized, and future generalized searches should take less and less time. ●

Information and Forms

Incorporation Checklist

Application for Reservation of Corporate Name

Articles of Incorporation

Articles Filing Letter

Bylaws (including Membership Provisions and Adoption of Bylaws clause)

Waiver of Notice and Consent to Holding of First Meeting of Board of Directors

Minutes of First Meeting of Board of Directors

IRS Form 1023-EZ: *Streamlined Application for Recognition of Exemption Under Section 501(c)(3) of the Internal Revenue Code*

Incorporation Checklist

Step	Location of Instructions
☐ Go Online to Your Secretary of State's Website	Chapter 6
☐ Choose a Corporate Name	Chapter 6
☐ Reserve Your Corporate Name	Chapter 6
☐ Perform a Name Search	Chapter 6
☐ Protect Your Name	Chapter 6
☐ Prepare Articles of Incorporation	Chapter 6
☐ File Articles of Incorporation	Chapter 6
☐ Prepare Bylaws	Chapter 7
☐ Prepare Membership Provisions	Chapter 7
☐ Prepare and File Your Federal Tax Exemption Application	Chapter 8
☐ Obtain State Corporate Income Tax Exemption	Chapter 9
☐ Set Up a Corporate Records Book	Chapter 9
☐ Prepare Minutes of First Board of Directors' Meeting	Chapter 9
☐ Place Minutes and Attachments in Corporate Records Book	Chapter 9
☐ Prepare Assignments of Leases and Deeds	Chapter 9
☐ File Final Papers for Prior Organization (existing groups only)	Chapter 9
☐ Notify Others of Your Incorporation (existing groups only)	Chapter 9
☐ File Assumed Business Name Statement	Chapter 9
☐ Apply for Federal Nonprofit Mailing Permit	Chapter 9
☐ Apply for Property Tax Exemptions	Chapter 9
☐ File Corporate Report Form	Chapter 9
☐ Register With Attorney General	Chapter 9
☐ Comply With Political Reporting Requirements	Chapter 9

Date: _____

_____

_____

_____

_____

Re: Corporate Name Reservation

Please reserve the following corporate name for my use for the allowable period specified under the state's corporation statutes.

_____

I enclose the required payment of $_____. My name, address, and phone number are included below if you wish to contact me regarding this request.

Name: _____

Address: _____

Phone: _____

Thank you for your assistance.

_____

Articles of Incorporation

Pursuant to the provision of the Nonprofit Corporation Act of this state, the undersigned incorporators hereby adopt the following Articles of Incorporation:

Article 1

The name of this corporation is: _____

_____

Article 2

The name and address of the registered agent and registered office of this corporation is: _____

_____

_____

Article 3

The purposes for which this corporation is organized are: _____

_____

_____

_____

_____

_____

_____

_____

_____

_____

_____

_____

_____

_____

_____

_____

_____

Article 4

The number of initial directors of this corporation is: _____ and the names and addresses

of the initial directors are as follows: _____

_____

_____

_____

_____

Article 5

The name(s) and address(es) of the incorporator(s) of this corporation is/are: _____

_____

_____

Article 6

The period of duration of this corporation is: _____

Article 7

The classes, rights, privileges, qualifications, and obligations of members of this corporation are as follows:

_____

_____

_____

_____

Article 8

Additional provisions (attach separate pages if necessary): _____

_____

_____

_____

_____

_____

_____

_____

_____

_____

_____

_____

_____

_____

_____

_____

_____

_____

_____

_____

_____

_____

_____

_____

_____

_____

_____

_____

_____

The undersigned incorporators hereby declare under penalty of perjury that the statements made in the foregoing Articles of Incorporation are true.

Dated: _____

_____

_____

_____

_____

Name and Address of Incorporator: _____

_____

_____

Name and Address of Incorporator: _____

_____

_____

Name and Address of Incorporator: _____

_____

_____

Name and Address of Incorporator: _____

_____

_____

_____

_____

_____

_____

Date: _____

_____

_____

_____

_____

Re: Articles of Incorporation Filing

I enclose an original and _____ copies of the proposed Articles of Incorporation of

_____.

Please file the Articles of Incorporation and return a Certificate of Incorporation (or file-stamped copy of the original Articles) to me at the above address.

A check/money order in the amount of $_____, made payable to your office, for total filing and processing fees is enclosed.

The above corporate name was reserved for my use pursuant to Reservation # _____ issued on

_____.

Sincerely,

_____

_____, Incorporator

Bylaws

of

_____

Article 1
Offices

Section 1. Principal Office

The principal office of the corporation is located in _____ County, State of

_____ .

Section 2. Change of Address

The designation of the county or state of the corporation's principal office may be changed by amendment of these bylaws. The board of directors may change the principal office from one location to another within the named county by noting the changed address and effective date below, and such changes of address shall not be deemed, nor require, an amendment of these bylaws:

New Address: _____

Dated: _____, 20_____

New Address: _____

Dated: _____, 20_____

New Address: _____

Dated: _____, 20_____

Section 3. Other Offices

The corporation may also have offices at such other places, within or without its state of incorporation, where it is qualified to do business, as its business and activities may require, and as the board of directors may, from time to time, designate.

Article 2
Nonprofit Purposes

Section 1. IRC Section 501(c)(3) Purposes

This corporation is organized exclusively for one or more of the purposes as specified in Section 501(c)(3) of the Internal Revenue Code, including, for such purposes, the making of distributions to organizations that qualify as exempt organizations under Section 501(c)(3) of the Internal Revenue Code.

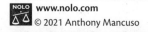

Section 2. Specific Objectives and Purposes

The specific objectives and purposes of this corporation shall be: _____

_____

_____

_____

_____

_____

_____

_____

_____

_____

_____

_____

_____

_____

_____

_____

_____

_____

_____

_____

_____

_____

_____

_____

_____

_____

_____

_____

_____

_____

_____

Article 3
Directors

Section 1. Number

The corporation shall have _____ directors and collectively they shall be known as the board of directors.

Section 2. Qualifications

Directors shall be of the age of majority in this state. Other qualifications for directors of this corporation shall be as follows: _____

_____

_____

_____

_____

_____

Section 3. Powers

Subject to the provisions of the laws of this state and any limitations in the articles of incorporation and these bylaws relating to action required or permitted to be taken or approved by the members, if any, of this corporation, the activities and affairs of this corporation shall be conducted and all corporate powers shall be exercised by or under the direction of the board of directors.

Section 4. Duties

It shall be the duty of the directors to:

a. Perform any and all duties imposed on them collectively or individually by law, by the articles of incorporation, or by these bylaws;

b. Appoint and remove, employ and discharge, and, except as otherwise provided in these bylaws, prescribe the duties and fix the compensation, if any, of all officers, agents, and employees of the corporation;

c. Supervise all officers, agents, and employees of the corporation to assure that their duties are performed properly;

d. Meet at such times and places as required by these bylaws;

e. Register their addresses with the secretary of the corporation, and notices of meetings mailed or telegraphed to them at such addresses shall be valid notices thereof.

Section 5. Term of Office

Each director shall hold office for a period of _____ and until his or her successor is elected and qualifies.

Section 6. Compensation

Directors shall serve without compensation except that a reasonable fee may be paid to directors for attending regular and special meetings of the board. In addition, they shall be allowed reasonable advancement or reimbursement of expenses incurred in the performance of their duties. Any payments to directors shall be approved in advance in accordance with this corporation's conflict of interest policy, as set forth in Article 9 of these bylaws.

Section 7. Place of Meetings

Meetings shall be held at the principal office of the corporation unless otherwise provided by the board or at such other place as may be designated from time to time by resolution of the board of directors.

Section 8. Regular Meetings

Regular meetings of directors shall be held on _____ at _____ _____.m., unless such day falls on a legal holiday, in which event the regular meeting shall be held at the same hour and place on the next business day.

If this corporation makes no provision for members, then, at the regular meeting of directors held on _____, directors shall be elected by the board of directors. Voting for the election of directors shall be by written ballot. Each director shall cast one vote per candidate, and may vote for as many candidates as the number of candidates to be elected to the board. The candidates receiving the highest number of votes up to the number of directors to be elected shall be elected to serve on the board.

Section 9. Special Meetings

Special meetings of the board of directors may be called by the chairperson of the board, the president, the vice president, the secretary, by any two directors, or, if different, by the persons specifically authorized under the laws of this state to call special meetings of the board. Such meetings shall be held at the principal office of the corporation or, if different, at the place designated by the person or persons calling the special meeting.

Section 10. Notice of Meetings

Unless otherwise provided by the articles of incorporation, these bylaws, or provisions of law, the following provisions shall govern the giving of notice for meetings of the board of directors:

a. **Regular Meetings.** No notice need be given of any regular meeting of the board of directors.

b. **Special Meetings.** At least one week prior notice shall be given by the secretary of the corporation to each director of each special meeting of the board. Such notice may be oral or written, may be given personally, by first class mail, by telephone or by facsimile machine, and shall state the place, date, and time of the meeting and the matters proposed to be acted upon at the meeting. In the case of facsimile notification, the director to be contacted shall acknowledge personal receipt of the facsimile notice by a return message or telephone call within twenty-four hours of the first facsimile transmission.

c. Waiver of Notice. Whenever any notice of a meeting is required to be given to any director of this corporation under provisions of the articles of incorporation, these bylaws, or the law of this state, a waiver of notice in writing signed by the director, whether before or after the time of the meeting, shall be equivalent to the giving of such notice.

Section 11. Quorum for Meetings

A quorum shall consist of _____ of the members of the board of directors.

Except as otherwise provided under the articles of incorporation, these bylaws, or provisions of law, no business shall be considered by the board at any meeting at which the required quorum is not present, and the only motion that the chair shall entertain at such meeting is a motion to adjourn.

Section 12. Majority Action as Board Action

Every act or decision done or made by a majority of the directors present at a meeting duly held at which a quorum is present is the act of the board of directors, unless the articles of incorporation, these bylaws, or provisions of law require a greater percentage or different voting rules for approval of a matter by the board.

Section 13. Conduct of Meetings

Meetings of the board of directors shall be presided over by the chairperson of the board, or, if no such person has been so designated, or in his or her absence, the president of the corporation, or in his or her absence, by the vice president of the corporation, or in the absence of each of these persons, by a chairperson chosen by a majority of the directors present at the meeting. The secretary of the corporation shall act as secretary of all meetings of the board, provided that, in his or her absence, the presiding officer shall appoint another person to act as secretary of the meeting.

Meetings shall be governed by _____, insofar as such rules are not inconsistent with or in conflict with the articles of incorporation, these bylaws, or with provisions of law.

Section 14. Vacancies

Vacancies on the board of directors shall exist (1) on the death, resignation, or removal of any director, and (2) whenever the number of authorized directors is increased.

Any director may resign effective upon giving written notice to the chairperson of the board, the president, the secretary, or the board of directors, unless the notice specifies a later time for the effectiveness of such resignation. No director may resign if the corporation would then be left without a duly elected director or directors in charge of its affairs, except upon notice to the Office of the Attorney General or other appropriate agency of this state.

Directors may be removed from office, with or without cause, as permitted by and in accordance with the laws of this state.

Unless otherwise prohibited by the articles of incorporation, these bylaws, or provisions of law, vacancies on the board may be filled by approval of the board of directors. If the number of directors then in office is less than a quorum, a vacancy on the board may be filled by approval of a majority of the directors then in office or by a sole remaining director. A person elected to fill a vacancy on the board shall hold office until the next election of the board of directors or until his or her death, resignation, or removal from office.

Section 15. Nonliability of Directors

The directors shall not be personally liable for the debts, liabilities, or other obligations of the corporation.

Section 16. Indemnification by Corporation of Directors and Officers

The directors and officers of the corporation shall be indemnified by the corporation to the fullest extent permissible under the laws of this state.

Section 17. Insurance for Corporate Agents

Except as may be otherwise provided under provisions of law, the board of directors may adopt a resolution authorizing the purchase and maintenance of insurance on behalf of any agent of the corporation (including a director, officer, employee, or other agent of the corporation) against liabilities asserted against or incurred by the agent in such capacity or arising out of the agent's status as such, whether or not the corporation would have the power to indemnify the agent against such liability under the articles of incorporation, these bylaws, or provisions of law.

Article 4
Officers

Section 1. Designation of Officers

The officers of the corporation shall be a president, a vice president, a secretary, and a treasurer. The corporation may also have a chairperson of the board, one or more vice presidents, assistant secretaries, assistant treasurers, and other such officers with such titles as may be determined from time to time by the board of directors.

Section 2. Qualifications

Any person may serve as officer of this corporation.

Section 3. Election and Term of Office

Officers shall be elected by the board of directors, at any time, and each officer shall hold office until he or she resigns or is removed or is otherwise disqualified to serve, or until his or her successor shall be elected and qualified, whichever occurs first.

Section 4. Removal and Resignation

Any officer may be removed, either with or without cause, by the board of directors, at any time. Any officer may resign at any time by giving written notice to the board of directors or to the president or secretary of the corporation. Any such resignation shall take effect at the date of receipt of such notice or at any later date specified therein, and, unless otherwise specified therein, the acceptance of such resignation shall not be necessary to make it effective. The above provisions of this section shall be superseded by any conflicting terms of a contract that has been approved or ratified by the board of directors relating to the employment of any officer of the corporation.

Section 5. Vacancies

Any vacancy caused by the death, resignation, removal, disqualification, or otherwise, of any officer shall be filled by the board of directors. In the event of a vacancy in any office other than that of president, such vacancy may be filled temporarily by appointment by the president until such time as the board shall fill the vacancy. Vacancies occurring in offices of officers appointed at the discretion of the board may or may not be filled as the board shall determine.

Section 6. Duties of President

The president shall be the chief executive officer of the corporation and shall, subject to the control of the board of directors, supervise and control the affairs of the corporation and the activities of the officers. He or she shall perform all duties incident to his or her office and such other duties as may be required by law, by the articles of incorporation, or by these bylaws, or which may be prescribed from time to time by the board of directors. Unless another person is specifically appointed as chairperson of the board of directors, the president shall preside at all meetings of the board of directors and, if this corporation has members, at all meetings of the members. Except as otherwise expressly provided by law, by the articles of incorporation, or by these bylaws, he or she shall, in the name of the corporation, execute such deeds, mortgages, bonds, contracts, checks, or other instruments that may from time to time be authorized by the board of directors.

Section 7. Duties of Vice President

In the absence of the president, or in the event of his or her inability or refusal to act, the vice president shall perform all the duties of the president, and when so acting shall have all the powers of, and be subject to all the restrictions on, the president. The vice president shall have other powers and perform such other duties as may be prescribed by law, by the articles of incorporation, or by these bylaws, or as may be prescribed by the board of directors.

Section 8. Duties of Secretary

The secretary shall:

Certify and keep at the principal office of the corporation the original, or a copy, of these bylaws as amended or otherwise altered to date.

Keep at the principal office of the corporation or at such other place as the board may determine, a book of minutes of all meetings of the directors, and, if applicable, meetings of committees of directors and of members, recording therein the time and place of holding, whether regular or special, how called, how notice thereof was given, the names of those present or represented at the meeting, and the proceedings thereof.

Ensure that the minutes of meetings of the corporation, any written consents approving action taken without a meeting, and any supporting documents pertaining to meetings, minutes, and consents shall be contemporaneously recorded in the corporate records of this corporation. "Contemporaneously" in this context means that the minutes, consents, and supporting documents shall be recorded in the records of this corporation by the later of (1) the next meeting of the board, committee, membership, or other body for which the minutes, consents, or supporting documents are being recorded, or (2) sixty (60) days after the date of the meeting or written consent.

See that all notices are duly given in accordance with the provisions of these bylaws or as required by law.

Be custodian of the records and of the seal of the corporation and affix the seal, as authorized by law or the provisions of these bylaws, to duly executed documents of the corporation.

Keep at the principal office of the corporation a membership book containing the name and address of each and any members, and, in the case where any membership has been terminated, he or she shall record such fact in the membership book together with the date on which such membership ceased.

Exhibit at all reasonable times to any director of the corporation, or to his or her agent or attorney, on request therefor, the bylaws, the membership book, and the minutes of the proceedings of the directors of the corporation.

In general, perform all duties incident to the office of secretary and such other duties as may be required by law, by the articles of incorporation, or by these bylaws, or which may be assigned to him or her from time to time by the board of directors.

Section 9. Duties of Treasurer

The treasurer shall:

Have charge and custody of, and be responsible for, all funds and securities of the corporation, and deposit all such funds in the name of the corporation in such banks, trust companies, or other depositories as shall be selected by the board of directors.

Receive, and give receipt for, monies due and payable to the corporation from any source whatsoever.

Disburse, or cause to be disbursed, the funds of the corporation as may be directed by the board of directors, taking proper vouchers for such disbursements.

Keep and maintain adequate and correct accounts of the corporation's properties and business transactions, including accounts of its assets, liabilities, receipts, disbursements, gains, and losses.

Exhibit at all reasonable times the books of account and financial records to any director of the corporation, or to his or her agent or attorney, on request therefor.

Render to the president and directors, whenever requested, an account of any or all of his or her transactions as treasurer and of the financial condition of the corporation.

Prepare, or cause to be prepared, and certify, or cause to be certified, the financial statements to be included in any required reports.

In general, perform all duties incident to the office of treasurer and such other duties as may be required by law, by the articles of incorporation of the corporation, or by these bylaws, or which may be assigned to him or her from time to time by the board of directors.

Section 10. Compensation

The salaries of the officers, if any, shall be fixed from time to time by resolution of the board of directors. In all cases, any salaries received by officers of this corporation shall be reasonable and given in return for services actually rendered to or for the corporation. All officer salaries shall be approved in advance in accordance with this corporation's conflict of interest policy, as set forth in Article 9 of these bylaws.

Article 5
Committees

Section 1. Executive Committee

The board of directors may, by a majority vote of its members, designate an Executive Committee consisting of _____ board members and may delegate to such committee the powers and authority of the board in the management of the business and affairs of the corporation, to the extent permitted, and, except as may otherwise be provided, by provisions of law.

By a majority vote of its members, the board may at any time revoke or modify any or all of the executive committee authority so delegated, increase or decrease but not below two (2) the number of the members of the executive committee, and fill vacancies on the executive committee from the members of the board. The executive committee shall keep regular minutes of its proceedings, cause them to be filed with the corporate records, and report the same to the board from time to time as the board may require.

Section 2. Other Committees

The corporation shall have such other committees as may from time to time be designated by resolution of the board of directors. These committees may consist of persons who are not also members of the board and shall act in an advisory capacity to the board.

Section 3. Meetings and Action of Committees

Meetings and action of committees shall be governed by, noticed, held, and taken in accordance with the provisions of these bylaws concerning meetings of the board of directors, with such changes in the context of such bylaw provisions as are necessary to substitute the committee and its members for the board of directors and its members, except that the time for regular and special meetings of committees may be fixed by resolution of the board of directors or by the committee. The board of directors may also adopt rules and regulations pertaining to the conduct of meetings of committees to the extent that such rules and regulations are not inconsistent with the provisions of these bylaws.

Article 6
Execution of Instruments, Deposits, and Funds

Section 1. Execution of Instruments

The board of directors, except as otherwise provided in these bylaws, may by resolution authorize any officer or agent of the corporation to enter into any contract or execute and deliver any instrument in the name of and on behalf of the corporation, and such authority may be general or confined to specific instances. Unless so authorized, no officer, agent, or employee shall have any power or authority to bind the corporation by any contract or engagement or to pledge its credit or to render it liable monetarily for any purpose or in any amount.

Section 2. Checks and Notes

Except as otherwise specifically determined by resolution of the board of directors, or as otherwise required by law, checks, drafts, promissory notes, orders for the payment of money, and other evidence of indebtedness of the corporation shall be signed by the treasurer and countersigned by the president of the corporation.

Section 3. Deposits

All funds of the corporation shall be deposited from time to time to the credit of the corporation in such banks, trust companies, or other depositories as the board of directors may select.

Section 4. Gifts

The board of directors may accept on behalf of the corporation any contribution, gift, bequest, or devise for the nonprofit purposes of this corporation.

Article 7
Corporate Records, Reports, and Seal

Section 1. Maintenance of Corporate Records

The corporation shall keep at its principal office:

a. Minutes of all meetings of directors, committees of the board, and, if this corporation has members, of all meetings of members, indicating the time and place of holding such meetings, whether regular or special, how called, the notice given, and the names of those present and the proceedings thereof;

b. Adequate and correct books and records of account, including accounts of its properties and business transactions and accounts of its assets, liabilities, receipts, disbursements, gains, and losses;

c. A record of its members, if any, indicating their names and addresses and, if applicable, the class of membership held by each member and the termination date of any membership;

d. A copy of the corporation's articles of incorporation and bylaws as amended to date, which shall be open to inspection by the members, if any, of the corporation at all reasonable times during office hours.

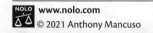

Section 2. Corporate Seal

The board of directors may adopt, use, and at will alter, a corporate seal. Such seal shall be kept at the principal office of the corporation. Failure to affix the seal to corporate instruments, however, shall not affect the validity of any such instrument.

Section 3. Directors' Inspection Rights

Every director shall have the absolute right at any reasonable time to inspect and copy all books, records, and documents of every kind and to inspect the physical properties of the corporation, and shall have such other rights to inspect the books, records, and properties of this corporation as may be required under the articles of incorporation, other provisions of these bylaws, and provisions of law.

Section 4. Members' Inspection Rights

If this corporation has any members, then each and every member shall have the following inspection rights, for a purpose reasonably related to such person's interest as a member:

a. To inspect and copy the record of all members' names, addresses, and voting rights, at reasonable times, upon written demand on the secretary of the corporation, which demand shall state the purpose for which the inspection rights are requested.

b. To obtain from the secretary of the corporation, upon written demand on, and payment of a reasonable charge to, the secretary of the corporation, a list of the names, addresses, and voting rights of those members entitled to vote for the election of directors as of the most recent record date for which the list has been compiled or as of the date specified by the member subsequent to the date of demand. The demand shall state the purpose for which the list is requested. The membership list shall be made available within a reasonable time after the demand is received by the secretary of the corporation or after the date specified therein as of which the list is to be compiled.

c. To inspect at any reasonable time the books, records, or minutes of proceedings of the members or of the board or committees of the board, upon written demand on the secretary of the corporation by the member, for a purpose reasonably related to such person's interests as a member.

Members shall have such other rights to inspect the books, records, and properties of this corporation as may be required under the articles of incorporation, other provisions of these bylaws, and provisions of law.

Section 5. Right to Copy and Make Extracts

Any inspection under the provisions of this article may be made in person or by agent or attorney and the right to inspection shall include the right to copy and make extracts.

Section 6. Periodic Report

The board shall cause any annual or periodic report required under law to be prepared and delivered to an office of this state or to the members, if any, of this corporation, to be so prepared and delivered within the time limits set by law.

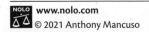

Article 8
IRC 501(c)(3) Tax Exemption Provisions

Section 1. Limitations on Activities

No substantial part of the activities of this corporation shall be the carrying on of propaganda, or otherwise attempting to influence legislation (except as otherwise provided by Section 501(h) of the Internal Revenue Code), and this corporation shall not participate in, or intervene in (including the publishing or distribution of statements), any political campaign on behalf of, or in opposition to, any candidate for public office.

Notwithstanding any other provisions of these bylaws, this corporation shall not carry on any activities not permitted to be carried on (a) by a corporation exempt from federal income tax under Section 501(c)(3) of the Internal Revenue Code, or (b) by a corporation, contributions to which are deductible under Section 170(c)(2) of the Internal Revenue Code.

Section 2. Prohibition Against Private Inurement

No part of the net earnings of this corporation shall inure to the benefit of, or be distributable to, its members, directors or trustees, officers, or other private persons, except that the corporation shall be authorized and empowered to pay reasonable compensation for services rendered and to make payments and distributions in furtherance of the purposes of this corporation.

Section 3. Distribution of Assets

Upon the dissolution of this corporation, its assets remaining after payment, or provision for payment, of all debts and liabilities of this corporation, shall be distributed for one or more exempt purposes within the meaning of Section 501(c)(3) of the Internal Revenue Code or shall be distributed to the federal government, or to a state or local government, for a public purpose. Such distribution shall be made in accordance with all applicable provisions of the laws of this state.

Section 4. Private Foundation Requirements and Restrictions

In any taxable year in which this corporation is a private foundation as described in Section 509(a) of the Internal Revenue Code, the corporation (1) shall distribute its income for said period at such time and manner as not to subject it to tax under Section 4942 of the Internal Revenue Code; (2) shall not engage in any act of self-dealing as defined in Section 4941(d) of the Internal Revenue Code; (3) shall not retain any excess business holdings as defined in Section 4943(c) of the Internal Revenue Code; (4) shall not make any investments in such manner as to subject the corporation to tax under Section 4944 of the Internal Revenue Code; and (5) shall not make any taxable expenditures as defined in Section 4945(d) of the Internal Revenue Code.

Article 9
Conflict of Interest and
Compensation Approval Policies

Section 1. Purpose of Conflict of Interest Policy

The purpose of this conflict of interest policy is to protect this tax-exempt corporation's interest when it is contemplating entering into a transaction or arrangement that might benefit the private interest of an officer or director of the corporation or any "disqualified person" as defined in Section 4958(f)(1) of the Internal Revenue Code and as amplified by Section 53.4958-3 of the IRS Regulations and which might result in a possible "excess benefit transaction" as defined in Section 4958(c)(1)(A) of the Internal Revenue Code and as amplified by Section 53.4958 of the IRS Regulations. This policy is intended to supplement but not replace any applicable state and federal laws governing conflict of interest applicable to nonprofit and charitable organizations.

Section 2. Definitions

a. Interested Person. Any director, principal officer, member of a committee with governing board delegated powers, or any other person who is a "disqualified person" as defined in Section 4958(f)(1) of the Internal Revenue Code and as amplified by Section 53.4958-3 of the IRS Regulations, who has a direct or indirect financial interest, as defined below, is an interested person.

b. Financial Interest. A person has a financial interest if the person has, directly or indirectly, through business, investment, or family:

1. An ownership or investment interest in any entity with which the corporation has a transaction or arrangement,

2. A compensation arrangement with the corporation or with any entity or individual with which the corporation has a transaction or arrangement, or

3. A potential ownership or investment interest in, or compensation arrangement with, any entity or individual with which the corporation is negotiating a transaction or arrangement.

Compensation includes direct and indirect remuneration as well as gifts or favors that are not insubstantial.

A financial interest is not necessarily a conflict of interest. Under Section 3, paragraph B, a person who has a financial interest may have a conflict of interest only if the appropriate governing board or committee decides that a conflict of interest exists.

Section 3. Conflict of Interest Avoidance Procedures

a. Duty to Disclose. In connection with any actual or possible conflict of interest, an interested person must disclose the existence of the financial interest and be given the opportunity to disclose all material facts to the directors and members of committees with governing board delegated powers considering the proposed transaction or arrangement.

b. Determining Whether a Conflict of Interest Exists. After disclosure of the financial interest and all material facts, and after any discussion with the interested person, he/she shall leave the governing board or committee meeting while the determination of a conflict of interest is discussed and voted upon. The remaining board or committee members shall decide if a conflict of interest exists.

c. Procedures for Addressing the Conflict of Interest. An interested person may make a presentation at the governing board or committee meeting, but after the presentation, he/she shall leave the meeting during the discussion of, and the vote on, the transaction or arrangement involving the possible conflict of interest.

The chairperson of the governing board or committee shall, if appropriate, appoint a disinterested person or committee to investigate alternatives to the proposed transaction or arrangement.

After exercising due diligence, the governing board or committee shall determine whether the corporation can obtain with reasonable efforts a more advantageous transaction or arrangement from a person or entity that would not give rise to a conflict of interest.

If a more advantageous transaction or arrangement is not reasonably possible under circumstances not producing a conflict of interest, the governing board or committee shall determine by a majority vote of the disinterested directors whether the transaction or arrangement is in the corporation's best interest, for its own benefit, and whether it is fair and reasonable. In conformity with the above determination, it shall make its decision as to whether to enter into the transaction or arrangement.

d. Violations of the Conflicts of Interest Policy. If the governing board or committee has reasonable cause to believe a member has failed to disclose actual or possible conflicts of interest, it shall inform the member of the basis for such belief and afford the member an opportunity to explain the alleged failure to disclose.

If, after hearing the member's response and after making further investigation as warranted by the circumstances, the governing board or committee determines the member has failed to disclose an actual or possible conflict of interest, it shall take appropriate disciplinary and corrective action.

Section 4. Records of Board and Board Committee Proceedings

The minutes of meetings of the governing board and all committees with board delegated powers shall contain:

a. The names of the persons who disclosed or otherwise were found to have a financial interest in connection with an actual or possible conflict of interest, the nature of the financial interest, any action taken to determine whether a conflict of interest was present, and the governing board's or committee's decision as to whether a conflict of interest in fact existed.

b. The names of the persons who were present for discussions and votes relating to the transaction or arrangement, the content of the discussion, including any alternatives to the proposed transaction or arrangement, and a record of any votes taken in connection with the proceedings.

Section 5. Compensation Approval Policies

A voting member of the governing board who receives compensation, directly or indirectly, from the corporation for services is precluded from voting on matters pertaining to that member's compensation.

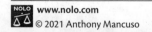

A voting member of any committee whose jurisdiction includes compensation matters and who receives compensation, directly or indirectly, from the corporation for services is precluded from voting on matters pertaining to that member's compensation.

No voting member of the governing board or any committee whose jurisdiction includes compensation matters and who receives compensation, directly or indirectly, from the corporation, either individually or collectively, is prohibited from providing information to any committee regarding compensation.

When approving compensation for directors, officers and employees, contractors, and any other compensation contract or arrangement, in addition to complying with the conflict of interest requirements and policies contained in the preceding and following sections of this article as well as the preceding paragraphs of this section of this article, the board or a duly constituted compensation committee of the board shall also comply with the following additional requirements and procedures:

a. the terms of compensation shall be approved by the board or compensation committee prior to the first payment of compensation;

b. all members of the board or compensation committee who approve compensation arrangements must not have a conflict of interest with respect to the compensation arrangement as specified in IRS Regulation Section 53.4958-6(c)(iii), which generally requires that each board member or committee member approving a compensation arrangement between this organization and a "disqualified person" (as defined in Section 4958(f)(1) of the Internal Revenue Code and as amplified by Section 53.4958-3 of the IRS Regulations):

   1. is not the person who is the subject of the compensation arrangement, or a family member of such person;

   2. is not in an employment relationship subject to the direction or control of the person who is the subject of the compensation arrangement;

   3. does not receive compensation or other payments subject to approval by the person who is the subject of the compensation arrangement;

   4. has no material financial interest affected by the compensation arrangement; and

   5. does not approve a transaction providing economic benefits to the person who is the subject of the compensation arrangement, who in turn has approved or will approve a transaction providing benefits to the board or committee member.

c. the board or compensation committee shall obtain and rely upon appropriate data as to comparability prior to approving the terms of compensation. Appropriate data may include the following:

   1. compensation levels paid by similarly situated organizations, both taxable and tax-exempt, for functionally comparable positions. "Similarly situated" organizations are those of a similar size, purpose, and with similar resources;

   2. the availability of similar services in the geographic area of this organization;

   3. current compensation surveys compiled by independent firms;

4. actual written offers from similar institutions competing for the services of the person who is the subject of the compensation arrangement.

As allowed by IRS Regulation 4958-6, if this organization has average annual gross receipts (including contributions) for its three prior tax years of less than $1 million, the board or compensation committee will have obtained and relied upon appropriate data as to comparability if it obtains and relies upon data on compensation paid by three comparable organizations in the same or similar communities for similar services.

d. the terms of compensation and the basis for approving them shall be recorded in written minutes of the meeting of the board or compensation committee that approved the compensation. Such documentation shall include:

1. the terms of the compensation arrangement and the date it was approved;

2. the members of the board or compensation committee who were present during debate on the transaction, those who voted on it, and the votes cast by each board or committee member;

3. the comparability data obtained and relied upon and how the data was obtained;

4. If the board or compensation committee determines that reasonable compensation for a specific position in this organization or for providing services under any other compensation arrangement with this organization is higher or lower than the range of comparability data obtained, the board or committee shall record in the minutes of the meeting the basis for its determination;

5. If the board or committee makes adjustments to comparability data due to geographic area or other specific conditions, these adjustments and the reasons for them shall be recorded in the minutes of the board or committee meeting;

6. any actions taken with respect to determining if a board or committee member had a conflict of interest with respect to the compensation arrangement, and if so, actions taken to make sure the member with the conflict of interest did not affect or participate in the approval of the transaction (for example, a notation in the records that after a finding of conflict of interest by a member, the member with the conflict of interest was asked to, and did, leave the meeting prior to a discussion of the compensation arrangement and a taking of the votes to approve the arrangement);

7. the minutes of board or committee meetings at which compensation arrangements are approved must be prepared before the later of the date of the next board or committee meeting or 60 days after the final actions of the board or committee are taken with respect to the approval of the compensation arrangements. The minutes must be reviewed and approved by the board and committee as reasonable, accurate, and complete within a reasonable period thereafter, normally prior to or at the next board or committee meeting following final action on the arrangement by the board or committee.

Section 6. Annual Statements

Each director, principal officer, and member of a committee with governing board delegated powers shall annually sign a statement that affirms such person:

a. has received a copy of the conflicts of interest policy;

b. has read and understands the policy;

c. has agreed to comply with the policy; and

d. understands the corporation is charitable and in order to maintain its federal tax exemption it must engage primarily in activities that accomplish one or more of its tax-exempt purposes.

Section 7. Periodic Reviews

To ensure the corporation operates in a manner consistent with charitable purposes and does not engage in activities that could jeopardize its tax-exempt status, periodic reviews shall be conducted. The periodic reviews shall, at a minimum, include the following subjects:

a. Whether compensation arrangements and benefits are reasonable, based on competent survey information, and the result of arm's-length bargaining.

b. Whether partnerships, joint ventures, and arrangements with management organizations conform to the corporation's written policies, are properly recorded, reflect reasonable investment or payments for goods and services, further charitable purposes, and do not result in inurement, impermissible private benefit, or in an excess benefit transaction.

Section 8. Use of Outside Experts

When conducting the periodic reviews as provided for in Section 7, the corporation may, but need not, use outside advisers. If outside experts are used, their use shall not relieve the governing board of its responsibility for ensuring periodic reviews are conducted.

Article 10
Amendment of Bylaws

Section 1. Amendment

Subject to the power of the members, if any, of this corporation to adopt, amend, or repeal the bylaws of this corporation and except as may otherwise be specified under provisions of law, these bylaws, or any of them, may be altered, amended, or repealed, and new bylaws adopted by approval of the board of directors.

Article 11
Construction and Terms

If there is any conflict between the provisions of these bylaws and the articles of incorporation of this corporation, the provisions of the articles of incorporation shall govern.

Should any of the provisions or portions of these bylaws be held unenforceable or invalid for any reason, the remaining provisions and portions of these bylaws shall be unaffected by such holding.

All references in these bylaws to the articles of incorporation shall be to the articles of incorporation, articles of organization, certificate of incorporation, organizational charter, corporate charter, or other founding document of this corporation filed with an office of this state and used to establish the legal existence of this corporation.

All references in these bylaws to a section or sections of the Internal Revenue Code shall be to such sections of the Internal Revenue Code of 2186 as amended from time to time, or to corresponding provisions of any future federal tax code.

[The following provisions are for use in your bylaws ONLY if you have chosen to adopt a membership structure for your corporation. If you have decided to form a nonmembership corporation (as most nonprofits do), you should not include the "Membership Provisions" clauses in your bylaws. Instead, delete them from this document.

NOTE: Take care not to delete the "Adoption of Bylaws" clause at the end of this document. This clause will be the last page of your bylaws, whether you include the "Membership Provisions" or not.]

[Optional]:
Membership Provisions of the Bylaws

of

_____

Article 12
Members

Section 1. Determination and Rights of Members

The corporation shall have only one class of members. No member shall hold more than one membership in the corporation. Except as expressly provided in or authorized by the articles of incorporation, the bylaws of this corporation, or provisions of law, all memberships shall have the same rights, privileges, restrictions, and conditions.

Section 2. Qualifications of Members

The qualifications for membership in this corporation are as follows: _____

_____

_____

_____

_____

Section 3. Admission of Members

Applicants shall be admitted to membership_____

_____

_____

_____

Section 4. Fees and Dues

a. The following fee shall be charged for making application for membership in the corporation:

    _____.

b. The annual dues payable to the corporation by members shall be _____.

Section 5. Number of Members

There is no limit on the number of members the corporation may admit.

Section 6. Membership Book

The corporation shall keep a membership book containing the name and address of each member. Termination of the membership of any member shall be recorded in the book, together with the date of termination of such membership. Such book shall be kept at the corporation's principal office.

Section 7. Nonliability of Members

A member of this corporation is not, as such, personally liable for the debts, liabilities, or obligations of the corporation.

Section 8. Nontransferability of Memberships

No member may transfer a membership or any right arising therefrom. All rights of membership cease upon the member's death.

Section 9. Termination of Membership

The membership of a member shall terminate upon the occurrence of any of the following events:

1. Upon his or her notice of such termination delivered to the president or secretary of the corporation personally or by mail, such membership to terminate upon the date of delivery of the notice or date of deposit in the mail.

2. If this corporation has provided for the payment of dues by members, upon a failure to renew his or her membership by paying dues on or before their due date, such termination to be effective thirty (30) days after a written notification of delinquency is given personally or mailed to such member by the secretary of the corporation. A member may avoid such termination by paying the amount of delinquent dues within a thirty (30) day period following the member's receipt of the written notification of delinquency.

3. After providing the member with reasonable written notice and an opportunity to be heard either orally or in writing, upon a determination by the board of directors that the member has engaged in conduct materially and seriously prejudicial to the interests or purposes of the corporation. Any person expelled from the corporation shall receive a refund of dues already paid for the current dues period.

    All rights of a member in the corporation shall cease on termination of membership as herein provided.

Article 13
Meetings of Members

Section 1. Place of Meetings

Meetings of members shall be held at the principal office of the corporation or at such other place or places as may be designated from time to time by resolution of the board of directors.

Section 2. Regular Meetings

A regular meeting of members shall be held on _____, _____, at _____ ____.m., for the purpose of electing directors and transacting other business as may come before the meeting. The candidates receiving the highest number of votes up to the number of directors to be elected shall be elected. Each voting member shall cast one vote, with voting being by ballot only. The annual meeting of members for the purpose of electing directors shall be deemed a regular meeting.

Other regular meetings of the members shall be held on _____, at _____ ____.m.,

If the day fixed for a regular meeting falls on a legal holiday, such meeting shall be held at the same hour and place on the next business day.

Section 3. Special Meetings of Members

Special meetings of the members shall be called by the board of directors, the chairperson of the board, or the president of the corporation, or, if different, by the persons specifically authorized under the laws of this state to call special meetings of the members.

Section 4. Notice of Meetings

Unless otherwise provided by the articles of incorporation, these bylaws, or provisions of law, notice stating the place, day, and hour of the meeting and, in the case of a special meeting, the purpose or purposes for which the meeting is called, shall be delivered not less than ten (10) nor more than fifty (50) days before the date of the meeting, either personally or by mail, by or at the direction of the president, or the secretary, or the persons calling the meeting, to each member entitled to vote at such meeting. If mailed, such notice shall be deemed to be delivered when deposited in the United States mail addressed to the member at his or her address as it appears on the records of the corporation, with postage prepaid. Personal notification includes notification by telephone or by facsimile machine, provided however, in the case of facsimile notification, the member to be contacted shall acknowledge personal receipt of the facsimile notice by a return message or telephone call within twenty-four hours of the first facsimile transmission.

The notice of any meeting of members at which directors are to be elected shall also state the names of all those who are nominees or candidates for election to the board at the time notice is given.

Whenever any notice of a meeting is required to be given to any member of this corporation under provisions of the articles of incorporation, these bylaws, or the law of this state, a waiver of notice in writing signed by the member, whether before or after the time of the meeting, shall be equivalent to the giving of such notice.

Section 5. Quorum for Meetings

A quorum shall consist of _____ of the voting members of the corporation.

Except as otherwise provided under the articles of incorporation, these bylaws, or provisions of law, no business shall be considered by the members at any meeting at which the required quorum is not present, and the only motion that the chair shall entertain at such meeting is a motion to adjourn.

Section 6. Majority Action as Membership Action

Every act or decision done or made by a majority of voting members present in person or by proxy at a duly held meeting at which a quorum is present is the act of the members, unless the articles of incorporation, these bylaws, or provisions of law require a greater number.

Section 7. Voting Rights

Each member is entitled to one vote on each matter submitted to a vote by the members. Voting at duly held meetings shall be by voice vote. Election of directors, however, shall be by written ballot.

Section 8. Action by Written Ballot

Except as otherwise provided under the articles of incorporation, these bylaws, or provisions of law, any action that may be taken at any regular or special meeting of members may be taken without a meeting if the corporation distributes a written ballot to each member entitled to vote on the matter. The ballot shall:

1. set forth the proposed action;

2. provide an opportunity to specify approval or disapproval of each proposal;

3. indicate the number of responses needed to meet the quorum requirement and, except for ballots soliciting votes for the election of directors, state the percentage of approvals necessary to pass the measure submitted; and

4. shall specify the date by which the ballot must be received by the corporation in order to be counted. The date set shall afford members a reasonable time within which to return the ballots to the corporation.

Ballots shall be mailed or delivered in the manner required for giving notice of membership meetings as specified in these bylaws.

Approval of action by written ballot shall be valid only when the number of votes cast by ballot within the time period specified equals or exceeds the quorum required to be present at a meeting authorizing the action, and the number of approvals equals or exceeds the number of votes that would be required to approve the action at a meeting at which the total number of votes cast was the same as the number of votes cast by ballot.

Directors may be elected by written ballot. Such ballots for the election of directors shall list the persons nominated at the time the ballots are mailed or delivered.

Section 9. Conduct of Meetings

Meetings of members shall be presided over by the chairperson of the board, or, if there is no chairperson, or in his or her absence, by the president of the corporation or, in his or her absence, by the vice president of the corporation or, in the absence of all of these persons, by a chairperson chosen by a majority of the voting members present at the meeting. The secretary of the corporation shall act as secretary of all meetings of members, provided that, in his or her absence, the presiding officer shall appoint another person to act as secretary of the meeting.

Meetings shall be governed by _____, as such rules may be revised from time to time, insofar as such rules are not inconsistent with or in conflict with the articles of incorporation, these bylaws, or with provisions of law.

[End option]

Adoption of Bylaws

We, the undersigned, are all of the initial directors or incorporators of this corporation, and we consent to, and hereby do, adopt the foregoing bylaws, consisting of _____ preceding pages, as the bylaws of this corporation.

Dated: _____

_____

_____

_____

_____

Waiver of Notice and Consent to Holding
of First Meeting of Board of Directors

of

_____

We, the undersigned, being all the directors of _____

_____, hereby waive notice of the first

meeting of the board of directors of the corporation and consent to the holding of said meeting at

_____, on

_____, 20_____, at _____ ____.m., and consent to the

transaction of any and all business by the directors at the meeting, including, without limitation, the

adoption of bylaws, the election of officers, and the selection of the place where the corporation's bank

accounts will be maintained.

Date: _____

_____

_____, Director

_____

_____, Director

_____

_____, Director

_____

_____, Director

_____

_____, Director

_____

_____, Director

_____

_____, Director

Minutes of First Meeting of Board of Directors

of

_____

The board of directors of _____

held its first meeting on _____, 20_____, at _____.m.

The following directors, constituting a quorum of the full board, were present at the meeting:

_____

_____

_____

_____

The following directors were absent:

_____

_____

_____

On motion and by unanimous vote, _____

was elected temporary chairperson and then presided over the meeting. _____

_____ was elected temporary secretary of the meeting.

The chairperson announced that the meeting was held pursuant to written waiver of notice signed by each of the directors. Upon a motion duly made, seconded, and unanimously carried, the waiver was made a part of the records of the meeting. It now precedes the minutes of this meeting in the corporate records book.

Articles of Incorporation

The chairperson announced that the articles of incorporation or similar organizing instrument of this corporation was filed with the office of _____

_____ on _____.

RESOLVED, that the secretary of this corporation is directed to see that a copy of the articles of incorporation or similar organizing instrument of this corporation, file-stamped or certified by the secretary of state or other appropriate state office or official, is kept at the corporation's principal office.

Bylaws

There was then presented to the meeting for adoption a proposed set of bylaws of the corporation. The bylaws were considered and discussed and, on motion duly made and seconded, it was unanimously

RESOLVED, that the bylaws presented to this meeting be and hereby are adopted as the bylaws of the corporation;

RESOLVED FURTHER, that the secretary of this corporation is directed to see that a copy of the bylaws is kept at the corporation's principal office.

Corporate Tax Exemptions

The chairperson announced that, upon application previously submitted to the Internal Revenue Service, the corporation was determined to be exempt from payment of federal corporate income taxes under Section 501(c)(3) of the Internal Revenue Code per Internal Revenue Service determination letter dated _____, 20_____. The chairperson then presented the federal tax exemption determination letter and the secretary was instructed to insert this letter in the corporate records book.

The chairperson announced that the corporation was exempt from applicable state corporate income, franchise, or similar taxes. The chairperson instructed the secretary to place a copy of any correspondence related to the corporation's state corporate tax exemption in the corporate records book.

Election of Officers

The chairperson then announced that the next item of business was the election of officers. Upon motion, the following persons were unanimously elected to the offices shown after their names:

_____ President

_____ Vice President

_____ Secretary

_____ Treasurer

Each officer who was present accepted his or her office. Thereafter, the president presided at the meeting as chairperson of the meeting, and the secretary of the corporation acted as secretary of the meeting.

Principal Office

After discussion as to the exact location of the corporation's principal office for the transaction of business in the county named in the bylaws, upon motion duly made and seconded, it was

RESOLVED, that the principal office of this corporation shall be located at _____

_____.

Bank Account

Upon motion duly made and seconded, it was

RESOLVED, that the funds of this corporation shall be deposited with _____

_____.

RESOLVED FURTHER, that the treasurer of this corporation be and hereby is authorized and directed to establish an account with said bank and to deposit the funds of this corporation therein.

RESOLVED FURTHER, that any officer, employee, or agent of this corporation be and is authorized to endorse checks, drafts, or other evidences of indebtedness made payable to this corporation, but only for the purpose of deposit.

RESOLVED FURTHER, that all checks, drafts, and other instruments obligating this corporation to pay money shall be signed on behalf of this corporation by any of the following persons:

_____

_____

_____

_____

RESOLVED FURTHER, that said bank be and hereby is authorized to honor and pay all checks and drafts of this corporation signed as provided herein.

RESOLVED FURTHER, that the authority hereby conferred shall remain in force until revoked by the board of directors of this corporation and until written notice of such revocation shall have been received by said bank.

RESOLVED FURTHER, that the secretary of this corporation be and hereby is authorized to certify as to the continuing authority of these resolutions, the persons authorized to sign on behalf of this corporation, and the adoption of said bank's standard form of resolution, provided that said form does not vary materially from the terms of the foregoing resolutions.

Compensation of Officers

There followed a discussion concerning the compensation to be paid by the corporation to its officers. Upon motion duly made and seconded, it was unanimously

RESOLVED, that the following annual salaries be paid to the officers of this corporation:

President	$_____
Vice President	$_____
Secretary	$_____
Treasurer	$_____

Corporate Seal

The secretary presented to the meeting for adoption a proposed form of seal of the corporation. Upon motion duly made and seconded, it was:

RESOLVED, that the form of corporate seal presented to this meeting be and hereby is adopted as the seal of this corporation, and the secretary of the corporation is directed to place an impression thereof in the space next to this resolution.

[Impress seal here]

Corporate Certificates

The secretary then presented to the meeting proposed director, sponsor, membership, or other forms of corporate certificates for approval by the board. Upon motion duly made and seconded, it was

RESOLVED, that the form of certificates presented to this meeting are hereby adopted for use by this corporation and the secretary is directed to attach a copy of each form of certificate to the minutes of this meeting.

Since there was no further business to come before the meeting, on motion duly made and seconded, the meeting was adjourned.

Dated: _____

_____

_____, Secretary

You must complete the Form 1023-EZ Eligibility Worksheet in the Instructions for Form 1023-EZ to determine if you are eligible to file this form. Form 1023-EZ is filed electronically **only** on Pay.gov.
Go to www.irs.gov/form1023ez for additional filing information.

| Form **1023-EZ** (June 2014) Department of the Treasury Internal Revenue Service | **Streamlined Application for Recognition of Exemption Under Section 501(c)(3) of the Internal Revenue Code** ▶ Do not enter social security numbers on this form as it may be made public. ▶ Information about Form 1023-EZ and its separate instructions is at *www.irs.gov/form1023*. | OMB No. 1545-0056 **Note:** *If exempt status is approved, this application will be open for public inspection.* |

☐ Check this box to attest that you have completed the Form 1023-EZ Eligibility Worksheet in the current instructions, are eligible to apply for exemption using Form 1023-EZ, and have read and understand the requirements to be exempt under section 501(c)(3).

Part I   Identification of Applicant

1a Full Name of Organization

b Address (number, street, and room/suite). If a P.O. box, see instructions.   **c** City   **d** State   **e** Zip Code + 4

2 Employer Identification Number   **3** Month Tax Year Ends (MM)   **4** Person to Contact if More Information is Needed

5 Contact Telephone Number   **6** Fax Number (optional)   **7** User Fee Submitted

8 List the names, titles, and mailing addresses of your officers, directors, and/or trustees. (If you have more than five, see instructions.)

First Name:	Last Name:	Title:	
Street Address:	City:	State:	Zip Code + 4:
First Name:	Last Name:	Title:	
Street Address:	City:	State:	Zip Code + 4:
First Name:	Last Name:	Title:	
Street Address:	City:	State:	Zip Code + 4:
First Name:	Last Name:	Title:	
Street Address:	City:	State:	Zip Code + 4:
First Name:	Last Name:	Title:	
Street Address:	City:	State:	Zip Code + 4:

9 a Organization's Website (if available):

b Organization's Email (optional):

Part II   Organizational Structure

1 To file this form, you must be a corporation, an unincorporated association, or a trust. **Check the box** for the type of organization.

☐ Corporation ☑ Unincorporated association ☐ Trust

2 ☐ **Check this box** to attest that you have the organizing document necessary for the organizational structure indicated above. (See the instructions for an explanation of **necessary organizing documents**.)

3 Date incorporated if a corporation, or formed if other than a corporation (MMDDYYYY): _____

4 State of incorporation or other formation: _____

5 Section 501(c)(3) requires that your organizing document must limit your purposes to one or more exempt purposes within section 501(c)(3).

☐ **Check this box** to attest that your organizing document contains this limitation.

6 Section 501(c)(3) requires that your organizing document must not expressly empower you to engage, otherwise than as an insubstantial part of your activities, in activities that in themselves are not in furtherance of one or more exempt purposes.

☐ **Check this box** to attest that your organizing document does not expressly empower you to engage, otherwise than as an insubstantial part of your activities, in activities that in themselves are not in furtherance of one or more exempt purposes.

7 Section 501(c)(3) requires that your organizing document must provide that upon dissolution, your remaining assets be used exclusively for section 501(c)(3) exempt purposes. Depending on your entity type and the state in which you are formed, this requirement may be satisfied by operation of state law.

☐ **Check this box** to attest that your organizing document contains the dissolution provision required under section 501(c)(3) or that you do not need an express dissolution provision in your organizing document because you rely on the operation of state law in the state in which you are formed for your dissolution provision.

For Paperwork Reduction Act Notice, see the instructions.   Catalog No. 66267N   Form **1023-EZ** (6-2014)

Part III   Your Specific Activities

1 Enter the appropriate 3-character NTEE Code that best describes your activities (See the instructions): _____

2 To qualify for exemption as a section 501(c)(3) organization, you must be organized and operated exclusively to further one or more of the following purposes. By checking the box or boxes below, you attest that you are organized and operated exclusively to further the purposes indicated. **Check all that apply.**

☐ Charitable   ☐ Religious   ☐ Educational

☐ Scientific   ☐ Literary   ☐ Testing for public safety

☐ To foster national or international amateur sports competition   ☐ Prevention of cruelty to children or animals

3 To qualify for exemption as a section 501(c)(3) organization, you must:

• Refrain from supporting or opposing candidates in political campaigns in any way.

• Ensure that your net earnings do not inure in whole or in part to the benefit of private shareholders or individuals (that is, board members, officers, key management employees, or other insiders).

• Not further non-exempt purposes (such as purposes that benefit private interests) more than insubstantially.

• Not be organized or operated for the primary purpose of conducting a trade or business that is not related to your exempt purpose(s).

• Not devote more than an insubstantial part of your activities attempting to influence legislation or, if you made a section 501(h) election, not normally make expenditures in excess of expenditure limitations outlined in section 501(h).

• Not provide commercial-type insurance as a substantial part of your activities.

☐ **Check this box** to attest that you have not conducted and will not conduct activities that violate these prohibitions and restrictions.

4 Do you or will you attempt to influence legislation? . . . .   ☐ Yes ☐ No

(If yes, consider filing Form 5768. See the instructions for more details.)

5 Do you or will you pay compensation to any of your officers, directors, or trustees? . . . .   ☐ Yes ☐ No

(Refer to the instructions for a definition of **compensation**.)

6 Do you or will you donate funds to or pay expenses for individual(s)? . . . .   ☐ Yes ☐ No

7 Do you or will you conduct activities or provide grants or other assistance to individual(s) or organization(s) outside the United States? . . . .   ☐ Yes ☐ No

8 Do you or will you engage in financial transactions (for example, loans, payments, rents, etc.) with any of your officers, directors, or trustees, or any entities they own or control? . . . .   ☐ Yes ☐ No

9 Do you or will you have unrelated business gross income of $1,000 or more during a tax year? . . . . .   ☐ Yes ☐ No

10 Do you or will you operate bingo or other gaming activities? . . . .   ☐ Yes ☐ No

11 Do you or will you provide disaster relief? . . . .   ☐ Yes ☐ No

Part IV   Foundation Classification

Part IV is designed to classify you as an organization that is either a private foundation or a public charity. Public charity status is a more favorable tax status than private foundation status.

1 If you qualify for public charity status, check the appropriate box (**1a – 1c** below) and skip to **Part V** below.

a ☐ **Check this box** to attest that you normally receive at least one-third of your support from public sources or you normally receive at least 10 percent of your support from public sources and you have other characteristics of a publicly supported organization. **Sections 509(a)(1) and 170(b)(1)(A)(vi).**

b ☐ **Check this box** to attest that you normally receive more than one-third of your support from a combination of gifts, grants, contributions, membership fees, and gross receipts (from permitted sources) from activities related to your exempt functions and normally receive not more than one-third of your support from investment income and unrelated business taxable income. **Section 509(a)(2).**

c ☐ **Check this box** to attest that you are operated for the benefit of a college or university that is owned or operated by a governmental unit. **Sections 509(a)(1) and 170(b)(1)(A)(iv).**

2 If you are not described in items **1a – 1c** above, you are a private foundation. As a private foundation, you are required by section 508(e) to have specific provisions in your organizing document, unless you rely on the operation of state law in the state in which you were formed to meet these requirements. These specific provisions require that you operate to avoid liability for private foundation excise taxes under sections 4941-4945.

☐ **Check this box** to attest that your organizing document contains the provisions required by section 508(e) or that your organizing document does not need to include the provisions required by section 508(e) because you rely on the operation of state law in your particular state to meet the requirements of section 508(e). (See the instructions for explanation of the section 508(e) requirements.)

Form 1023-EZ (6-2014)

Go to www.irs.gov/form1023ez for additional filing information.

Page 3

Part V Reinstatement After Automatic Revocation

Complete this section only if you are applying for reinstatement of exemption after being automatically revoked for failure to file required annual returns or notices for three consecutive years, and you are applying for reinstatement under section 4 or 7 of Revenue Procedure 2014-11. (Check only one box.)

1 ☐ **Check this box** if you are seeking retroactive reinstatement under section 4 of Revenue Procedure 2014-11. By checking this box, you attest that you meet the specified requirements of section 4, that your failure to file was not intentional, and that you have put in place procedures to file required returns or notices in the future. (See the instructions for requirements.)

2 ☐ **Check this box** if you are seeking reinstatement under section 7 of Revenue Procedure 2014-11, effective the date you are filing this application.

Part VI Signature

☐ I declare under the penalties of perjury that I am authorized to sign this application on behalf of the above organization and that I have examined this application, and to the best of my knowledge it is true, correct, and complete.

PLEASE SIGN HERE

▶ _____
(Type name of signer)

_____
(Type title or authority of signer)

▶ _____
(Signature of Officer, Director, Trustee, or other authorized official)

_____
(Date)

Form **1023-EZ** (6-2014)

Index

A

Accountants. See Record keeping; Tax advisers

Accounting period, 137, 142, 160, 183

Activities of nonprofits
articles of incorporation and clause limiting, to purposes of organization, 36, 104–105
authorization to engage in, 118
bylaws and limitations on, 124–125
bylaws detailing, 116–118
NTEE Codes, 138, 148
out-of-state, 18
questions about, IRS website for answers to, 49–50
See also Exempt activities support test for public charity status; Goods, services, or funds provided to the public; Purposes of nonprofits; Unrelated business income; *specific activities and purposes*

Activities of nonprofits, and IRS Form 1023, 145–155
automatic qualification for public charity status, 147
consumer credit counseling, 152
fictitious business name, explanation of using, 148
as fiscal agent, 173–174
foreign-based nonprofits, 143, 173
fundraising/financial support, 146–148, 149–155
grants or loans to other nonprofits, 152–153
honesty about, 146
intellectual property ownership and/or use, 149–152

limitation of benefits to a segment of the community, 148
narrative description, 145–148
NTEE Codes, 148
political activities, 148–149
special nonprofit organizations, 132, 166
unrelated business activities, 146, 147

Advance ruling/five-year support test, 159

Advertising rates, discounted, 11

Advisers. *See* Supporters/sponsors/ patrons/contributors/advisers

Advisers to nonprofit. *See* Lawyers; Tax advisers

Affordable Care Act (ACA), 154

Agent of corporation, registered, 98, 108

Aging. *See* Elderly persons

Agricultural research organizations, 166

Amateur sports organizations, 37

Animal welfare groups, 37

Annual information returns. *See* Information returns (federal); State nonprofit corporate reports

Antiterrorism, 138–139, 153

Articles of incorporation, 94–105
acceptance by the secretary of state, 106
for California, 97
checklist for filing, 95
customizing, 107
date filed, 137, 142, 167, 170
delayed effective date, 143, 170
directors named in, 101–102, 108
directors not named in, 173, 174
directors, special appointments of, 107

filing, 105–106
filing letter, 105–107, 110
filing online, 94, 95
formatting of articles, 95, 96–97
forms for, 83, 94–96, 105, 106
for Iowa, 95–96
as IRS Form 1023 attachment (PDF upload), 141, 142, 168
and IRS Form 1023-EZ submission, 137
and IRS Form 1023 narrative about activities, 146
lawyer for, 106
in minutes of first board meeting, 174
name changes after filing, 85
and name of corporation reserved, signatures for, 90
name of nonprofit checked via filing of, 88
for Nebraska, 95, 96
Nolo's Online Nonprofit formation service, 95
nomenclature differences between states, 82
notarization of, 109
organizational test of purposes/ activities in, 38b
problems with, returned by secretary of state, 106
retyping of, guidelines for, 95, 97
sample articles filing letter, 110
sample completed articles, 108–109
signing, 90, 95, 106, 109
state corporate filing websites and, 94–95
state-level filing, and advance tax payments, 76
state-level filing, and tax-exempt status, 76
successor organizations and, 143

of information returns, 114,
133, 183
at office of the nonprofit, 133
penalties for failure to permit,
133
private foundations and
(Form 990-PF), 184
private foundations not subject
to, 133
of tax-exempt application
(Form 1023), 114, 132–133
written requests for, 133
Publicly supported
organizations, use of term by
IRS, 63, 162
See also Public support test for
public charity status
Public safety organizations, 55
Public safety testing
organizations, 166
Public service announcements
(PSAs), 11
Public support. *See* Exempt
activities support test for
public charity status; Public
support test for public charity
status
Public support test for public
charity status
overview, 53, 55–56
additional "attraction of public
support" requirement, 56, 60,
61–63
defined, 162
disqualified persons for, 64, 66,
156, 163–164, 165
government unit support
received as, 58, 59
and IRS Form 990,
Schedule A, 183
and IRS Form 1023, 147,
162–163
and IRS Form 1023-EZ, 139

letting IRS decide which test,
53, 56, 63, 162, 166–167
membership dues and fees and,
60, 63
"normally" met criteria, 55–56,
57
online resources on, 56
public charities as support
source, 58, 59
qualified public support defined
for, 57
ratio of public support to total
support (one-tenth or one-
third), 56–57, 61
sources not considered public
support for purposes of, 56,
60–61
2% limit for one contributor,
58–60, 163
unusual grants and, 59–60,
160–161
See also Exempt activities
support test for public charity
status; Public charity status
Publishing
by educational organizations,
43, 146–147, 149–150, 151–152
by literary purpose
organizations, 42
Publishing and lectures
organizations, 100
Purposes of nonprofits
articles of incorporation and
clause limiting activities to,
36, 104–105
articles of incorporation and
dedication of assets to,
103–104, 144–145
articles of incorporation and
statements of, 98–101, 108,
144
bylaws and statements of,
116–118

charitable purpose
organizations, 37–39
educational purpose
organizations, 42–44,
117–118
on IRS Form 1023, 144
on IRS Form 1023-EZ,
137–139
literary purpose organizations,
42
more than one allowed, 36
non-allowable purposes as not
valid, 36
organizational test for, 36
overview, 6–7
political action in statements
of, 49
religious purpose organizations,
39–41
scientific purpose
organizations, 41–42
special purpose groups not
covered in text, 6, 37, 132
See also Activities of nonprofits;
Public charity status; *specific
purposes and activities*

Q

Quorum rules
for directors, 25, 26, 122
initial quorum rule, 26
for membership nonprofits, 34,
128–129

R

Raffle tickets, 73
Real estate. *See* Property
Record keeping
accountant setting up, 13, 192
balance sheet, 161
as burden, and choice to
become nonprofit, 12–13, 82